Chambers ghosts and spirits

Chambers

CHAMBERS
An imprint of Chambers Harrap Publishers Ltd
7 Hopetoun Crescent
Edinburgh
EH7 4AY

www.chambers.co.uk

First published by Chambers Harrap Publishers Ltd 2008

This book contains material previously published in *Chambers Dictionary of the Unexplained* © Chambers Harrap Publishers Ltd 2007

A CIP catalogue record for this book is available from the British Library.

ISBN: 978 0550 10393 2

Designed and typeset by Chambers Harrap Publishers Ltd, Edinburgh
Printed in Dubai by Oriental Press

Contents

Contributors

Editor
Kate Sleight

Consultant
Una McGovern

Contributors
Lorna Gilmour
Simon Hill
Peter Lamont
Una McGovern
Michael Munro
Alan Murdie
Gordon Rutter

Editorial Assistance
Katie Brooks
Stuart Fortey

Picture Research
Kate Sleight

Prepress
Nicolas Echallier
Becky Pickard

Publishing Manager
Hazel Norris

INTRODUCTION

Ghosts and Spirits explores the evidence for continued existence after death, a notion that has intrigued people for centuries. As well as featuring classic ghost stories, such as the Brown Lady of Raynham Hall, and tales of famously haunted buildings like Hampton Court Palace (where the spirits of two of Henry VIII's ill-fated wives are said to roam), the book delves into a range of topics related to the afterlife.

In addition to individual cases, various types of ghostly phenomena are described, from phantom coaches and poltergeists to spectral armies and apparitions. Also featured are spirits in folklore, like the mischievous mine spirits known by different names in several parts of Europe. The history of spiritualism is thoroughly examined; coverage includes biographies of mediums who claimed to be able to communicate with the dead, as well as of those who tried to expose them as frauds. Possible evidence of reincarnation, including personal accounts of supposed past lives, is reviewed. The book also looks at the attempts made, from ghost hunting to psychical research, to find a rational explanation for these baffling, apparently supernatural occurrences.

Cross-references to other relevant entries in the book are signified in the text by the use of small capitals. A glossary is provided to supply further explanation of some of the terms used, while a thematic index enables particular areas of interest to be found quickly and easily.

While it is not possible to include every case study and aspect of the debate, we hope we have succeeded in examining the subject from a variety of angles, in a considered and unbiased way. As well as serving as a useful and informative guide, the book should prove both fascinating and entertaining, and hopefully will whet readers' appetites to find out more.

A

Adelphi Theatre

A theatre in the Strand, London, said to be haunted by the ghost of a popular Victorian actor.

On 16 December 1897, the actor William Terriss was murdered as he entered the Adelphi Theatre – stabbed to death by fellow actor Richard Prince. Terriss, best known for his roles in melodramas, was appearing in *Secret Service* with his mistress Jessie Millward, and some claim that as he lay dying in her arms, he uttered the words 'I'll be back'. Prince was tried and convicted of the murder, and found 'criminally insane'. Terriss had, apparently, tried to help Prince several times, but had also been responsible for his dismissal on one occasion.

Terriss's ghost, which is also said to haunt the London Underground (see LONDON UNDERGROUND GHOSTS), was not reported until some years after his death. At some point in the 1920s, a visitor to London described seeing a man dressed in Victorian clothes walking along Maiden Lane – the road which Terriss walked along in order to enter the theatre. The figure was described as being almost glowing, and fabulously handsome. Further sightings were reported, and witnesses were apparently able to identify the apparition as Terriss from photographs of the actor. The ghost has also been

The stage door at the Adelphi Theatre, London, where William Terriss was murdered in 1897. (© TopFoto)

known to cause disturbances in the dressing room once used by Jessie Millward. At least one actor has heard mysterious rapping sounds which some suggest are similar to those made when the actor was alive, when he was in the habit of tapping on Millward's door with his cane. Some have also reported the ghost of Terriss manifesting as a glowing greenish light.

aerial phantoms

Apparitions that appear in the sky, often taken to have a symbolic or prophetic meaning.

Many cultures hold a belief in APPARITIONS appearing in the sky, usually as signs or portents. Some interpret these aerial phantoms as manifestations of gods, angels or important human personages elevated to spiritual form.

The archetypal aerial phantom in European mythology is the WILD HUNT of Odin. Norse tradition held that the god Odin rode across the sky on a phantom horse, Slepinir, followed by a pack of spectral hounds, chasing lost souls. The influence of Christianity changed the leader of the hunt to the Devil snatching up the souls of sinners and unbaptized babies. In later stories the leader of the hunt changed to historical or quasi-historical figures such as Barbarossa or King Arthur. Still later versions transform the hunt into a PHANTOM COACH. Underlying the belief in such appearances is the magical notion of correspondences and the idea that the heavenly realm may mirror upheavals upon earth.

Accounts of aerial phantoms enjoyed a particular vogue in the 16th and 17th centuries. The German writer Ludwig Lavater, in *Of Ghosts and Spirits Walking by Night* (1572), wrote:

> Before alterations and changes of kingdoms and in time of wars, seditions and other dangerous seasons, there most commonly happen very strange things in the air ... swords, spears and such like innumerable; there are heard in air or upon earth whole armies of men, encountering together, and when one part is forced to fly, there is heard horrible cries, and great clattering of armour.

In England at around this time, numerous accounts of galloping horses, strange emblems, dragons and SPECTRAL ARMIES appearing in the skies were circulated in pamphlets, particularly during periods of national crisis such as the English Civil War. A pamphlet held in the Ashmolean Museum, Oxford, contains a typically bizarre example of such a report. In its description of the vision of two country women who witnessed an aerial battle and angels on 16 April 1651, the angels are said to be 'of a blueish colour having faces ... like owls'. A decade earlier, the BATTLE OF EDGEHILL (1642) was said to have been re-enacted in the skies on successive Christmas Eves, with witnesses recognizing deceased soldiers. These events were allegedly investigated by a Royal Commission under the instructions of Charles I, but modern scholarship has found no corroboration for this. Reports found in pamphlet

An engraving depicting Odin's Wild Hunt. (© Mary Evans Picture Library)

literature must be approached with caution. Even attempts to reinterpret them as misperceptions of naturally occurring phenomena (such as lightning or meteors) might themselves attribute a greater level of veracity to the testimony than it perhaps deserves, since the authors regularly recycled entirely hearsay stories, embellishing them for their own religious, political or financial reasons.

Expanding scientific knowledge of the universe led to fewer accounts of aerial phantoms from the 18th century onwards, with the exception of a brief revival during World War I with the ANGELS OF MONS. Perhaps the only classic cases of any significance recorded in the 20th century are the reports of Marian apparitions at Fátima in 1917 and at Zeitoun, Egypt, in 1968. However, it is arguable that elements of ufology such as modern flying saucer accounts represent a new evolution of the tradition. See also CRISIS APPARITIONS; RE-ENACTMENT GHOSTS.

aeroplanes, phantom *see* PHANTOM AEROPLANES

afterlife

The continuation of some form of existence, usually spiritual, after the death of the body; a belief in life after death is fundamental to many religions, although ideas as to its nature vary greatly.

Most cultures, both past and present, subscribe to a belief in some kind of afterlife. The idea that a form of existence, usually spiritual, continues after the death of the body predates recorded history, and is fundamental to many religions and belief systems. However, ideas about what happens to the soul, or spiritual part of the individual, after death vary greatly from religion to religion. Many testimonies as to the reality of an afterlife have been advanced throughout the ages; some people claim to have died for a short time and then been sent back to this life after NEAR-DEATH EXPERIENCES, which are frequently characterized by the person's seeing a long tunnel with a light at the end and being met by their departed loved ones before being instructed to return to life. Others claim to have visited the afterlife while unconscious, in OUT-OF-BODY EXPERIENCES, and some say they can remember past lives or have seen visions of the afterlife. Many people believe it is possible to communicate with the dead through SPIRITUALISM, and there are countless stories of the recently dead appearing to friends and family to tell them that they are well and happy in another world.

Most cultures have some concept of a land of the dead, which is located either in the sky, under the earth, across a body of water or in the West, and the afterlife is typically regarded as a time when people will be rewarded or punished according to how they lived their lives on earth. This idea of the afterlife was also found in ancient Greek and Roman religions and various Asian belief systems, and is generally restricted to humans; animals are not held responsible for their actions. The belief in the afterlife determines many of the customs associated with death and burial, which are designed to help the soul attain eternal bliss. For example, the ancient Egyptian Book of the Dead describes the many hymns and rituals to be performed for the dead. It also provides the spells, charms, passwords, magical numbers and formulas necessary to guide the deceased through the various trials they would encounter before reaching the Underworld. In ancient Egypt, food, drink and money were also provided for the dead person's journey to the afterlife. Many tribal societies include sacrifices to the dead as part of their funeral rites; in Hinduism, cremation is thought to be a means of releasing the spirit for REINCARNATION, while other cultures, such as those of the Native Americans, believe that the spirit cannot attain peace in the afterlife if the body is destroyed or dismembered.

agency

The active force, entity or process (human or otherwise) through which a paranormal event is brought about.

In the field of PARAPSYCHOLOGY the word 'agent' is used specifically to refer to a person who apparently produces, or is attempting to produce, a paranormal event. The effects are brought about through their 'agency'. For example, in experiments to investigate telepathy, the agent is the person who attempts to transmit information to another individual (known as the 'percipient'), and in experiments investigating PSYCHOKINESIS, the agent is the individual attempting to influence the outcome of the experiment by, for example, levitating an object or bending a piece of metal using only the power of their mind.

The word 'agency' can also be more generally applied to phenomena occurring in SPIRITUALISM, in POLTERGEIST cases and in other areas of the paranormal – the person, or other entity, through which the effects are thought to be produced generally being called the agent (although the words are interchangeable to some extent in common usage, so they may also be referred to as the agency).

In the case of poltergeist phenomena, if they cannot easily be explained by simple fraud or natural causes, the question arises as to their origin. Many poltergeists appear to show signs of a limited intelligence, and so it is contended that they must either involve a living, human agent or a discarnate agent such as a SPIRIT. The majority of parapsychologists who accept the reality of poltergeist effects consider them to be examples of RECURRENT SPONTANEOUS PSYCHOKINESIS – originating in the unconscious mind of a living human agent. However, a minority entertain the hypothesis that they occur through the agency of a discarnate entity (for example, the spirit of a deceased person or even a non-human entity) – a view shared by many spiritualists and spiritists. A survey of 500 poltergeist cases conducted in 1979 by British psychical researchers Alan Gauld and Tony Cornell suggested that up to 25 per cent of poltergeist cases might be long-term, place-centred phenomena, rather than person-centred phenomena giving support to the notion that (at least in these instances) they are not due to the agency of a living human.

agent *see* AGENCY

American Society for Psychical Research

The oldest psychical research organization in the USA.

The American Society for Psychical Research (ASPR) was formed in Boston in 1885, making it the oldest psychical research organization in the USA. Since its inception the ASPR has used scientific methodology to investigate alleged paranormal and PSYCHIC claims.

After a period as a branch of the SOCIETY FOR PSYCHICAL RESEARCH the ASPR became independent in 1905. It opened a headquarters in New York, with an extensive library and archive. In 1907 the ASPR started to publish the *Journal of the American Society for Psychical Research*, which is still published quarterly. The society managed to recover from an internal split in the 1920s and has continued to maintain its strong scientific credentials ever since – despite its somewhat embarrassing involvement in a number of cases over the years that were initially identified as genuine but later exposed as fraudulent.

The ASPR has an international membership and over the years a number of prominent scientists and psychologists have been actively involved with the society. The ASPR still funds research programmes into many areas of PARAPSYCHOLOGY and acts as a repository of knowledge and past research. A regular newsletter is produced, and all members are free to use the society's meeting rooms and resources.

Amityville

Famous alleged haunting in Amityville, USA, which led to a bestselling book and numerous films.

The house at 112 Ocean Avenue, Amityville, Long Island, New York, first acquired its gruesome reputation in November 1974, when a 23-year-old man called Ronnie Defeo shot and killed his parents and four siblings there. A year later the property was bought by George and Kathleen Lutz at a very cheap price and they moved into the house in December 1975 with their three young children. After only 28 days the family left the property, claiming to the media that they could no longer endure the bizarre and terrifying experiences they had suffered there: APPARITIONS of a talking pig; menacing figures in hoods; sinister voices; infestations by flies; sounds of a marching band; putrid smells and green slime running down the walls. Family members allegedly underwent physical and behavioural changes and visitors to the house were also affected – Father Ralph Pecoraro (a local priest) reportedly suffered a debilitating illness after a disembodied voice ordered him to 'get out' while he was blessing the house with holy water.

In 1977 *The Amityville Horror: A True Story*, by Jay Anson, was published by Prentice Hall, ostensibly as a non-fiction book. It rapidly became a bestseller, eventually selling over six million copies, although scrutiny of the 'non-fiction' text revealed numerous factual errors and the inclusion of material drawn from the author's own imagination (with the implicit approval of the Lutzes who were part-credited with authorship in the early editions).

The credibility of *The Amityville Horror* was further damaged when, in 1979, Ronnie Defeo's attorney, William Webber, claimed that he had had the idea of the hoax haunting. When the Lutzes proceeded with the plan on their own he sued for a share of the royalties. The Lutzes countersued, still claiming that the haunting had really occurred. The trial judge, Jack Weinstein, stated for the record that 'the evidence shows fairly clearly that the Lutzes during this entire period were considering and acting with the thought of having a book published'. Further litigation followed – the subsequent purchasers of the house (tiring of constant sightseers) sued Anson, the Lutzes and Prentice Hall and received an out-of-court settlement; Father Ralph Pecoraro also sued the Lutzes for invasion of privacy and distortion of his role and received an out-of-court settlement. The story, however, continued to gain fame through film treatments such as *The Amityville Horror* (1979), *Amityville II: The Possession* (1982), *Amityville 3-D* (1983) and *The Amityville Horror* (2005) – a remake of the original film.

Subsequent occupiers have not reported any psychic manifestations, only disturbances from curiosity-seekers drawn to the house because of its reputation.

Angels of Mons

Aerial phantoms that allegedly appeared in support of Allied forces during World War I.

Following the Battle of Mons in August 1914, rumours spread that ghostly knights had appeared on the battlefield in support of the retreating

French and British soldiers and that these APPARITIONS had counter-attacked the approaching German army. Later versions of what became known as the Angels of Mons legend had the Allies assisted by angels, St Michael, Joan of Arc or St George. Many now believe that these rumours stemmed from a short story – *The Bowmen* by journalist Arthur Machen – in which spectral English archers from the Battle of Agincourt join British soldiers in resisting a German advance. First published in the *London Evening News* on 14 September 1914, the story circulated widely – first among civilians in Britain and then across the Channel to soldiers in France. In his autobiography, *Goodbye to All That* (1929), Robert Graves recalls hearing the claims about the Angels of Mons while serving on the Western Front but notes that he never met any first-hand witnesses. For his part, Machen

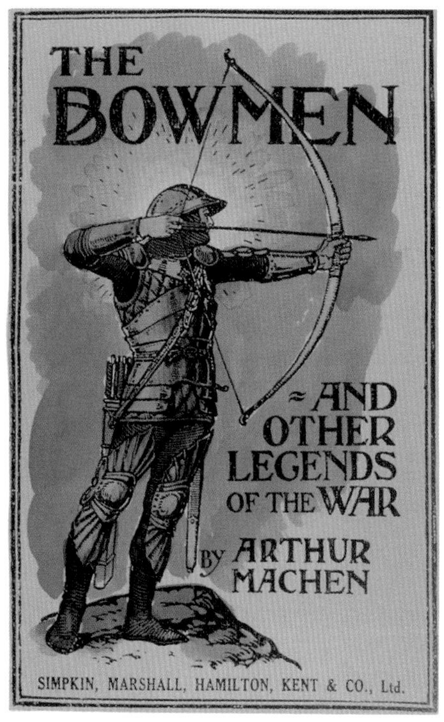

The cover of Arthur Machen's *The Bowmen and Other Legends of the War*, the title story of which is often cited as the origin of the legend of the Angels of Mons. (© 2003 Charles Walker/TopFoto)

fervently denied there was any truth in his story, but it continued to be retold as truth (and with embellishments) throughout the war and after, suiting the patriotic public mood.

Contemporary testimony from soldiers present at Mons fails to corroborate anything resembling the apparitions. Although numerous service personnel and their relatives reported psychic experiences during World War I, these were primarily premonitions, CRISIS APPARITIONS or 'ordinary' GHOSTS. However, the tale of the Angels of Mons may be seen as a rare 20th-century equivalent of the AERIAL PHANTOMS reported at times of national crisis in earlier centuries.

animal ghosts

Ghosts that appear in the form of an animal.

Stories of animal ghosts are found throughout the world, often linked with specific religious and magical traditions. Although tales of animal ghosts are widespread, they have been little studied as a specific category by psychical researchers, largely because sightings of animal ghosts are relatively rare. The whole area is complicated by the existence of accounts of supernatural animals such as BLACK DOGS and other bizarre creatures which, although they might be considered to fall within the province of cryptozoology, sometimes exhibit ghost-like behaviour and lack of physical form. Furthermore, in some traditions the ghost may appear as an animal but be regarded by witnesses as the transmogrified spirit of a deceased human.

One popular study, *Animal Ghosts* (1913) by Elliot O'Donnell, dutifully records stories of phantom dogs, cats, horses, rabbits, wolves, bears and birds together with legends of more exotic creatures such as phantom tigers, but the majority of accounts are at best folkloric. Outside the realm of folklore, a nationwide survey of hauntings in Great Britain conducted between 1967 and 1973 by the *Journal of Paraphysics* revealed that animal ghosts accounted for an average of 2–5 per cent of all reported APPARITIONS annually, and there is no reason to believe this statistic has changed. Generally, in the Western cultural tradition, only domestic animals such as dogs, cats and horses are said to appear as ghosts. The implication may be that some kind of emotional association with humans is necessary for an animal to manifest as a ghost, or it might simply be that it would be difficult to distinguish between sightings of physical or discarnate wild animals. See also GHOST DOGS.

apparitions

Visual appearances of people, animals or objects that are not materially present.

Apparitions have been reported around the world for thousands of years. Every culture appears to have a belief both in the survival of the dead and in appearances of the deceased to the living. However, apparitions should not automatically be equated with the SPIRITs of the dead since they can include the forms of still-living people (see GHOSTS OF THE LIVING) and animals and also inanimate objects or scenery. Apparitions are usually of short duration and are characterized by an ability to appear and disappear without explanation. They are generally visible to only a limited number of people and rarely leave any physical traces. Apparitions may sometimes be interpreted as relating to past, present or future occurrences. It has been noted that not all people report seeing them (even in instances where others do), suggesting that there may be a subjective element to the process – ranging from some form of extrasensory perception through to non-paranormal processes such as hallucination or misperception caused by expectation – although it is often claimed that certain mammals, particularly dogs, cats and horses, also appear to react to their appearance.

The most extensive collection of apparition reports was undertaken by the SOCIETY FOR PSYCHICAL RESEARCH (SPR) in its *Census of Hallucinations* in 1894. Collectors were sent out to obtain answers to the following question (among others):

> Have you ever, when believing yourself to be completely awake, had a vivid impression of seeing or being touched by a living being or inanimate object, or of hearing a voice; which impression, so far as you could discover, was not due to any external physical cause?

Of the 17,000 answers received, 2,272 were in the affirmative – although it is important to note that the question does not express, or invite, any opinion as to the source of the perception. Of those who had experienced impressions, 32 per cent reported seeing the form of a living person, 14 per cent had seen those of dead persons and 33 per cent persons who remained unidentified. Most were remarkably normal in appearance, although occasionally figures were partly formed or luminous. Extrapolating from the figures obtained from the census as a whole, one in six people in England believed in the existence of GHOSTs while one in fourteen believed they had seen one. The findings of the SPR surveys indicated that 'apparitions' were primarily a hallucinatory phenomenon, but with the curious elements that they could sometimes be seen by more than one percipient on the same occasion, or seen by different people on separate occasions. Much thought was given to the idea that the experience of seeing a ghost could be (at least partly) to do with some form of telepathy between the living.

Surveys in the 20th century have tended to confirm these patterns. Again, the types of apparitions reported were remarkably mundane in appearance. In some cases the apparition was described as appearing to have a purpose (to impart information, to give a warning or to say farewell) but in the majority of cases it appeared to have no discernible motive or meaning.

Classifying apparitional reports is difficult because of the complexity and variety of the experiences described. In addition to apparitions of human beings, the following categories can be listed:

Animal apparitions – either real or symbolic animals (see ANIMAL GHOSTS).

Religious apparitions – appearances of deities or religious persons such as Christ, the Virgin Mary, individual saints, or religious symbols or emblems (eg crosses, flaming hearts).

Humanoid – apparitions with a superficial resemblance to a human being but incorporating features suggesting such things as a supernatural entity (for example, an angel or fairy), a hybrid terrestrial species or an extraterrestrial form of life.

Inanimate objects or transport – including vehicles such as ships, cars or planes (see GHOST SHIPS; PHANTOM AEROPLANES).

Scenic apparitions – phantom scenery, such as buildings and gardens that do not exist, or wholesale re-enactments of scenes such as battles (see SPECTRAL ARMIES).

Occasionally apparitions also feature in POLTERGEIST cases but this is very much the exception rather than the rule.

There are many competing theories as to the causes of apparitions and what they may represent. The most detailed theory was that offered by G N M Tyrell (1879–1953), who proposed, in his book *Apparitions* (1942), that the subconscious mind receives PSYCHIC impressions and acts as 'stage carpenter' by creating an apparitional figure in the form of a visual hallucination. Alternatively, it has been suggested by others that apparitional experiences involve interaction between the mind and a 'deeper level of reality'. However, it is equally possible that the range of reports loosely grouped together as 'sightings of apparitions' may be brought about through a number of different mechanisms – including (and some might say limited to) a number of processes recognized by mainstream psychology. However, such things as COLLECTIVE APPARITIONS present more of a difficulty for those who wish to explain them away in entirely 'non-paranormal' terms – and the fact that there is still a huge amount that we do not understand about human perception, and the processing of sensory information, will ensure that the debate remains alive for some time to come.

apparitions, collective *see* COLLECTIVE APPARITIONS

apparitions, crisis *see* CRISIS APPARITIONS

apparitions, recurrent *see* RECURRENT APPARITIONS

apport

The supposed transport or sudden appearance of material objects without the involvement of a material agency.

The appearance of an apport (meaning 'to bring', from Latin via French) is an example of a MATERIALIZATION, although the implication is usually that the object has been brought from somewhere else. The word was originally used in connection with SÉANCES. When apports appeared at spiritualist séances they were said to have been physically manifested by SPIRITS and were offered as proof of the reality of spirit communication. The word 'apport' is also sometimes used to refer to the unseen movement or sudden appearance of objects in POLTERGEIST cases.

One of the earliest records of the appearance of an apport comes from a séance in Paris in 1819. During the séance a dove was reportedly seen flying around with a package in its beak. The package was then deposited on the table, and upon inspection it was found to contain pieces of paper with small fragments of bone and the names of saints. One of the most famous producers of apports was the 19th-century MEDIUM Agnes Guppy. Mrs Guppy was renowned for the variety of objects that 'materialized' on her séance table – flowers, plants and food were all known to appear – although sceptics suggested that it might just be possible that these were hidden in advance in the medium's ample petticoats. Mrs Guppy's best-known feat occurred at a séance conducted in London by fellow mediums Frank Herne and Charles Williams. At this séance, someone apparently jokingly requested that Mrs Guppy be made to appear. After much debate as to whether this would be possible, in view of her size, there was a great thump on the table to the accompaniment of screams. A light was struck, and there was Mrs Guppy. One witness said, 'She was not by any means dressed for an excursion, as she was without shoes, and had a memorandum book in one hand and a pen in the other. The last word inscribed in her book was "onions", the ink of which was wet.' While many believed that Mrs Guppy had truly been transported across London, the less exciting possibility that she had been hidden in the room all along has also been suggested.

Sceptics point to the fact that apports can be easily explained as examples of sleight of hand and misdirection. Some former séance leaders have confessed that even sleight of hand was not always required – the simple throwing of objects into the air was often enough to convince the unwary that an apport had taken place.

armies, spectral *see* SPECTRAL ARMIES

Ash Manor

A haunted house in Sussex, England, investigated by psychoanalyst and psychical researcher Nandor Fodor.

Ash Manor, in Sussex, was originally built in the 13th century. The structure was much changed over the years, but part of the original building still stood when it was purchased in 1934 by a family who were later given the pseudonym Keel by the psychical researcher NANDOR FODOR. Mr and Mrs Keel, their 16-year-old daughter and their servants moved into the property on 24 June. Soon after, they heard strange stamping noises coming from the attic. Some months later, Mr Keel was woken in the night by three loud knocks on his bedroom door. He went to his wife's bedroom, and she confirmed that she had also heard the sound but was unable to explain it. The same unexplained noises were heard on the following two nights. Mr Keel then went away on business for a few days. Nothing happened during his absence, but on his return he was again woken in the night, this time by a single loud knock on his bedroom door. He claimed that when he sat up, he could see a figure standing in the doorway, later described as 'a little oldish man, dressed in a green smock, very muddy breeches and gaiters, a slouch hat on his head and a handkerchief around his neck'. Keel questioned the figure, but got no reply. Keel said he then got out of bed and reached out to grab the man, but his hand went straight through him. Keel found himself in his wife's room, and she went to fetch him some brandy. Allegedly she then also saw the figure, and on trying to strike him found that her hand went through him as if he was not there.

The 'green man' continued to appear, most often to Mr Keel, and usually in front of the chimney in his bedroom. The strange noises also continued, the Keels now attributing them to the ghost. The family were most distressed, and servants apparently left their jobs in fear, so the Keels decided to take action. A series of exorcisms were held, but these did not help – in fact the family believed that the attempts of a priest had actually made the phenomena worse. Nandor Fodor became involved in the case in 1936, at the invitation of an author who wished to include Ash Manor in a book he was researching. Fodor stayed in the house without witnessing any unusual phenomena, before asking the medium EILEEN GARRETT to join the investigation.

With the help of her CONTROL, Uvani, Garrett apparently learnt that the 'green man' was called Charles Edward. He claimed that his lands had been stolen by the Earl of Huntingdon, he had been betrayed by a man named only as 'Buckingham', and he had finally been left to die in a nearby jail. Charles Edward wanted revenge. The ghost was informed that he was dead and was asked to leave, which seemingly he did, albeit reluctantly. However, Mr Keel witnessed the apparition again on the following day. It is claimed that Mr Keel seemed happy that the exorcism had failed. Another sitting was held, without the Keels, and this time Uvani revealed that the ghost had returned because it was used by Mr and Mrs Keel as a means of embarrassing each other. There was a great deal of tension between the couple, and Mrs Keel informed Fodor that her husband was homosexual. The ghost finally disappeared when Mr Keel admitted that he had wanted it to stay.

Whatever the truth of the reported happenings at Ash Manor, Fodor concluded that while it was possible that the ghost had been created by Mr Keel's subconscious, it seemed that some truly paranormal phenomena had occurred at the house – his justification being that the ghost had been witnessed by several people. Fodor believed that suppressed sexual energies had created an atmosphere which had attracted the ghost, and the haunting phenomena had ceased when this tension had been relieved by the couple's admitting the problem.

ASPR *see* AMERICAN SOCIETY FOR PSYCHICAL RESEARCH

astral projection

A system of movement of the spirit outside of the body that forms part of some mystical and religious belief systems.

Astral projection (sometimes just referred to as 'projection') might be described as a form of OUT-OF-BODY EXPERIENCE or a proposed explanation for such experiences. During astral projection it is said that the astral double, or 'astral body', leaves the physical host and is taken to the 'astral plane' (a realm of existence just beyond the physical world), from which it is then free to travel anywhere. The astral double is usually defined as being an

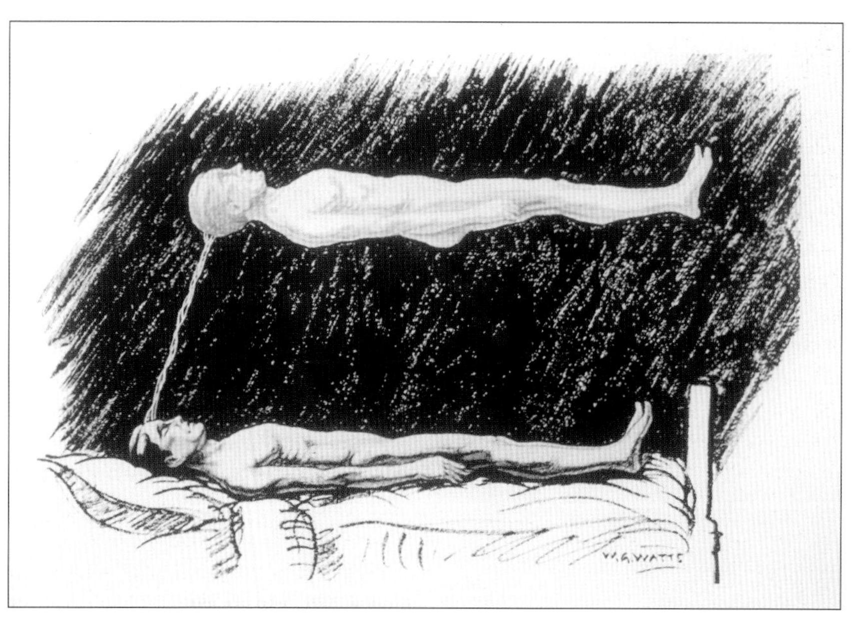

The astral body floating above the physical body, connected by a silver cord – from *The Projection of the Astral Body* (1929) by Sylvan Muldoon and Hereward Carrington. (© Mary Evans Picture Library)

exact duplicate of a human being, but one that is not usually encountered on the normal plane of existence, while the astral body is said to be a SPIRIT form of our living bodies, although the two terms are often used interchangeably. During projection, the astral double is usually described as remaining connected to the physical body by a silver cord. In some movements, 'astral double' is used to describe the spirit of a deceased person, and this can appear after death.

The term astral projection is frequently treated as interchangeable with the term 'astral travelling', although during astral travelling the astral body has to make its own way back to the physical body. Some spiritualists claim to be able to control their astral bodies – allowing them to roam free in the astral plane under their conscious control.

auditory hallucinations

The phenomenon of experiencing the sensation of hearing sounds where there is no identifiable external cause.

Many individuals report experiencing sounds which have no apparent external cause. These may include such things as voices, breathing sounds, and the sounds of animals, birds or music. How such experiences come about is not entirely agreed upon, and to dismiss them as 'imaginary' is to fail to address the complexity of the mechanisms involved (paranormal or otherwise). In some cases, it is widely accepted that the sounds are wholly generated by the brain of the person, even though they may be believed by them to be external in origin – such as is the case in some psychological disorders or where the subject is using some form of hallucinogen. However, it is important to note that such voices or sounds can also occasionally occur in people who are not suffering from any condition that would usually be identified as a mental or physical illness. It has even been observed by some that there are cases where hearing such voices and sounds appears to be linked with creativity, leading to the suggestion that they may serve some perfectly ordinary functional purpose.

How such experiences are interpreted is often determined by the culture in which the individual lives. By some people they may be considered to be the voices of (or signals from) gods or SPIRITS, or to be other messages with a PSYCHIC or supernatural origin. To psychical researchers certain auditory hallucinations may even be evidence for the existence of extrasensory perception, its being postulated that they arise from the exercise of a psi faculty or power, leading to the generation of an auditory hallucination which is perceived by the conscious mind. However, the use of the phrase 'auditory hallucination' now usually carries with it the implication that the sound experiences are generated only through a process in the brain, and when the phrase is used by sceptics it is often taken by them to embody a complete and internally consistent alternative to a paranormal explanation.

automatic art

The production of a piece of artwork without the person who is making it being aware of what is being produced.

Automatic art is a form of AUTOMATISM and is related to AUTOMATIC SPEECH and AUTOMATIC WRITING. It is often, but not always, produced at SÉANCES by MEDIUMS, who will produce works of art (of varying quality) while purportedly in the control of SPIRITS. The medium is said to be CHANNELLING the artistic ability of whoever is controlling them.

Often, automatic art is produced by scribbling at great speed on a sheet of paper, often with the pen or pencil remaining in constant contact with the sheet. Once the work has been finished, if the process has been successful, it should be found to be a recognizable picture. Mediums often claim that the automatic art that they produce is in the style of a particular dead artist.

automatic speech

Speech which apparently comes from an individual but over which they seemingly have no control.

Automatic speech, like AUTOMATIC WRITING and AUTOMATIC ART, is a form of AUTOMATISM. As such it is alleged that the apparent originator of the speech has no control over the words that are being spoken; they are instead merely a conduit for communication from SPIRITS or other beings. The process is usually carried out by a MEDIUM who enters a trance, during which the speech is channelled (see CHANNELLING and TRANCE, MEDIUMISTIC).

In its modern form, automatic speech can be traced back to the spiritualists of the 19th century. However, much earlier examples can be found in the stories of ecstatics speaking in tongues reported in the Christian Bible. See also XENOGLOSSY.

automatic writing

The production of written material supposedly without the conscious control of the person who is writing it down.

Automatic writing is a form of AUTOMATISM like AUTOMATIC SPEECH and AUTOMATIC ART. To produce it, a pen or pencil is held over a piece of paper and (if the process has been successful) it will begin to write, apparently without the conscious control of the person holding it. It is normally carried out by a MEDIUM, who may enter a trance – the pen or pencil is then supposedly being directed by SPIRITS.

Using this technique, mediums have supposedly produced written material from once-living individuals, such as new works by Beethoven, for example, or new creeds on how to live life by Jesus Christ (see *A COURSE IN MIRACLES*). One medium in the late 19th century, HÉLÈNE SMITH, even produced complex documents describing life on Mars. They were written in Martian, which, fortunately, bore a striking resemblance to the medium's native French. See also CHANNELLING.

automatism

Behaviour on the part of an individual that occurs without their apparent intervention or conscious control.

Within the realms of SPIRITUALISM and other spiritual belief systems, automatism is behaviour that is supposedly born out of an individual's ability to receive and channel messages from SPIRITS without their being aware of what is happening. The most frequently encountered forms of automatism are AUTOMATIC WRITING, AUTOMATIC SPEECH and AUTOMATIC ART.

The term 'automatism' (or, more commonly, 'automatic behaviour') is also used to describe the spontaneous production of verbal or motor behaviour without conscious self-control which is associated with some medical conditions and with sleepwalking. See also MEDIUM; CHANNELLING.

B

Bachelor's Grove Cemetery

A small abandoned graveyard near the Chicago suburb of Midlothian, claimed by some to be the most haunted cemetery in the world.

The area around Bachelor's Grove, close to the modern Chicago suburb of Midlothian, was settled in the 1820s and 1830s, and the cemetery there, originally known as Everdon's, was set aside some time after that. The one-acre site is relatively small, and burials decreased there in the 1960s, in which decade the road that leads to the cemetery was officially closed to traffic. The last recorded burial there was in 1989, although by that time the graveyard had essentially been abandoned for many years. Vandals have overturned the gravestones and graves have been opened and desecrated, and it is thought that allegedly satanic rituals have been held on the site. The unsavoury reputation of the area is further fuelled by stories that a small lagoon around the cemetery was used by Chicago gangsters as a dumping ground for dead bodies in the 1920s and 1930s.

Stories of hauntings at Bachelor's Grove first circulated in the 1960s, and reports of ghostly phenomena reached a peak in the 1970s and 1980s. There have been claims of APPARITIONS, DISEMBODIED VOICES, GHOST LIGHTS and strange creatures. One of the most frequently reported apparitions is that of a 'phantom house', generally described as being white, with a pillared veranda, a swing and a soft light burning within. While witnesses seem to agree on what the house looks like, it seems to appear in different places, although it always disappears when people try to approach it. There is no historical evidence that such a house has ever existed near the cemetery. The apparition of a two-headed man has also been reported, as has a WHITE LADY. Also referred to as the 'Madonna of Bachelor's Grove', the White Lady is said to be seen wandering around the cemetery during a full moon, sometimes carrying a baby in her arms. While popular lore has it that the ghost is that of a woman who is buried in the graveyard next to her baby, no historical records support this theory.

Many ghost investigators have attempted to record evidence of the phenomena at Bachelor's Grove, including members of the Ghost Research Society (GRS). In 1991, Mari Huff took photographs in the graveyard while she was there with other investigators from the GRS. Using infrared film to photograph an area that the group was interested in, Huff took a picture which remains controversial. It shows the semi-transparent figure of a woman, wearing white old-fashioned clothes, sitting upon a broken gravestone. According to Huff and her colleagues, no such figure was visible to them when the photograph was taken. Supporters believe this is a genuine GHOST PHOTOGRAPH, while sceptics claim that it is either an accidental double exposure or a deliberate fake. And, while the abandoned cemetery continues to attract many amateur ghost hunters, some believe that the reports of its haunted nature are simply fabrications or urban legends.

Ballechin House

A property in Perthshire, Scotland, that was the subject of a controversial haunting in the 19th century. It was once dubbed 'the most haunted house in Scotland'.

The alleged haunting of Ballechin House in Perthshire, Scotland, was investigated by members of the SOCIETY FOR PSYCHICAL RESEARCH in 1897. Many ghostly phenomena were said to occur at the house – particularly strange noises, an APPARITION of a nun, and an apparition of a spectral dog – leading to the property being dubbed 'the most haunted house in Scotland' (a title later adapted for BORLEY RECTORY in England).

The Society for Psychical Research (SPR) took out a tenancy on the isolated building (a method later employed by HARRY PRICE at Borley Rectory), and a team of investigators stayed at the property over a period of several months. Attempts at SÉANCE communication were made and vigils were conducted in the hope of experiencing manifestations. However, adverse publicity followed in *The Times* in June 1897 when it was alleged that members of the SPR had not disclosed their intentions to the property's owners when taking on the lease – the owners claimed that they had been deceived. Further criticism of the approach of one of the leading investigators, Ada Goodrich-Freer, followed, leading to the investigation being prematurely abandoned – members of the SPR tactfully avoided discussion of the case thereafter.

Goodrich-Freer went on to write a detailed book on the case, in conjunction with the Marquess of Bute, entitled *The Alleged Haunting of B----- House* (published in 1899, with an updated edition appearing the following year). Although no serious allegations of fraud were made concerning Ballechin, many of the accounts in the book were considered dubious – for example, the strange noises were dismissed as the product of minor earth tremors in what is a seismically active area. Appreciation of the book was also handicapped by the lengths taken in the text to preserve the anonymity of witnesses. Apart from a nursery block, Ballechin House was entirely demolished in the 20th century. However, the case may well merit re-assessment.

Baltimore Poltergeist

A famous 20th-century poltergeist case from the USA.

What became known as the 'Baltimore Poltergeist' wreaked havoc in a house in Baltimore, USA, in early 1960. The house was occupied by Mr and Mrs Jones, their daughter and son-in-law Mr and Mrs Pauls, and their grandson Ted Pauls, who was 17 years old at the time. The POLTERGEIST activity started in the middle of January, and continued until early February. The first reported incident was the explosion of 15 miniature pottery pitchers that occupied a shelf in the dining room. Over the following weeks, the family claimed that other items mysteriously jumped off shelves, pictures fell from the walls and furniture moved – classic features of many poltergeist cases. They also claimed that kindling stored in the cellar exploded, and said they were forced to remove as many objects as they could from the house in order to get some peace.

Family members became local celebrities when the media became interested in the case, and a number of theories were put forward to explain the phenomena. Many believed that Ted Pauls, a high-school dropout who spent his time reading science fiction and editing and writing his own newsletter, was the obvious culprit – but his family rejected the idea that he could be perpetrating a hoax. It was also suggested that earth tremors or high-frequency soundwaves were to blame, but on investigation there was no evidence to support either. The psychoanalyst and psychical researcher NANDOR FODOR investigated the case and came to the conclusion that Ted was at the centre of the disturbances, but as an unconscious agent (see AGENCY) rather than as a hoaxer. Fodor believed that by increasing Ted's feelings of self-worth his unconscious mind would no longer cause the disturbances. When the phenomena ceased, Fodor believed he had found the way to 'cure' the poltergeist outbreak, but the family maintained that it was not Fodor but a plumber who found the solution. Coincident or not, on the night that the phenomena ceased a plumber suggested that the hot air furnace was the cause of the problems, and the family removed the storm windows and opened a window in the dining room at his suggestion, to 'equalize the pressure'. Sceptics contend that the disturbances ended when Ted decided to stop causing them.

Barghest *see* BLACK DOGS

Battle of Edgehill *see* EDGEHILL, BATTLE OF

Battle of Naseby *see* NASEBY, BATTLE OF

Bell Witch

A 19th-century poltergeist case from Tennessee, USA, characterized by claims of extremely aggressive behaviour on the part of the entity involved.

There are several versions of the story of the Bell Witch POLTERGEIST, which afflicted John Bell, his wife and their eight children at a farm near Adams, Tennessee, in 1817. The main details of the occurrences were allegedly recorded in the diary of one of the sons, Richard Williams Bell.

The case is considered dubious, partly because of the extreme and long-running nature of the disturbances. The forms taken by the manifestations varied widely. Strange APPARITIONS were supposedly witnessed, followed by alarming noises. The poltergeist was also said to have launched violent attacks upon twelve-year-old Betsy Bell, who was slapped, pinched and later harassed to the point where she broke off an engagement with a man of whom the poltergeist apparently disapproved. The poltergeist acquired a voice and delighted in cursing and shouting abuse. The voice claimed variously to be a demon or the SPIRITS of deceased persons, and allegedly uttered prophecies. It finally adopted the persona of Kate Betts, a woman who was living locally and was known to have a grudge against John Bell. It was thereafter referred to as 'Kate'. Physical phenomena were supposedly witnessed by amateur exorcists and by sightseers who were drawn to the property – among them General Andrew Jackson.

The disturbances continued for three years, during which the poltergeist persecuted several, but not all, of the members of the family. John Bell was a particular target, to the point that his health failed – when this happened the poltergeist still cursed him continuously as he lay sick in bed. On the morning of 19 December 1820 John Bell was found lying in a stupor and a strange bottle was found in his medicine cabinet. Its contents were tested upon a cat, which went into convulsions and died, whereupon 'Kate' declared she had poisoned John Bell. As he lay dying she sang rowdy songs in triumph.

After the death of John Bell the disturbances declined in severity, and 'Kate' declared she would depart and return in seven years' time to wreak further havoc. Seven years later the manifestations were limited to noises and the disturbance of bedclothes, but 'Kate' was said to have visited John Bell Jnr and pledged a further return in 107 years. No phenomena were experienced by descendants of the Bell family when the supposed return date was finally reached in 1935.

Various theories have been advanced as to the source of the Bell Witch poltergeist (in addition to the possibilities of exaggeration, hoax and deliberate acts on the part of one or more of the family members). Psychoanalyst NANDOR FODOR suggested that it arose from the subconscious minds of one or more of the Bell daughters, with its behaviour being shaped by repressed conflicts within the family (see RECURRENT SPONTANEOUS PSYCHOKINESIS). Another theory, containing a popular theme in interpretations of US haunting cases, was put forward by Troy Taylor, who suggested in *Season of the Witch* (1999) that a disturbed Native American burial mound in the area might be a factor.

Berkeley Square

An address in London's Mayfair, 50 Berkeley Square, long associated with stories of a haunting.

The property at 50 Berkeley Square, London, has long had a reputation as a haunted house, a reputation which seemingly arose at some time in the 1840s or 1850s. Various legends are attached to the house, but many feel stories of the haunting began with the occupation of the house by an eccentric recluse called Mr Myers. It is said that Mr Myers was jilted by his beautiful fiancée on the eve of his wedding, and was made so distraught by this incident that he lost his mind and lived in only one room of the house, letting the rest fall into decay. Some hypothesize that his candle-lit wanderings in the night caused the first rumours of a haunting. In the 1870s a series of letters relating to the house appeared in the magazine *Notes and Queries*:

> The story of the haunted house in the heart of Mayfair can be recapitulated in a few words ... The house in Berkeley Square contains at least one room of which the atmosphere is supernaturally fatal to body and mind. A girl saw, heard, or felt such horror in it that she went mad, and never recovered sanity enough to tell how or why.
>
> A gentleman, a disbeliever in ghosts, dared to sleep in it and was found a corpse in the middle of the floor after frantically ringing for help in vain. Rumour suggests other cases of the same kind, all ending in death, madness or both as a result of sleeping, or trying to sleep in that room.

The supposed events at Berkeley Square have appeared in so many fictional writings that it is difficult to distinguish which, if any, of the elements have a basis in fact. One often recounted tale involves two sailors who broke into the then deserted house in order to sleep there. One of them encountered something so unspeakably hideous that he leapt from the window and died, impaled on the railings below. His companion variously lives to tell the tale, or goes quite mad.

The building now houses an antiquarian book shop, and the room rumoured to be at the centre of the disturbances is an office.

Berry Pomeroy Castle

A ruined 15th-century castle near Totnes, Devon, associated with a number of hauntings and a legend of buried treasure.

The now ruined Berry Pomeroy Castle was built in the 15th century for the

The privy tower at Berry Pomeroy Castle.
(© English Heritage/HIP/TopFoto)

Pomeroy family. They sold the castle in 1547 to Edward Seymour, whose sister, Jane Seymour, had married Henry VIII in 1536. However, the tales of ghosts and treasure associated with Berry Pomeroy are linked to the original owners.

One of the castle's ghosts is said to haunt the battlements of a certain tower, known as Lady Margaret's Tower. The legend goes that Lady Margaret Pomeroy loved the same man that her sister, Lady Eleanor, did. Through absolute jealousy and a desire to get her man, Lady Eleanor imprisoned Lady Margaret for 19 years, and in some of the more colourful versions of the story Lady Margaret either starved to death or perished after being walled up alive within the fabric of the castle. It is often said that the ghost of Lady Margaret now rises and walks on the ramparts on certain nights, although some disagree and say it is the ghost of Lady Eleanor, whose evil deed left her with an unquiet soul. Unfortunately, the Pomeroy family tree does not reveal sisters named Eleanor and Margaret, but stories relating to an APPARITION on Lady Margaret's Tower persist.

A further Berry Pomeroy ghost is said to be that of another member of the Pomeroy family, although she is not named. Her legend is included in the memoirs of the eminent physician Sir Walter Farquhar (1738–1819). Farquhar claimed that, when attending to the wife of the castle's steward, he witnessed the ghost of richly dressed woman, who hurried past him, wringing her hands. Farquhar learned from the steward that the appearance of this ghost was an omen of death and, accordingly, Farquhar's patient died.

The buried treasure of Berry Pomeroy Castle is supposed to have been hidden in 1549. The story goes that two brothers, Pomeroy heirs, fearing the castle would be captured by enemies, hid the family treasure, then mounted blindfolded horses and rode to their deaths over a nearby precipice, knowing that in this way torture would never force them to reveal the hiding place. Unfortunately for the storytellers, the castle had already changed hands in 1549, and the simultaneous deaths of two Pomeroy brothers is not documented. Whether the brothers haunt the castle, guarding their treasure, is not recorded.

Bettiscombe Manor

A 17th-century manor house near Bridport in Dorset, home to Britain's most famous screaming skull.

The earliest known account of Bettiscombe's famous SCREAMING SKULL dates to 1847, when Mrs Anna Maria Pinney, whose family owned the house, described it as being kept on a beam in the attic, near the chimney – left there for good luck and to prevent supernatural attack upon the house. The skull was later kept in a niche in the attic and, in more recent times, lodged for a while in a shoe box in the study.

Family legend states that the skull is that of a black male servant of the Pinney family, who was brought to the house in the 17th or 18th century – it is said that Azariah Pinney was exiled to the West Indies for his part in the Monmouth Rebellion, but flourished there, and either he or his descendant was able to return to Bettiscombe in triumph. It is claimed that soon after his arrival in Dorset, the servant became ill, and requested on his deathbed that his body be returned to his native Nevis for interment. The wish was disregarded, and the servant was buried in the local churchyard. It is said that screams and moans were heard coming from the grave, and the house was plagued by bad luck. The Pinneys were forced to have the body disinterred and (for reasons that are unclear) the skull was preserved in the house. This, apparently, put a stop to the troubles.

Traditionally, attempts to bury or otherwise dispose of the skull have led to psychic disturbances and ill fortune. It is said that one resident of the Manor threw the skull into a pond, but constant screams and moans forced him to retrieve the skull and place it once again in the house. On another occasion, it is claimed that the skull was buried in a deep hole, but within a few days it was found inexplicably sitting on top of the ground (or, in some versions of the story, on the doorstep).

By the 20th century, stories circulated which claimed that the servant had not died of natural causes, but had been beaten to death by his master. An alternative version claimed that the skull was not that of the servant, but of a young girl who had been kept prisoner in the attic, although there is no evidence to support this. Further lore associated with the skull suggests that it sweats blood at times of national calamity, having done so in 1914 prior to the outbreak of World War I.

An examination of the Bettiscombe skull carried out in 1963 indicated that it was that of a European female and that it might be 2,000 or more years old. This has led some to believe that in earlier times it was venerated at a Celtic shrine, or was originally kept by the family as an archaeological curio.

bilocation

The act of appearing in two different places simultaneously.

The ability to appear in two different places at the same time is a phenomenon that has been reported throughout history by holy men, sages and saints, and is also described as occurring in cases involving GHOSTS OF THE LIVING.

According to one occult theory, the effect is caused by the separation of the astral body (see ASTRAL PROJECTION), or etheric body, from the physical. In cases of so-called CRISIS APPARITIONS, telepathy is also offered as an explanation. The phenomenon is also linked with the folkloric concept of the DOPPELGÄNGER, which is sometimes said to presage the death of the individual concerned. See also DOUBLES.

Black Dogs

Large black spectral dogs said to haunt places such as crossroads and churchyards; legends of Black Dogs are common all over the British Isles, with each area calling the apparition by a different name.

Many places in the British Isles have traditions of spectral Black Dogs, known by a variety of local names. In East Anglia, the Black Dog is known as Black Shuck or Old Shuck; in Lancashire, there are tales of the Bogey Beast, also known as Trash or Skriker; in Yorkshire, it is called the Barghest or Padfoot; in Somerset, the Gurt (Great) Dog; in Ireland, the Pooka; on the Isle of Man, the Mauthe Dog; in Wales, the Gwyllgi ('dogs of the dusk'); and in Cumbria, the Cappel or Cappelthwaite.

Black Dogs have a number of characteristics that set them apart from the phantoms of domestic dogs (see GHOST DOGS) and from normal domestic animals. These include their great size (they are frequently described as being as big as a calf) and their eyes, which are large and luminous, often described as blazing red saucers.

The Black Dog is often described as walking through solid objects, and its appearance is frequently said to be accompanied by lightning or a fire or explosion; it may vanish or fade gradually from view or disappear with a bang or flash if the person who sees it lets their gaze wander or tries to touch it. It is usually seen at night. It leaves no tracks, and makes no sound as it walks. Occasionally it is described as having the head or limbs of another animal or a human being, or as being headless, and although it is generally reported to be black and shaggy, there have been a few reported sightings in which it is white or (particularly in Scotland) green. In some stories Black Dogs have supposedly left physical traces in the form of burns or scratches on places or people, most famously at the churches of Blythburgh and Bungay in Suffolk during a thunderstorm in August 1577.

The appearance of a Black Dog is often interpreted as an omen of impending death or disaster for the person witnessing it – although in some areas, such as Essex, they traditionally have a protective function. Stories of such creatures have been told in one form or another for centuries, both in ballad and pamphlet form and in oral tradition. While in some legends the Black Dog is a manifestation of the devil (leading to another popular name for the phenomenon, 'Devil Dog') or the transmogrified spirit of a wicked human being, the majority of Black Dog apparitions have no such accompanying legend to 'explain' their appearance. It is possible that the name of Shuck, by which the Black Dog is generally known in East Anglia, is derived from *scucca*, the Anglo-Saxon world for demon. Legends of a ghostly Black Dog at Cromer in Norfolk are said to have provided the inspiration for SIR ARTHUR CONAN DOYLE's *The Hound of the Baskervilles* – although Dartmoor in Devon, the setting for the story, also has its own rich tradition of demonic dog folklore.

Perhaps surprisingly, there is a considerable amount of 20th-century testimony for the appearance of Black Dogs at different locations, although these more recent appearances have been somewhat less dramatic than those in earlier stories. Country roads, churchyards, ancient monuments and parish and county boundaries have historically been the favourite haunts of Black Dogs, with their appearance being celebrated in some local place names (eg Black Dog Lane, Uplyme on the Devon/Dorset border; Dogland and Shuckmoor in Coventry, Warwickshire). Black Dogs are rarely reported inside or close to buildings and a study conducted in the 1970s by a Lowestoft-based researcher called Ivan Bunn suggested that Black Dogs have an affinity for bodies of water such as rivers, streams and the sea.

Black Monk

Archetypal form of hooded apparition.

Hooded APPARITIONS falling within the type generally described as 'Black Monk' appear in reports from locations throughout Britain. They are also a common feature of numerous folk stories and legends: a hooded figure with a skeletal face is said to haunt Beacon Hill at Woodhouse Eaves in Leicestershire; a monk in black was said to walk the route of a secret tunnel at Binham in Norfolk; and a black monk apparition known as the 'Goblin Friar' was said to act as a harbinger of disaster to the Byron family at NEWSTEAD ABBEY in Nottinghamshire – the poet Lord Byron referred to the spectre in his poem *Don Juan* (1819–24), and was even said to have seen it himself. Many more examples could also be listed.

Originally it was thought that such apparitions were simply the GHOSTS of deceased monks, who in their lives had been attached to one of the many monastic sites that existed in England and Wales until the Reformation. This view has now been challenged by the idea that, in at least some cases, the Black Monk figure is better understood as an archetypal figure linked with particular landscapes. If so, the Black Monk may have more in common with other symbolic apparitions such as the WHITE LADY and the BLACK DOG rather than resulting from manifestations connected with deceased individuals. There are also rare examples of hooded forms connected with POLTERGEIST outbreaks, notably the so-called 'Black Monk of Pontefract' case in 1966, in which the well-witnessed disturbances were attributed to the ghost of a monk from a Cluniac monastery who was supposedly executed in the reign of Henry VIII (although this theory was rejected by Colin Wilson, who reviewed the case in 1980).

Although the Black Monk is a common ghost motif in Britain, it is much rarer in other European countries, particularly in those that did not embrace Protestantism and remained mainly Catholic. It is also known in Latin American countries but does not appear in folklore or reports of hauntings from the USA.

Black Shuck *see* BLACK DOGS

Blickling Hall

A Jacobean mansion in Norfolk, associated with the legend of a phantom coach.

Blickling Hall was at one time owned by Sir Thomas Boleyn, who was the father of Anne Boleyn – the second wife of Henry VIII. Legend has it that the ghost of Sir Thomas regularly travels from Blickling in a PHANTOM COACH, as described by a contributor to *Notes and Queries* in 1850:

> The spectre of this gentleman is believed by the vulgar to be doomed, annually, on a certain night in the year, to drive, for a period of 1,000 years, a coach drawn by four headless horses, over a circuit of twelve bridges in the vicinity ... Sir Thomas carries his head under his arm, and flames issue from his mouth.

It is also said that should a witness to this APPARITION speak to Sir Thomas, he will carry them away.

Some say that the phantom coach appears on the anniversary of Anne Boleyn's execution, and claim that Sir Thomas is carrying out a 1,000-year penance in atonement for his part in his daughter's death. Others have stated that the ghostly vision can be witnessed on any night, and have also changed the locations of the twelve bridges from early versions, making the circuit longer. In more recent times it is often cited that the coach carries not Sir Thomas, but Anne herself, a written description of which apparition dates to 1877. She is said to be seen in a hearse-like coach, sitting with her bloody severed head in her lap. She has a coachman and attendants, and these are also headless. In some versions she returns to Blickling, the coach and horses disappear, and the ghost of Anne, dressed in white and carrying her head, enters the building and roams the hallways until dawn.

Bloxham tapes

A series of recorded interviews purporting to offer proof of the reality of reincarnation.

The Bloxham tapes were first brought to the attention of the public in a 1976 BBC television documentary entitled *The Bloxham Tapes*. This was followed, in the same year, by the inevitable tie-in book by the programme's producer, Jeffrey Iverson – *More Lives than One? The Evidence of the Remarkable Bloxham Tapes*.

Cardiff-based hypnotherapist Arnall Bloxham spent 20 years hypnotizing and regressing over 400 men and women. He claimed that audio recordings from these sessions offered definite proof of REINCARNATION, and some of his best cases were investigated in the television documentary and subsequent book.

Jane Evans, while visiting Bloxham for relief from rheumatism, apparently gave detailed descriptions of six former lives under hypnosis. These included a Roman housewife (Livonia), a Jew from the York Massacres of the 12th century (Rebecca), a medieval servant to a French prince (Alison), a maid of honour to Catherine of Aragon (Anna), a servant in the early 18th century (Ann Tasker) and a 19th-century American nun (Sister Grace). Many of the facts that Evans gave were instantly verifiable, although they were also relatively easy to ascertain from a number of history books. As Rebecca, Evans claimed to have died in the cellar of a church in York. For the filming of the BBC documentary, a York church was used, which may have been the one referred to by Rebecca. When the church was located it was found to have no cellar. However, six months later restoration work uncovered a cellar. Unfortunately, this was only one of three possible churches uncovered by the BBC, and it was used for filming simply because it was the easiest to gain permission to shoot in. Further evidence against the claims included the fact that the former personifications of Evans seemed to have forgotten some rather important details; for example, Alison knew nothing of her master Jacques Couer's

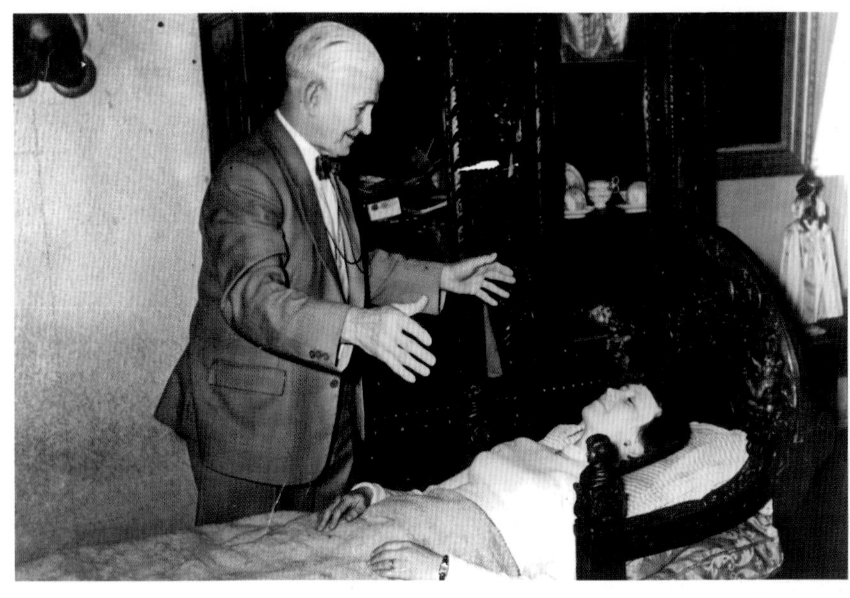

Hypnotherapist Arnall Bloxham at work. (© Topham Picturepoint)

wife or five children – although she was well aware of the layout of the house. Similar gaps appeared throughout all of the accounts. In the case of Alison, many aspects of her master's life can be found in a 1948 novel – *The Money Man* by Thomas Costain – in which, for reasons of dramatic artistry, the family of Couer had been written out. Couer's house is also one of the most photographed houses in France and many books have carried pictures of it.

In the case of Evans and the others involved in Bloxham's work, verifiable facts could easily have been read prior to the hypnotic regressions. How much of this apparent 'memory recall' was brought about by leading questions, or through their merely remembering previously read novels, is unclear, but no evidence was found to indicate that Bloxham or any of the participants deliberately engaged in fraud.

Blue Bell Hill

A stretch of road between Maidstone and Chatham, in Kent, famously associated with a haunting.

The A229 at Blue Bell Hill in Kent is perhaps Britain's most famously haunted road, associated with stories of a SPECTRAL PEDESTRIAN and a PHANTOM HITCH-HIKER.

In the late 1960s, researcher Tom Herber was the first to collect stories relating to this stretch of road. He claimed that a number of motorists reported picking up a phantom hitch-hiker there – in each case at around

11 o'clock at night, the motorist would pick up a hitch-hiking girl at the bottom of Blue Bell Hill and she would sit in the back seat of the car, only to vanish mysteriously when the journey continued. Harber's findings were reported in the local press, and the legend that Blue Bell Hill was haunted grew.

The first known encounter with a spectral pedestrian at Blue Bell Hill was a dramatic event reported in 1974. Maurice Goodenough arrived at the police station in Rochester in the early hours of 13 July. He told officers that he had been driving on Blue Bell Hill when a girl walked out in front of his car. He had not been able to avoid hitting her, and had left her wrapped in a car rug at the side of the road while he came to summon help. Goodenough estimated that the girl was around 10 years old. The police hastened to the scene, but when they arrived there they found the rug, but no sign of the girl. A search ensued, and Goodenough remained convinced that he had hit a girl with his car. However, the police could find no trace of her, and there were none of the signs of damage to the car that would have been expected if Goodenough had been involved in a collision. In local lore, the two APPARITIONS, the hitch-hiker and the pedestrian, became the same ghost.

Periodic sightings of the ghost of Blue Bell Hill continued to be reported, but the story truly came to prominence again in 1992, when the local press covered a series of incidents involving motorists who believed they had run someone over on Blue Bell Hill. At around midnight on 8 November, a motorist reported hitting a young woman who had appeared in front of his vehicle, running towards it before disappearing under the front of the car. Again, there was no evidence that any incident had occurred, although the motorist seemed to be genuinely shaken. The story was picked up by the national press, and the fame of Blue Bell Hill spread.

Two weeks later, another similar incident occurred. A teenage motorist reported that he had run over a young woman who had appeared in front of his car. He described what happened to him:

> She ran in front of the car. She stopped and looked at me. There was no expression on her face. Then I hit her and it was as if the ground moved apart and she went under the car. I thought I had killed her because it wasn't as if she were see-through or anything. She was solid – as real as you are.

Again, the motorist seemed to be genuinely distressed by the experience, but the police found no trace of a victim, and no damage to the car.

In local lore, the ghost of Blue Bell Hill is associated with an accident that occurred there on 19 November 1965. Two cars collided, and three out of the four women travelling in one of the vehicles were killed. One of the women who died was due to be married the following day, and another was her bridesmaid. It is said that the ghost is that of the bridesmaid, although, inevitably, there have been a number of fatal accidents on Blue Bell Hill, and some investigators believe that the link to that particular incident was established by the local press, simply to add an element of tragic romance to the story.

Borley Rectory

Famously dubbed 'the most haunted house in England'.

The notorious Borley Rectory in Essex, known as 'the most haunted house in England', was the scene of unrivalled paranormal activity between its construction in 1863 and its destruction by fire in February 1939. Five successive rectors and their families claimed to have experienced a wide range of GHOST and POLTERGEIST phenomena in and around the rectory, as did locals, visitors and investigators attracted to the site. It has been claimed that in excess of 200 people witnessed strange events in and around the rectory over the years.

Ghostly phenomena reported at Borley Rectory included the frequent APPARITION of a nun, a PHANTOM COACH and horses in the grounds, a headless man and a spectral cat. The sounds of footsteps, galloping horses and DISEMBODIED VOICES were also heard, and numerous poltergeist incidents were apparently witnessed. The majority of the poltergeist activity occurred between 1927 and 1935, and was said to include bell-ringing, the movement and breakage of objects, APPORTS which included bottles and religious medals, and pencilled wall writings calling for 'help', 'light', 'mass' and 'prayers'.

The fame achieved by Borley Rectory largely stems from two bestselling books – *The Most Haunted House in England* (1940) and *The End of Borley Rectory* (1946), both written by the flamboyant PSYCHICAL RESEARCHer HARRY PRICE. Price investigated the case for nearly 20 years, following national publicity in the *Daily Mirror* newspaper in 1929 – although his relationship with the various occupants of the rectory was not always good. Price rented the house in 1937 and, in a year-long effort at experimental investigation, moved in teams of observers recruited through *The Times*. SÉANCEs were also held, including one in 1937 when the participants supposedly communicated with someone called 'Marie Lairre'. It was claimed that she was a nun, murdered at Borley on 17 May 1667, and that her remains lay buried under the building.

Following the end of the Price tenancy in 1938, the rectory was sold to a Captain Gregson. On 11 February 1939 the building was destroyed by fire, exactly eleven months after a séance prediction that a ghost calling itself Sunex Amures would burn it down. The fire was supposedly caused by a paraffin lamp falling over. There were suspicions of deliberate arson by Gregson, although the insurance claim was ultimately settled.

In 1943 the cellar floor of the ruined rectory was excavated and a jaw bone, supposedly that of the ghostly

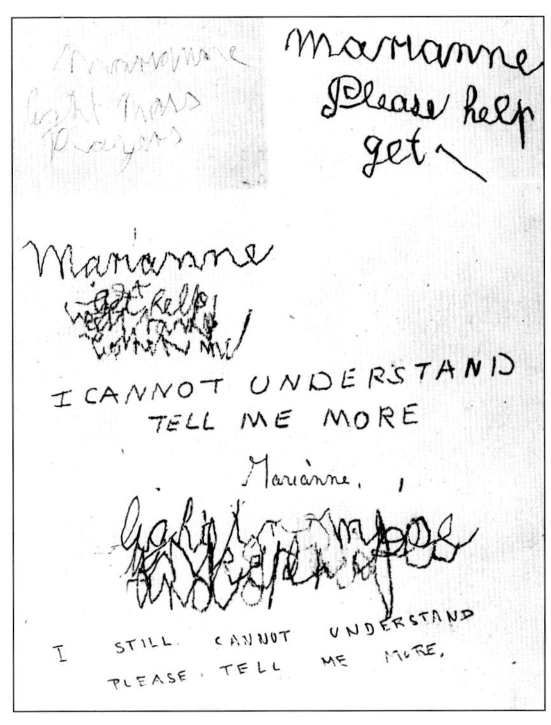

Attempted correspondence with 'ghostly' graffiti on a wall at Borley Rectory, 'the most haunted house in England', photographed in 1931.
(© 2004 Fortean/TopFoto)

nun or even 'Marie Lairre', was discovered; this was buried at Liston Churchyard in 1945. The remains of the rectory were demolished in 1944. Further digging occurred on the site in 1954 and 1955, organized by Philip Paul – but nothing was revealed beyond the remains of a 17th-century wall, suggesting an earlier building had once stood there.

With no physical remains of the rectory left to investigate, researchers turned to re-examining the testimony and background of the original witnesses. A sceptical tone was set in *The Haunting of Borley Rectory* (1956) by E J Dingwall, K M Goldney and T H Hall. The book was severely critical of Price, his methods and his treatment of incidents at the rectory. Particularly damning was the discovery that a photograph published in *Life* magazine of a brick apparently hovering in midair on the rectory site was a hoax, set up as the building was being demolished. This had been passed off by Price as a genuine manifestation. Since then attention has focused on the lives of some of Borley Rectory's colourful inhabitants, and the question of to what extent phenomena were helped along by trickery and self-deception. Elaborate theories have been debated back and forth in books and articles on the case. Some maintain that the haunting has now transferred to the nearby church, but the existence of a large crypt prone to flooding, which was found beneath the building in 1988, may account for many of the strange noises that have been heard there.

Assessing the truth about Borley is difficult amid the wealth of claims and counterclaims. Any final verdict necessarily rests upon the view taken as to the reliability of human testimony. Nonetheless, an arguable case can be made for Borley being haunted both before and after the periods in which Price was involved.

Brocken spectre *see* SPECTRE

Brown, Derren (1971–)

English mentalist and psychological illusionist.

Derren Brown was born in Croydon in 1971. He studied Law and German at Bristol University, and in his first year there he was impressed by a show performed by a hypnotist, and became interested in the subject. On leaving university, Brown went on to perform magic in restaurants and bars, and also gave some stage hypnosis shows. In 2000, his first television show was broadcast, *Derren Brown: Mind Control*, and he became famous for his 'mind-reading' act. Brown himself does not claim to have any PSYCHIC powers, but says he amazes audiences through 'a mixture of magic, suggestion, psychology, misdirection and showmanship'.

Further television shows have followed, including the infamous *Russian Roulette* (2003), *Derren Brown: Séance* (2004), *Messiah* (2005), and *The Gathering* (2005). His performances have brought him into conflict with spiritualists and self-professed psychics, as he sceptically recreates apparently supernatural feats through natural means. In *Séance*, he described some of the manipulations he had used, but he rarely reveals many of his techniques.

During the course of his television shows, Brown is known for having made shoppers raise their right arms, apparently by giving a sales patter over a loudhailer (when the patter actually disguised the command, 'come right arm up'), and for having replicated Uri Geller's spoon-bending (the viewer saw no change to the cutlery, but Brown made the people he was with believe it had become bent).

Brown has written a number of books, including *Tricks of the Mind* (2006), also the name of one of his television series. When not performing, he is well known for painting caricatures of the famous.

See also MENTALISM.

Possibly the most famous ghost photograph ever taken; first published in *Country Life* magazine on 26 December 1936. It shows what appears to be a phantom figure descending a staircase at Raynham Hall, Norfolk. (© 2004 Fortean/TopFoto)

Brown Lady of Raynham Hall

A female apparition said to haunt Raynham Hall in Norfolk, England; the Brown Lady was made famous by a 'ghost photograph'.

The Brown Lady is the name given to a female APPARITION said to have haunted Raynham Hall in Norfolk, which was for many generations the home of the Townsend family. The name of the apparition refers to the brown brocade dress which she is said to have worn. It has been claimed that the Brown Lady was the GHOST of Dorothy Walpole, sister of the first British prime minister Sir Robert Walpole, as Dorothy died of smallpox at Raynham Hall in 1729. The apparition was frequently reported at the Hall in the 19th and early 20th centuries.

In September 1936 two photographers, Indira Shira and Captain Provand, working on a commission for *Country Life* magazine, took a picture of a glowing figure descending a staircase at the hall. This was immediately held to be an image of the Brown Lady and has been widely considered one of the best GHOST PHOTOGRAPHS ever taken. On investigation no evidence of deliberate trickery was found and researchers who interviewed Shira and Provand considered them truthful, Provand being a sceptic who was at a loss to explain how the image had appeared. In 1937 C V C Herbert investigated the photograph for the SOCIETY FOR PSYCHICAL RESEARCH. Herbert suspected camera malfunction, but found it curious that this should occur at the same moment one of the photographers believed he saw the ghost. While some still champion the picture as a genuine example of a ghost photograph, others now believe that although there is little to suggest deliberate fraud, close scrutiny of the full photograph presents evidence of double exposure.

A portrait of Anne Griffith, attributed to Marc Gheeraerts. (©TopFoto)

Burton Agnes Hall

An Elizabethan manor house near Driffield in East Yorkshire, associated with the legend of a screaming skull.

Burton Agnes Hall is said to contain the SCREAMING SKULL of Anne Griffith. One version of the legend has it that the house was built by Anne and her two sisters, but that before the house was completed, Anne was set upon by robbers. She was left seriously ill, and greatly distressed that she would never see the hall. On her deathbed, she is supposed to have asked that her head be removed from her body and placed in the house when her sisters took up residence there. The sisters agreed, but after Anne's death they buried her without fulfilling their promise.

Nothing untoward occurred until the remaining sisters moved into the finished Burton Agnes Hall; then, it is claimed, for the next two years the house was beset with strange moans and noises, and no servants would stay. Eventually, the sisters had Anne's body disinterred and the skull was placed upon a table in the hall. All disturbances ceased until, some years later, a maid threw the skull from the house. It is said that until the skull was retrieved, the whole house shook. Other traditions claim that the skull was removed on several occasions, but that each time it 'screamed' until it was returned.

In 1654 the Boynton family succeeded to Burton Agnes by marriage. They are believed to have built a niche in the wall to take the skull and keep it safe, and either they or their successors are said to have bricked the niche up. Modern lore has it that the skull is still there, behind the panelling in one of the bedrooms, its exact location a secret.

Although Anne's original wish was eventually fulfilled, it is said that her ghost, known locally as 'Owd Nance', haunts the hall, seen by some as an APPARITION, and sensed by many others who stay there.

While Anne Griffith is not mentioned in contemporary family records, Burton Agnes Hall was actually built by Sir Henry Griffith, who may have been her father.

C

channelling

The process whereby a spirit apparently communicates through a human medium.

Channelling involves a person (usually described as a MEDIUM) being willingly possessed by a SPIRIT, and allowing the spirit to communicate through them. Channelling was popular within the SPIRITUALISM movement in the Victorian era. This alleged phenomenon came to modern prominence in 1963 when Jane Roberts claimed to have been possessed by a spirit called Seth and dictated a book to her husband, Robert Butts, supposedly under its guidance. In 1970 they published *The Seth Material*, which popularized this form of spirit communication. With the death of Jane Roberts in 1984, Seth apparently started to speak through Jean Loomis. Other celebrated channelled spirits include John (co-creator of the world with God), Ramtha (a 35,000-year-old Cro-Magnon warrior), Buddha, Vishnu, Jesus Christ (see *A COURSE IN MIRACLES*) and Mark Twain. All are apparently interested in the welfare of humans and generally preach that love and understanding is the way forward.

HARRY HOUDINI spent much of his later life debunking psychics and channellers. Houdini believed that channellers employed standard stage magicians' techniques such as cold reading (giving out general statements and then adapting the next piece based on the reaction of the audience member) or hot reading (gaining knowledge of the person who is having the reading carried out, without their knowledge).

Practices that might be described as channelling also form a part of many religious belief systems. It can be seen as essentially a similar phenomenon to benign possession. See also AUTOMATISM.

Chingle Hall

Reputed to be the oldest brick house in Britain, Chingle Hall in Cheshire attracted the epithet 'most haunted house in England' during the 1990s.

The manor house of Chingle Hall in Cheshire was one of a number of sites promoted as the most haunted house in England during the 1990s. Said to date back to 1260, the house is reputedly haunted by a phantom monk (see BLACK MONK), unusual temperature variations and unexplained footsteps. There are many stories of investigators hearing strange noises in the hall, or experiencing camera malfunctions or equipment breakdowns while carrying out their work. In recent years some owners have sought to make money from the reputation of the house by charging individuals and groups to spend a night there, and charity events have also taken place at the house. See also BORLEY RECTORY; HAUNTINGS.

clairaudience

The claimed ability to hear things which normal humans cannot.

Clairaudience (from the French for 'clear hearing') could be described as a form of extrasensory perception, as it purportedly involves 'hearing' sounds that others cannot – suggesting that the sound experience in the percipient's brain originates other than through the normal physical process. Clairaudience is sometimes talked about as a form of CLAIRVOYANCE (which involves seeing) but strictly speaking they are not the same thing. However, for obvious reasons, they are often described as being experienced together.

Clairaudience is one of a range of phenomena that it is claimed are experienced by some PSYCHICS or MEDIUMS at a SÉANCE, through which they pass on messages that are allegedly from SPIRITS of the dead. Watching people who claim to have this ability is indeed like watching a conversation of which one is aware of only one side.

clairsentience

The claimed ability to receive information about people or objects just by touching them.

Clairsentience (from the French for 'clear feeling') might be described as the ability to receive information through a PSYCHIC sense of touch. Merely by holding an object or by touching a person, a clairsentient claims to be able to gain and relate information about their history. A clairsentient claims also to be able to tell details about previous owners of any objects held and some, but not all, claim to be able to see the future for a person or object by touch.

clairvoyance

Strictly, the claimed ability to see things which are not normally visible. However, the term is more generally used to include any form of discerning information that is beyond the normal range of sense or perception.

Clairvoyance (from the French for 'clear seeing') has long been claimed as a technique for gaining information other than via the normal senses. As such, the word describes a form of extrasensory perception. It is a skill claimed by many MEDIUMS, PSYCHICS and other individuals who might simply refer to themselves as 'clairvoyants', and is an ability that is often claimed to be employed during a SÉANCE (in which instance the information is supposedly obtained from SPIRITS of the dead).

Clairvoyance is a skill that has also historically been associated with many religious and magical practices, in which the source of the information is usually understood to be spirits, gods or other supernatural beings. See also CLAIRAUDIENCE.

coaches, phantom *see* PHANTOM COACHES

Cock Lane ghost

Famous 18th-century poltergeist case in London which became a euphemism for fraud.

The Cock Lane ghost was supposedly active between 1762 and 1764 at a tiny house in Smithfield, London, which was occupied by a family named Parsons. Strange knocks were heard in a small room occupied by twelve-year-old Elizabeth Parsons and, by means of questions and rapped answers, a form of crude communication was established with the alleged entity. The ghost apparently identified itself as the SPIRIT of a woman named Frances Lynes, who claimed to have been poisoned by her lover. The culprit was identified by the ghost as William Kent, a stockbroker and former tenant of the house, with whom Elizabeth's father had an on-going dispute over money.

The ghost was given the nickname 'Scratching Fanny', and sightseers flocked to the house, Dr Samuel

Cock-Lane, Humbug.

THE town it long has been in pain
About the phantom in Cock-Lane,
To find it out they ſtrove in vain
Not one thing they neglected ;
They ſearched the bed and room com-
To ſee if there was any cheat, (pleat.
While little Miſs that looks ſo ſweet,
Was not the leaſt ſuſpected.

Then ſoon the knocking it begun
And then the ſcratching it wou'd come
'Twas pleaſed to anſwer any one,
And that was done by knocking ;
If you was poiſon'd tell us true,
For yes knock one, for no knock two,
Then ſhe knock'd I tell to you, (ing.
Which needs muſt making it ſhock-

On Friday night as many know,
A noble Lord did thither go,
The Ghoſt in knocking wou'd not ſhow
Which made the Gueſt to mutter :
They being gone then one was there
Who always called it my dear,
Fanny was pleas'd 'tis very clear,
And then began to flutter.

The Ghoſt ſome Gentlemen did tell,
If they would go to Clerkenwell,
Into the Vault where ſhe did dwell,
That they three knocks ſhould hear fir
On Monday night away they went
The man accus'd he was preſent,
But all as death it was ſilent.
The de'll a knock was there fir

The Gentlemen return'd again,
And told young miſſy flat and plain,
She was the Agent of Cock-Lane,
Who knock'd and ſcratch'd for Fanny
'Twas falſe each perſon did agree,
Miſs begg'd to go with her daddy
And then went into the Country
To knock and ſcratch for Fanny.

A ballad inspired by the Cock Lane ghost – the case was a great source of entertainment for the public in 1762. (© 2004 Fortean/TopFoto)

Johnson among them. Suspicions soon grew that the Cock Lane ghost was a fraud. It was noticed that when Elizabeth was restrained the knocks would cease. Also, when the spirit promised to make raps in the vault of a local church where Frances Lynes was buried, nothing was forthcoming.

Amid growing public hysteria, William Kent issued proceedings through the Guildhall Court to restrain the slanders on his character. A number of individuals were convicted, including some who had helped publicize the communications. Elizabeth's father was sentenced to the pillory and imprisonment.

The story was satirized in a print by Hogarth, and for many years the phrase 'Cock Lane ghost' became a euphemism for deception and credulity in cases of alleged paranormal phenomena. However, the possibility that at least some of the claims were genuine has not been wholly discounted.

collective apparitions

The name given to apparitions that are perceived simultaneously by two or more people.

The majority of GHOSTS and APPARITIONS are reported by single witnesses. Nonetheless, a significant number of cases involve apparitions that are perceived simultaneously by two or more witnesses, apparently either seeing the same thing or sharing the same hallucination. At least two hundred well-attested examples had been accumulated by the societies for PSYCHICAL RESEARCH in Great Britain and the USA by 1940, and this figure has continued to increase in the years since.

In such cases the shared nature of the perception has been taken by some to be evidence of the occurrence of a paranormal event – either that there must have been an entity external to the brains of the observers, or that some form of telepathy must have taken place between them. Sceptics would contend that the 'entity' could still quite easily have been something mundane that was misperceived by all of the observers or that their interpretations of their experience may have been (consciously or subconsciously) shaped by their subsequent communication with the others involved.

control

A spirit helper who supposedly assists a medium to communicate with the dead.

Many MEDIUMS claim that they use a 'control', also known as a 'spirit guide', as a go-between for their communications within the realm of the dead. Controls are also sometimes referred to as 'spirit helpers', and they supposedly ensure a safe passage within the world of the spirits and pass messages or 'fetch' other spirits to speak to the medium.

In the 19th century, Native American SPIRITS regularly featured as controls at SÉANCES, and the spirit Katie King (sometimes together with her father,

John King, said to be the pirate Henry Morgan) supposedly assisted countless mediums throughout London – the most famous being FLORENCE COOK. Even today, the popular British television medium Derek Acorah claims to use a control called Sam.

DIRECT VOICE MEDIUMS sometimes speak in what is allegedly the voice of their control, whereas MENTAL MEDIUMS appear to hold conversations with their control, with the audience only being able to hear the medium's contribution.

Some people claim that everyone has a control or spirit guide, and the term spirit guide is often used interchangeably with 'GUARDIAN SPIRIT'.

Cook, Florence (1856–1904)

A 19th-century medium famous for apparently being able to produce full-body materializations of her control, Katie King.

Florence Cook began her career as a medium in her early teens by conducting SÉANCES for the amusement of her family and friends. With the support of a wealthy patron, she went on to perform for a great many sitters over a number of years. Initially she specialized in making faces appear at an opening in a cabinet in which she was tied up, although it was pointed out by some people at the time that the faces all bore a remarkable similarity to her own.

In 1872, she allegedly materialized a full-body SPIRIT for the first time. The figure she materialized was called Katie King – supposedly the daughter of John King, a popular 'spirit CONTROL' (that it was also claimed was the spirit of the pirate Henry Morgan) apparently manifested during many séances since the 1850s. After this initial appearance Cook continued to materialize King at séances for the public, and she was investigated thoroughly by the scientist SIR WILLIAM CROOKES (along with DANIEL DUNGLAS HOME and Kate Fox – see FOX SISTERS).

Manifestations of Katie King were carried out in poor lighting – the spirits apparently preferred this. Florence Cook would be tied up in a spirit cabinet (just a large box to hide her from sight) and eventually, after sufficient time had passed for Cook to 'build up her PSYCHIC energies' (or, as some more cynical people might suggest, free herself from the ropes and get changed into her Katie King costume), the spirit of Katie King would walk out of the cabinet. King would walk around talking to participants in the séance and allowing them to touch her. Eventually, after this display King would return to the cabinet, in which Cook would be found still bound. Over the course of his investigations Crookes produced many photographs of King and of Cook, confirming to many people the similarities between the facial features of the two. Photographs purported to be of the pair together show signs of double exposure or reflections in mirrors or do not clearly show both faces – one of them usually being covered by what was said to be ECTOPLASM.

In 1875, Katie King apparently announced that she would be leaving Florence Cook and that her time on

The medium Florence Cook lies in a trance while an alleged spirit form manifests behind her. The photograph was taken during a séance at the home of the scientist William Crookes in 1874. (© Mary Evans Picture Library)

earth was nearing an end. However, Cook returned to the world of the séance in 1880, with a new spirit named Marie. During one sitting a member of the séance noticed that Marie appeared to be wearing a corset under her spirit garb. He grabbed hold of her and opened the door to Cook's cabinet, to find it empty. He was in fact holding onto the struggling figure of Florence Cook. After this her séances dropped off in frequency and she eventually retired to Monmouthshire to live out the last of her days. Katie King, however, apparently continued to put in appearances at séances – initially in the United States, but more recently in Rome in 1974.

Corpus Christi

A college of Cambridge University, said to be haunted by Dr Butts, a former master and vice-chancellor.

The Old Court of Corpus Christi College, Cambridge, has long been linked with stories of a haunting. The GHOST is generally said to be that of Dr Henry Butts, who was master of the college from 1626 to 1632, and was also vice-chancellor when the university was struck by the plague in 1630.

It is known that Dr Butts had suffered a great deal of stress and feelings of isolation at the time of the plague – he had remained at the college when the majority of his colleagues and students had fled. As he wrote to the High Steward of Cambridge, 'It is no little ease to pour out our painful passions and plaints into such a bosom. Myself am alone; a destitute and forsaken man: not a Scholler with me in College; not a Scholler seen by me without'. Dr Butts was due to preach before the college on Easter Sunday 1632, but failed to appear. When his rooms were checked, he was found hanging by his garters, having committed suicide. His ghost is said to have haunted these rooms since that time.

It is claimed that in 1904, an undergraduate was working in his rooms one afternoon around Easter time when he became uneasy. He looked towards the rooms opposite, which had been occupied by Butts, and saw the head and shoulders of a man leaning out of an upper window. He went upstairs to get a better view, but the mysterious and hostile face had gone. The undergraduate then went across Old Court to investigate, but the rooms were locked, and he later discovered that they had been empty and locked all afternoon.

The long-haired apparition was apparently seen again, and the story goes that a group of students held a SÉANCE in order to make contact with it. It is said that while only two of the students saw the ghost, it did appear – a mistiness was seen in the air that gradually took on the form of a man with a gash across his throat. The two who could see the ghost moved towards it with a crucifix, but were repelled by an invisible force. A further séance was held, but again the students were unable to banish the ghost.

While the ghost of Corpus Christi is usually ascribed to Butts, there is another version of the tale which holds that the college is haunted by the unfortunate lover of the daughter of another previous master, Dr James Spencer. It is said that Spencer did not approve of his daughter Elisabeth's relationship with a young student, and they were forced to conduct their affair in secret. One day they were surprised by Dr Spencer, and the lover hid in a cupboard, little knowing that it could only be opened from the outside. Dr Spencer whisked his daughter away on a trip, and the lover starved to death in the cupboard. Elisabeth died some short time later, presumably of a broken heart, and while some claim that the ghost of the lover haunts the college, others say that Elisabeth haunts it too, and that the two have been seen wandering around the college together.

Cortachy, Drummer of *see*

DRUMMER OF CORTACHY

Course in Miracles, A

A book that was allegedly dictated by Jesus to Helen Schucman.

From 1965 to 1972 the New York City-based psychologist Helen Schucman claimed she had had a series of symbolic dreams. Urged to write down the content of these by her colleague, William Thetford, Schucman apparently found that when she started to do so the dreams changed and took the form of a subconscious dictation of text. When Schucman started to write, the fully-fledged text appeared in her mind, with the first words being:

> This is a course in miracles. Please take notes.

Schucman would take notes and dictate text; Thetford would then put these two sources together and type up the result. When Thetford died in early 1972 his place was taken by Kenneth and Gloria Wapnick. Later, in 1983, the Wapnicks also started the Foundation for A Course in Miracles, an organization designed to spread the word and sell the book.

The book has sold over one and a half million copies in 15 languages since its publication in 1976. It consists of three parts, the largest section is the text itself; this is then followed by a manual for students and finally a manual for teachers. Written in the first person, it claims to be the words of Jesus Christ, and the central message is essentially one of forgiveness, which will in turn lead to a greater openness to love, and to love itself.

Schucman and associates edited the book from 1973 to 1975, removing material regarded as too personal and rearranging certain sections. Several different versions of *A Course in Miracles* exist with only minor differences between them. The names of those responsible for the book do not appear on the cover as they believed it should stand on its own merits, and Schucman and her collaborators wished to avoid a cult following, preferring people to listen to their own 'inner teacher'. The Foundation offers a number of courses and there are over 2,000 self-help groups for those having difficulty following their inner teacher.

A Course in Miracles is an example of a book which has apparently been produced by CHANNELLING.

crisis apparitions

Ghosts of living individuals seen elsewhere at the moment of their death or when they are suffering a trauma.

The term 'crisis apparition' appears to have been coined by researcher D J West in 1946 when he was examining some sixty years of testimony accumulated by the SOCIETY FOR PSYCHICAL RESEARCH. In such cases the APPARITION of a person who is dying or suffering a trauma is seen or sensed by a relative or friend many miles away. Hundreds of such cases were collected by members of the society and published in a two-volume work entitled *Phantasms of the Living* (Edmund Gurney, Frederic Myers and Frank Podmore, 1886). The 19th-century reports often contained symbolic elements – such as water dripping from the body of an apparition representing a person who had drowned at sea. Of the cases recorded in *Phantasms of the Living*, many involved family relationships and in nearly a third of cases the death would be classed as sudden. Reports of crisis apparitions are now far rarer than in the 19th century – the apparitions have generally been replaced by stories of dreams or vague feelings of unease at the time of the death of a friend or relative.

William Crookes took this photograph of the spirit 'Katie King', who supposedly manifested during a séance held at his home. (© Mary Evans Picture Library)

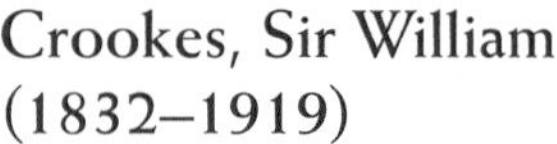

Crookes, Sir William (1832–1919)

English chemist and physicist who was also interested in psychic abilities and spiritualism.

William Crookes was born in London in 1832. He was a pupil and assistant of August Hoffman at the Royal College of Chemistry, then superintended the meteorological department of the Radcliffe Observatory, Oxford. From 1855 he lectured in chemistry at the Science College, Chester. He isolated the new metallic element thallium in 1861, and promoted electric lighting, and his work on the improvement of vacuums made the discovery of X-rays possible. He was knighted in 1897. Crookes was president of the Chemical Society (1887–89), of the Institution of Electrical Engineers (1890–94) and of the SOCIETY FOR PSYCHICAL RESEARCH (1897).

His involvement with organizations such as the Society for Psychical Research (SPR) was viewed as controversial within scientific circles. Perhaps prompted by the death of a brother, Crookes attended SÉANCES, and became convinced that some MEDIUMS showed genuine PSYCHIC abilities. He subjected Scottish psychic DANIEL DUNGLAS HOME to several tests, and was convinced that Home was a genuine medium, equipped with a number of paranormal skills. He submitted a paper to the Royal Society on the subject, but it was rejected on the grounds that the experimental procedures had been insufficiently rigorous. Crookes then reported his findings in his own publication, the *Quarterly Journal of Science*. Perhaps most controversial was Crookes's support of the medium FLORENCE COOK. Cook was famous for apparently being able to produce a full-body materialization of her CONTROL, Katie King, and while Crookes stood by the photographs he produced of King and Cook together, to others they simply showed that the two were the same person, and sceptics would suggest that the images were produced through double exposure.

Sir William Crookes was not the only scientist of the day to believe in SPIRITUALISM, but many scientists rejected it as fraudulent. Crookes retained his beliefs until the end of his life, and supported psychical research despite the criticism of his contemporaries. His best-known work in the area is *Researches in the Phenomena of Spiritualism* (1874).

cross correspondence

A proposed way to test the truth of mediumistic messages.

In the early part of the 20th century a particular series of tests was carried out in an attempt to prove or disprove the reality of the 'communications' conducted by MEDIUMS. The theory was that, if the information a medium communicates is true, then potentially any medium could, independently, communicate the same information. This agreement was described as 'cross correspondence' and, assuming of course that there was no normal means by which the parties could have gained access to the same information, examples of such agreement would be taken as confirmation of the mediums' claims.

From 1901 to 1930 a series of apparent cross correspondences between several mediums who utilized AUTOMATIC WRITING was investigated. A simple cross correspondence would involve the same words or phrase being produced, a complex cross correspondence would contain messages which would need to be interpreted and, finally, an ideal cross correspondence would involve incomplete messages which would have to be put together like a puzzle (part of the final complete message coming from each medium and, in itself, being meaningless). Some claimed these cross correspondences were indeed caused by several mediums communicating with the same SPIRIT; others claimed that this was actually evidence of telepathy. The SOCIETY FOR PSYCHICAL RESEARCH, investigated many of the cases, and tended towards the hypothesis of communication with the dead. However, despite some claims that it had produced strong evidence, the study of cross correspondences has fallen out of favour.

crossroads

The folkloric belief that crossroads are particularly haunted by supernatural entities.

In European folklore crossroads are said to have a peculiar attraction for GHOSTS and other supernatural entities, a notion perpetuated in the 20th century through the prolific writings of Elliot O'Donnell (1872–1965). Although road ghosts (see HAUNTED HIGHWAYS) are regularly reported, there is little to suggest that crossroads are actually more prone to generating such reports than other locations.

In England the uncanny reputation of crossroads was undoubtedly fuelled by their choice, until the early 19th century, as the burial place for those who had committed suicide. This was possibly due to a folk belief that the four roads would confuse any restless SPIRIT that had thwarted other traditional precautions (such as the driving of a stake through the body in order to bind it to the spot). In a Christian society the shape of the cross might also have been thought to neutralize harmful influences.

Crossroad burials were condemned in Parliament in 1813 and rendered superfluous in 1821 by an Act requiring all churchyards to have a section of unconsecrated ground reserved for the bodies of suicides. Nonetheless, the uncanny reputation of crossroads is also found in many other European cultures, including the mythology of ancient Greece, in which crossroads were sacred to Hecate, the goddess of witches. It is also noticeable that ghost lore worldwide often invests meeting points and various kinds of man-made or natural boundaries with supernatural significance.

cryptomnesia

The concept that memories can be 'hidden' in the mind in such a way that they cannot be consciously accessed.

Swiss psychologist Théodore Flournoy (1854–1920) coined the word 'cryptomnesia' to describe the (now controversial) idea of 'hidden memory' or 'concealed recollection'. The supposed hidden memories referred to cannot be consciously recalled, although some people believe that they can be recovered through processes such as hypnosis.

It is claimed that these hidden memories may be evidence for a number of paranormal phenomena, particularly REINCARNATION (see PAST-LIFE REGRESSION). However, in the case of the supposed reincarnation of BRIDEY MURPHY, many of the events recalled under regression hypnosis were found to relate to tales that Virginia Tighe had heard as a child from an Irish neighbour; so, even if the memories were 'hidden', they had quite possibly come from a mundane source. Some people have also suggested cryptomnesia as an alternative mechanism for the phenomena produced during such processes as AUTOMATIC WRITING and the apparent CHANNELLING of spirits.

Curran, Pearl *see* WORTH, PATIENCE

cyclic ghosts

Ghosts that are said to manifest repeatedly on a particular date or anniversary.

In popular tradition the GHOSTs of the dead are prone to manifest regularly on specific dates, usually the anniversary of the date on which their life ended. This is generally an annual cycle, but occasionally longer periods are claimed (eg 6, 20 or 50 years). An extensive list of examples could be compiled. For instance: Anne Boleyn is said to appear at BLICKLING HALL in Norfolk on 19 May, the anniversary of her execution; a ghostly monk named Rahere is said to appear at St Bartholomew's Church in Smithfield, London, on 1 July; on 27 July a ghostly glow is said to be seen at Killiecrankie in Perthshire on the anniversary of a battle; on 28 July a phantom nun is said to walk at BORLEY RECTORY in Essex; and on 2 August the ghost of King William Rufus is said to materialize by the Rufus Stone in the New Forest, Hampshire. Many SPECTREs are said to venture forth on Hallowe'en, but this date is soundly beaten by Christmas Eve, on which ghosts are said to appear at over 150 different locations throughout the British Isles.

Henry VIII's second wife, Anne Boleyn, is said to appear at Blickling Hall on the anniversary of her execution. (© TopFoto/HIP)

Despite the proliferation of such stories, there is little reliable evidence to suggest that ghosts follow annual anniversary cycles or come to order. GHOST HUNTING vigils organized for the specified date are notoriously disappointing for participants, and detailed research often fails to reveal any historical basis for such legends. There is no doubt that many famous anniversary ghosts (particularly those associated with the Norfolk and Suffolk Broads – see *GHOSTS OF THE BROADS*) are pure invention. Problems might also be posed by the switch from the Julian to the Gregorian calendar in 1752. This would have required many alleged anniversary ghosts to accommodate an artificial shift of eleven days into their cycle.

Nonetheless, there are indications of shorter cyclic periods at work with some better-attested ghosts. Occupants of haunted houses may note that their ghosts are more active at certain times of the day or week. Ghosts are rarely seen at breakfast time but the frequency of sightings seems to increase as the day progresses, with a peak after midnight and into the early hours of the morning. These features may simply point to the fact that the human mind is more open to PSYCHIC impressions at certain periods than at others. Subconscious expectation or other purely psychological factors may also play a crucial part. Another popular, and slightly more esoteric, suggestion is that reports of manifestations are more prevalent at the time of the waning moon. However, any firm connection with the lunar cycle has yet to be demonstrated.

D

Davenport brothers

American brothers who became well known for holding séances in both the USA and Britain in the 1860s.

Ira (1839–1911) and William (1841–77) Davenport were born in Buffalo, New York. They first held SÉANCES at home, their policeman father apparently having been intrigued by reports of SPIRIT RAPPINGS in a nearby town. The young brothers held their first public performances in around 1855. These included TABLE-TURNING and musical instruments played by the 'spirits', and the brothers soon added escapology to their repertoire. Their CONTROL was named as the popular John King, alleged father of Katie King, the control made famous by FLORENCE COOK.

While performing in New York, the brothers added their famous spirit cabinet to their show. Ostensibly introduced to prevent the Davenports from colluding with accomplices in the audience, it actually allowed the brothers to work on stage but in secret, inside the darkness of a large closet. During the course of a Davenport séance, the brothers would be placed in the spirit cabinet, and bound hand and foot, often by members of the audience. A number of items, such as musical instruments, would be placed in the cabinet with them. Once the doors to the cabinet were shut, music would be heard – apparently played by the spirits. 'Spirit' hands would also wave through a specially built aperture. The doors of the spirit cabinet would then be opened, revealing the brothers tied up as they had been at the start of the show.

The Davenports created quite a sensation – while critics thought they were nothing more than conjurers, many spiritualists embraced their abilities, believing the brothers were genuine MEDIUMS who were providing proof of spirit intervention in the living world. The brothers toured widely, acquiring an international reputation.

During a tour of Britain in 1865, the Davenports performed in Cheltenham, with the magician JOHN NEVIL MASKELYNE in the audience. Maskelyne believed he had spotted how the trick was done – he thought that the brothers

The Davenport brothers, depicted using their famous 'spirit cabinet'. (© 2003 Charles Walker/TopFoto)

escaped from their ropes, performed all the 'spirit' feats themselves, then retied the ropes before the cabinet was opened. For eight years Maskelyne toured the country, often repeating the tricks used at séances in order to discredit them.

The Davenports continued touring, taking in much of Europe before eventually travelling to Australia, where William suddenly died. Ira returned to New York, and gave up performing. While at the time many accepted the Davenports as genuine mediums, it is now generally accepted that they were clever conjurers.

dematerialization

The apparent unexplained disappearance of an object – usually used for situations where this is supposedly brought about by psychic means.

A dematerialization, or 'deport', is the opposite of a MATERIALIZATION (or APPORT) – it is the paranormal disappearance of a material object. Dematerializations of objects can reputedly occur during séances, and there have also been claims that parts of mediums have dematerialized. However, sceptics would point out that similar 'disappearances' can appear to occur in simple conjuring tricks.

devil dogs *see* BLACK DOGS

direct voice medium *see* MEDIUM, DIRECT VOICE

discarnate entity

An entity with mental attributes which exists independently of a physical body.

The concept of independent non-material beings possessing mental attributes is found in all societies. Often termed SPIRITS, they are considered to exist within the material body during life and to be capable of maintaining an independent existence after the death of the physical body. This surviving, non-material portion of an individual is considered to retain mental attributes including intention, emotion, memory and a degree of personality and self-awareness.

Discarnate entities are believed to be capable of interacting with living humans and are often proposed as the explanation for many PSYCHIC phenomena including GHOSTS, POLTERGEISTS, possession states and many spiritualist manifestations – the 'discarnate entity theory'. They also form a part of many religious and occult traditions and in some belief systems spirits are joined by various other classes of non-human discarnate entities such as angels, demons and elementals.

From a materialist perspective, there are major scientific and philosophical objections to the idea of discarnate entities, not least the question of how mental processes of any sort could be maintained in the complete absence of a body, brain or nervous system. Even as an explanation for many psychic phenomena, the concept of the discarnate entity runs into problems. For example, at SÉANCES discarnate entities are deemed capable of responding to verbal questions from sitters. But by what mechanism could a discarnate being actually hear such questions being put and, indeed, if there is a non-physical mechanism through which it receives the question, why must the questions be spoken aloud at all? There is also the general question of how a discarnate entity would interact with the physical world to produce raps, APPARITIONS or other physical phenomena.

However, many people would also argue that the materialist model of human consciousness offered by mainstream science is still incomplete, and so the possibility of forms of consciousness existing outside the living human brain cannot be unreservedly dismissed. It must also be said that many traditions do not recognize firm distinctions between material and discarnate forms of existence, and accept both as aspects of a single spiritual reality. Even some of the theories of modern physics ultimately challenge the simplistic, commonsense concept of the solid, material world – leaving scope for forms of non-physical or even (as yet uncomprehended) physical existence to be postulated.

disembodied voices

Anomalous voices which occur without identifiable physical cause.

Human-sounding voices lacking any identifiable physical cause are a class of spontaneous manifestation common in PSYCHIC literature. They are reported at HAUNTED HOUSES and other locations, during SÉANCE communications and in the form of anomalous recordings obtained on magnetic tape, where they are known as ELECTRONIC VOICE PHENOMENA (EVP).

In HAUNTINGS, disembodied voices are often reported as appearing to re-enact past events. Typical is the 1888 account of a Mrs Gilby who heard a voice declare 'Oh do forgive me' three times in her bedroom in a rented house in Brighton, accompanied by unexplained sounds including human sobs and cries. She was apparently neither the first nor the last occupant to experience strange sounds in the house, and the occurrences eventually drove her and her children from the property. The SOCIETY FOR PSYCHICAL RESEARCH collected reports of strange noises from five other sets of residents but at no point did any entity attempt to communicate, suggesting to them that it was an echo of a past tragedy in the house.

In other cases, disembodied voices seem to be directed at living human persons. Such voices may enter into apparent communication, give warnings, guidance or commands or impart information. As with AUDITORY HALLUCINATIONS (the category that some would argue many apparent disembodied voice manifestations fall into), such voices may be interpreted in many ways – as messages from SPIRITS, angels, demons or even extraterrestrial beings for example. Alternatively, it has been proposed that such voices may represent examples of telepathy or psychic projections from the subconscious minds of living persons.

doppelgänger

A term which comes from Germanic folklore and refers to an apparitional double of a still living person.

The term 'doppelgänger' is a German word meaning 'double-goer'. The best-known doppelgänger story from German literature is that of the 18th-century poet and dramatist Johann Wolfgang von Goethe, who is said to have met his own double while out riding one day. His double was wearing a grey suit with gold embroidery, which Goethe did not then possess. It did not foretell his death; rather it seemed to be a representation of his future state – some eight years later Goethe found himself riding at the same spot wearing identical clothing.

Some authorities restrict the term doppelgänger to those cases where the double is seen only by the person of whom it is an image, and usually only where it is in close proximity. In

Arthur Rackham's illustration of the character William Wilson meeting his doppelgänger, from Edgar Allan Poe's *Tales of Mystery ...* (1935 edition). (© Mary Evans Picture Library)

folklore, seeing one's doppelgänger is sometimes (but not always) considered to be an omen of death. The category would appear to merge with other classes of apparitional DOUBLES, GHOSTS OF THE LIVING and the phenomenon of BILOCATION. However, on the strict understanding of the term given above, it may well be difficult ever to establish that doppelgängers are a genuine paranormal phenomenon. In addition to the problem of corroborating the testimony of witnesses, it is also the case that people with a number of conditions, including epilepsy, migraines and certain neurological disorders, sometimes report encounters with a hallucinatory second self, appearing either whole or in part, among their symptoms. See also FETCH.

doubles

Apparitions of a living person which are exact duplicates.

'Doubles' is the term used for GHOSTS OF THE LIVING where the phantom 'copy' is perceived to be exactly the same as the original – even to the point of being dressed like them. Traditionally such doubles were considered to be an outward manifestation of the idea that each human individual possesses a non-physical component in the form of a SPIRIT or soul, or what some occultists might call an etheric or astral body (see ASTRAL PROJECTION). In Scotland such doubles were known as 'co-walkers', and in *The Secret Commonwealth* (1691), Rev Robert Kirk describes them as being 'in every way like the Man, as a Twin brother and companion, haunting him as a shadow, both before and after the original is dead'.

Stories of apparitional doubles were common during the 19th century. In 1810 Sir Robert Peel believed he saw his friend Lord Byron walking in a London street. Later he saw him again while in the company of the poet's brother, who also agreed that it was him. In fact Byron was in Turkey at the time. The most celebrated case from the period is that of a 32-year-old French schoolteacher named Amelie Saegee, who taught in Latvia and was reputedly seen as a double by pupils on a number of occasions. Such stories continued to be popular through to the 1890s. Examples were discussed at length in the spiritualist magazine *Borderland*, whose editor, W T Stead, claimed to have witnessed a number of doubles himself.

There also exists a collection of (mostly 19th-century) cases suggesting that individuals may be able to project themselves in the form of an APPARITION visible to others (see ASTRAL PROJECTION). However, as with CRISIS APPARITIONS, such cases have declined in the 20th century – some might contend that this is due to lack of experimentation. See also DOPPELGÄNGER; BILOCATION.

Doyle, Sir Arthur Conan (1859–1930)

Famous Scottish author who was greatly interested in all aspects of the paranormal.

Sir Arthur Conan Doyle is best known as a writer, particularly for his creation of the detective Sherlock Holmes, but he was also a committed spiritualist and defender of many paranormal claims – to the extent that when Margaret Fox, of the FOX SISTERS, confessed that their SÉANCES were faked, he stated that there was nothing they could say that would change his opinion of the reality of the spiritual world. He was a close friend of HARRY HOUDINI, despite their polar views on the subject of SPIRITUALISM – Houdini was a confirmed sceptic. In *The Edge of the Unknown* (1930), Conan Doyle states his belief that Houdini had PSYCHIC powers but would simply not admit it.

Conan Doyle's wife Jean was said to be an accomplished MEDIUM, and she conducted a séance for Houdini in which his mother was supposedly called from the spirit world. Conan Doyle took Houdini's mood afterwards to be one of shock at having his beliefs torn apart – it was in fact fury at his great friend. Houdini had not wanted the séance to take place and, when it did, he was angered by the use of his mother – she communicated in perfect English using Christian imagery, neither of which would be likely for a Hungarian Jew.

Conan Doyle's interest in spiritualism had been greatly increased by the death of his son in World War I, and in his later years it took on the form of an evangelical crusade. It has been observed that Conan Doyle, famous for creating the ultimate investigator, could be quite 'unobjective' when confronted with disagreeable evidence himself.

Drummer of Cortachy

Ghostly drumming heard at Cortachy Castle, Scotland, said to presage the death of a member of the Ogilvy family.

Cortachy Castle, in Angus, Scotland, is the family seat of the Ogilvys, the Earls of Airlie. According to a legend that dates back to medieval times, a messenger arrived at the castle one day only to be stuffed into his own drum and thrown down from the castle walls – whether because he had arrived with unpleasant news or due to his affiliation with an enemy clan is not known. The legend states that before the drummer perished, he vowed to haunt the Ogilvys for evermore, and it is claimed that for hundreds of years after this the family was haunted by his ghostly drumming, always heard shortly before a member of the family died.

Most famously, the drumming was allegedly heard at the Christmas of 1844. A Miss Dalrymple was staying at the castle, and as she prepared herself for dinner she heard the drummer, and later asked her hosts, the Earl of Airlie and his wife the Countess of Airlie, where the sound had come from. They told her of the legend, and when Miss Dalrymple heard the sound of drumming again on the following day she is said to have been so afraid that she ended her visit early and left the castle. The Countess of Airlie died six months later, in Brighton, and some claim that she had believed that the drumming was for her.

Another guest at the castle is said to have heard the drumming in 1849, the day before the 9th (or 4th) Earl of Airlie died. However, no one claimed to hear the sound of the drum before the death of the 11th (or 6th) Earl of Airlie in 1900, when he was killed in action in the Boer War, and no further claims exist of the ghostly drummer. Some believe that the curse had run its course, others that the drumming had been an example of POLTERGEIST activity that simply ceased, and there are those that hold that the Drummer of Cortachy is nothing more than a family legend.

Drummer of Tedworth

A famous 17th-century English poltergeist case.

The 17th-century case of the Demon Drummer of Tedworth (now Tidworth)

An illustration depicting the Drummer of Tedworth, from Joseph Glanvill's *Saducismus Triumphatus* (first published in 1861). (© Topfoto)

in Wiltshire is one of the more convincing early modern POLTERGEIST accounts.

The occurrences began in March 1661 at the house of John Mompesson, a local magistrate, who had recently tried an itinerant conjurer named William Drury. A drum possessed by Drury was confiscated and, on being banished from the area, he supposedly uttered curses against Mompesson and his household. Soon after this, Mompesson's house was disturbed by rapping and booming sounds followed by a range of other phenomena that would now be recognized as typical of alleged poltergeist cases. Objects were moved, children were pestered and levitated from their beds and unexplained animal noises were heard in the house. A DISEMBODIED VOICE was reportedly heard crying 'a witch, a witch' over a hundred times and the raps and knocks became particularly intense, with drumming sounds continuing for days on end. There were also a number of other bizarre incidents, such as the coins in the pockets of a visitor to the house being turned black.

The disturbances at the house lasted more than a year and were investigated by the royal chaplain Joseph Glanvill, who visited the house and heard the noises for himself. Glanvill also traced other witnesses and related the events in his book *Saducismus Triumphatus* (1681), which is now hailed as a classic of early PSYCHICAL RESEARCH. The phenomena were attributed at the time to sorcery on the part of Drury, who was duly tried as a witch and transported. According to later tales, the penal ship carrying him abroad was supposedly disturbed by storms conjured by him in further acts of witchcraft.

Many modern psychical researchers cite the Drummer of Tedworth as a classic poltergeist case because the phenomena occurred in the presence of young children approaching puberty (a common theme in more recent cases). There have also been a number of other theories based on the suggestions that Drury was of Roma ancestry, or possibly even a Siberian shaman, who possessed knowledge of how to induce fits and trance states by means of ritual drumming.

Drury Lane *see* THEATRE ROYAL

ectoplasm

Ectoplasm is a hypothetical substance of which it is suggested materializations of spirits within the physical world are constituted.

The word 'ectoplasm' comes from the Greek *ektos*, meaning 'outside', and *plasma*, meaning 'something moulded'. It is the hypothetical substance which allows ghosts to materialize and interact with the world of the living. An early name for this material was 'teleplasmic mass' – 'ectoplasm' was coined in the latter part of the 19th century by either the German doctor Albert Freiherr von Schrenck-Notzing or the Nobel Prize-winning French physiologist Charles Richet.

During 19th- and early 20th-century SÉANCES, ectoplasm (which was generally white) regularly appeared from every orifice of many physical mediums (see MEDIUM, PHYSICAL), and was taken by many spiritualists as proof of the existence of spirits. MATERIALIZATIONS took many forms – ranging from amorphous blobs and strings through to hands and eventually full figures with faces. It was believed that the spirits could mould the ectoplasm as it emanated from the body of the medium. Some of the ectoplasm glowed in the dark, and one investigator who attended a séance found that after being tapped by an ectoplasmic hand he had a spot on his arm which continued to glow some 20 minutes later.

Spiritualism and photography achieved prominence at a similar time, and many new photographic techniques were employed in an attempt to photograph ectoplasm and thus prove (or disprove) its existence (see SPIRIT PHOTOGRAPHY). Many photographs of ectoplasm were taken and hailed by some spiritualists as proof positive of the existence of the spirit world. However, it has been suggested that many mediums were unaware of the capabilities of the cameras that were used, as the ectoplasm in photographs showed more clearly than it did in the darkened séance room, and many of these photographs appear preposterous, with the

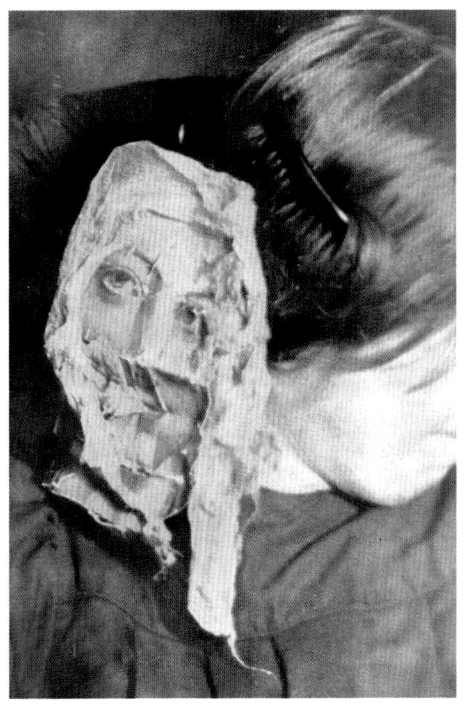

A medium manifesting a face during a séance in 1912. It was claimed that the spirit image was formed from ectoplasm which had been exuded from her ear.
(© TopFoto/Fortean)

ectoplasmic spirit looking very similar to various man-made concoctions – often cardboard and muslin.

From the 1930s onwards, scientific investigations into ectoplasm meant mediums were thoroughly searched to ensure that no material had been secreted about their person prior to the séance. To reduce embarrassment, a séance garment was invented which covered everything except the head of the medium. However, this did not help when ectoplasm was fraudulently produced via regurgitation or with the aid of an accomplice in the séance room. From around the same time as these investigations, the appearance of ectoplasm at séances became less and less frequent.

Edgehill, Battle of

The first major battle of the English Civil War; fought at Edgehill, between

Banbury and Stratford-upon-Avon, it is said to have been re-enacted in the sky at subsequent Christmas-times.

The Battle of Edgehill took place on 23 October 1642. In January 1643 a pamphlet appeared describing the ghostly re-enactment of the battle, as witnessed by shepherds on Christmas Eve:

> Between twelve and one of the clock in the morning was heard by some sheepherds, and other countrey-men, and travellers, first the sound of drummes afar off, and the noyse of souldiers, as it were, giving out their last groanes; at which they were much amazed ... But then, on the sudden ... appeared in the ayre those same incorporeall souldiers that made those clamours, and immediately, with Ensignes display'd, Drummes beating, Musquets going off, Cannons discharged, horses neyghing (which also to these men were visible), the alarum or entrance to this game of death was struck up ... Till two or three in the morning, in equal scale continued this dreadful fight.

According to the pamphleteer, the witnesses reported the vision of these AERIAL PHANTOMS to a clergyman and a magistrate, swearing oaths that they were telling the truth:

> And so, suspending their judgements till the next night about the same houre, they, with the same men, and all the substantiall Inhabitants of that and neighbouring parishes, drew thither; where, about halfe an houre after their arrivall, on Sunday, being Christmas night, appeared in the same tumultuous warlike manner, the same two adverse Armies, fighting with as much spite and spleen as formerly; and so departed the Gentlemen and all the spectatours, much terrified with these visions of horrour, withdrew themselves to their houses, beseeching God to defend them.

The pamphlet goes on to say that when Charles I heard of the events, he sent men to investigate, but no reliable record or account of this has ever been discovered. While some claim that the battle can still, periodically, be witnessed in the sky above Edgehill (particularly it now seems on the anniversary of the battle rather than at Christmas), and witnesses have reported seeing individual ghosts on the battlefield, many investigators believe that it is simply a ghost story. See also NASEBY, BATTLE OF; SOUTHER FELL; SPECTRAL ARMIES.

Edinburgh's vaults

Supposedly haunted underground passageways and chambers in Edinburgh that were chosen for experiments in 2003.

The South Bridge Vaults in Edinburgh were selected in 2003 for a series of experiments, conducted by Dr Richard Wiseman of the University of Hertford, to record the reactions of people in supposedly haunted places. The vaults are one of a number of sites that are reputed to be haunted, in a city which claims a high spectral population. Celebrated GHOSTs above and below the city are said to include Major Weir (who was a 17th-century witch), a phantom monk, a sad-looking beggar, a woman in 18th-century costume and an invisible entity dubbed 'the McKenzie poltergeist' at the Greyfriars Cemetery. These and other stories have featured in numerous ghost tours conducted around the city since 1985 – with particularly spine-chilling manifestations being associated with the vaults beneath the city. Built in the late 18th century, the vaults are said to be haunted by a boy who pulls at clothing and by a 'Mr Boots' who pushes people and whispers obscenities.

Some 250 volunteers took part in the tests, and the results were published in May 2003 in the *British Journal of Psychology*. The findings suggested that a substantial number of people were prone to interpret areas with naturally occurring cold spots, poor lighting or strong magnetic fields as haunted locations. Some participants reported strong feelings of anxiety but little was recorded in the way of visual APPARITIONS. Similar experiments were also conducted at HAMPTON COURT PALACE. Wiseman postulated that ghost experiences might be a form of warning triggered by a person's subconscious mind in response to claustrophobic situations or to slight sensory perceptions which indicate a possible danger. Added to the effects of suggestion, this theory may explain the many complaints of distressing sensations and hysteria experienced by visitors in a vault in the Greyfriars Cemetery since the end of the 1990s.

While it confirms that people may feel uneasy in spooky locations, the theory fails to address the fact that reported ghost encounters are more likely to occur in mundane settings (such as ordinary houses or offices) than in romantic and dramatic locations (such as stately homes or castle dungeons). Furthermore, in accounts of apparitions (for example, the MORTON GHOST) they usually appear when least expected and not when observers are agitated.

electronic voice phenomena

Apparently mysterious voices captured using electronic audio equipment.

Electronic voice phenomena (EVP) are voices that appear on audio recording media (originally tape) for which there is no known source and which some claim to be voices from the spirit world.

In the 1920s, Thomas Edison suggested in an interview for *Scientific American* that it might be possible to construct a machine that could record the voices of the spirit world. Little was done in this field until 1959, when the Latvian-born Swedish singer, painter and film producer Friedrich Jürgenson made a recording of nocturnal bird song. When he played the tape back he heard what he believed to be a Norwegian voice discussing the nocturnal habits of birds, when no one had been present. At the time, Jürgenson believed he had inadvertently picked up a radio broadcast, but some time later he believed he had recorded the DISEMBODIED VOICE of his dead mother speaking directly to him. Jürgenson went on to make hundreds of recordings, and in 1964 published his findings in *Voices from the Universe*. The Latvian psychologist Konstantin Raudive heard of this work, and he too began recording 'spirit' voices. He did much to popularize this area and for a time EVP were known as 'Raudive voices'.

Latvian psychologist Konstantin Raudive with the apparatus he used to record electronic voice phenomena. (© TopFoto/Fortean)

Recordings are made either by simply allowing audio equipment to record, or by recording a radio which has been detuned, in other words when it is picking up only static or white noise. Such recordings are then listened to carefully, often at different speeds, until the 'voices' are picked up. Thousands of alleged voices have been recorded in experiments in Europe and the USA over the last four decades. The voices are difficult to hear and interpret and even the language being spoken is in doubt in many cases. Messages are frequently short, nonsensical or banal in content, though occasionally researchers have reported receiving lucid and coherent statements in response to spoken questions.

Sceptics maintain that the voices can be explained without recourse to the paranormal: they could represent interference from various radio sources, previously recorded material not fully erased from the tape or simply the desire of the listener to hear voices when none are there.

Instrumental Transcommunication (ITC) is the term used to cover all forms of attempted electronic communication with the dead. See also SPIRICOM.

Enfield Poltergeist

Famous British poltergeist case from the late 1970s that attracted a great deal of media interest.

What is probably the best-known British POLTERGEIST event took place in a semi-detached council house in Enfield, North London, in 1977 and

1978. Its fame stems mostly from the fact that, as the following bizarre events unfolded, they were covered in great detail by the media.

The occupants of the house were the Harper family – Mrs Harper (a divorcée in her forties), her two sons and her two daughters. The occurrences that were to turn into an ordeal lasting some 14 months started on 31 August 1977, when the younger daughter, Janet, and her brother, Pete, told their mother that their beds had been shaken and furniture had moved by itself. Mrs Harper later saw for herself the movement of a heavy dresser, which then stubbornly refused to be replaced in its original position. The Harpers went to their neighbours for help, and the police were called – one of the officers later offering a statement to the effect that they had heard a strange knocking sound and witnessed the mysterious movement of a chair.

The phenomena continued – furniture slid around the floors, knocks came from the walls and toys flew through the air. The Harpers and their neighbours turned unsuccessfully to the local vicar, MEDIUMS, the council and again to the police. Finally they contacted the tabloid newspaper the *Daily Mail*. Despite being assaulted by flying marbles, a reporter and photographer from the newspaper

Investigator Maurice Grosse with a collection of the objects involved in the Enfield Poltergeist case. (© TopFoto/Fortean)

spent several days covering the story, which eventually made the front page (under the title 'The House of Strange Happenings') on 10 September. One of the *Daily Mail* reporters contacted the SOCIETY FOR PSYCHICAL RESEARCH on the family's behalf. Investigators Maurice Grosse and Guy Lyon Playfair reported witnessing many of the unusual occurrences first-hand (recording over 400 in total), although unexplained malfunctions in their hi-tech equipment interfered with their results and prevented them obtaining any conclusive photographs.

It became clear from the investigation that this was very much a 'classic' poltergeist case in that the events appeared to be centred on an adolescent girl, in this case Janet (aged 11) and to a lesser extent her older sister Rose (aged 13). A wide range of phenomena were recorded, including knocking sounds (with which the investigators were able to establish a form of communication by asking questions and receiving a set number of knocks for yes or no), moving objects, flying objects, spontaneous fires, falls of coins, flows of water, electrical disturbances affecting recording equipment and a force which could throw the girls from their beds. *Daily Mail* photographer Graham Morris did manage to achieve some success in capturing these goings-on, including a famous sequence of frames showing the bedclothes apparently being pulled by unseen hands from one of the girl's beds as she lay beneath them.

As the investigation progressed an entity (or entities) apparently manifested itself (or themselves) in the form of a deep, gruff voice which appeared to emanate from Janet. Opinion was divided among the investigators (including a ventriloquist called in by the *Daily Mail*) as to how the voice was produced and as to whether Janet was producing it deliberately. It seems likely that the voice came from a part of the larynx known as the false vocal folds. However, if this was the case, how an adolescent girl could sustain the voice for hours on end (when it would normally hurt after just a few seconds) remains something of a mystery. The voice regularly used obscene language and on at least one occasion implied that it belonged to a deceased local resident.

The occurrence of the phenomena, whether produced as a hoax by the children (as they certainly were on occasion later in the investigation) or of supernatural origin, seemed to be exacerbated by the tension within the family. This was added to greatly by the constant intrusive presence of the investigators and the intense media interest (the case was even reported on by the prime-time BBC programme *Nationwide*). The phenomena reached a peak at around the time of Janet's first period, on the first day of which she was reportedly seen flying round her bedroom by several passers-by in the street outside. She also claimed to have gone through the wall to the house next door (where one of her books was later found by the neighbour).

The poltergeist activity, and the media interest, gradually waned over the months that followed. The true cause of the occurrences remains a matter for debate.

epicentre

The person or object upon which paranormal phenomena are centred, particularly in poltergeist cases.

In the majority of POLTERGEIST cases a living human individual (quite often a person under stress), rather than a place, seems to be the focus for disturbances (see HAUNTED PEOPLE). For example, in the case of the MIAMI POLTERGEIST in 1967, the US researcher William Roll concluded that the epicentre of the disturbances in a warehouse was a 19-year-old Cuban refugee named Julio, who was working as a shipping clerk. After studying the flight paths of displaced objects, Roll tentatively suggested that the force moved in an anti-clockwise direction around the focus. The phenomena may even follow the individual from place to place. For example, in *Apparitions* (1942), G N M Tyrrell cites the case of an English cook who seemed to be accompanied by crashing sounds in successive homes.

In other cases the epicentre may be an object with alleged supernatural significance, but reliable evidence for such effects is scarce. See also AGENCY.

Epworth Parsonage Poltergeist

A well-attested 18th-century poltergeist which afflicted the family of John Wesley, the founder of Methodism.

The mysterious noises at Epworth Parsonage, Lincolnshire, the home of the Wesley family, occurred during December 1716 and January 1717. The events were recorded in family letters and in the diary of Rev Samuel Wesley, John Wesley's father. There were a number of extraordinary noises, including numerous raps, rumblings, vibrations and groans and a noise 'like a nightgown sweeping along the ground'. The knocks interrupted family prayers, and it is recorded that these

'Old Jeffrey's' room at Epworth Parsonage. (© 2005 Charles Walker/ TopFoto)

included prayers for the King. Animal APPARITIONS were also apparently witnessed.

The sceptical writer Trevor Hall proposed that the disturbances were caused by a servant prankster who was never detected – but this theory is hard to reconcile with an account by Jack Wesley, who recorded that the noises '... very often seemed in the air in the middle of a room, nor could they [the household] ever make such themselves by any contrivance'. The phenomena were variously attributed to SPIRITS or witchcraft, and the entity was dubbed 'Old Jeffrey'. Samuel Wesley rebuffed suggestions that the family should flee the house, and his judgement proved to have been sound when the phenomena ceased within two months. Sacheverell Sitwell noted in his book *Poltergeists* (1940) that a number of classic POLTERGEISTS were given names which were variants of Jeff or Jeffrey (see also GEF THE TALKING MONGOOSE) and suggested that the case encouraged a tradition of poltergeists in non-conformist Christian households.

EVP *see* ELECTRONIC VOICE PHENOMENA

Fancher, Mollie (1848–1916)

Known as 'The Brooklyn Enigma' or 'The Fasting Girl', Mollie Fancher apparently ate very little for 50 years and some claim that she channelled five different personalities.

Mollie Fancher led a relatively uneventful life until she was removed from her school, the Brooklyn Heights Seminary, in 1864. She was suffering from dyspepsia – extreme indigestion – as well as probable anorexia and fainting spells. After a prescribed cure of rest was unsuccessful a doctor recommended the opposite – exercise. During this course of exercise Fancher was thrown from a horse, breaking two ribs and striking her head in the process. In June 1865, after her convalescence, Mollie suffered a second, more serious accident, when her dress was caught on the streetcar she was alighting from and she was dragged along for a considerable distance.

After a brief spell when she was not bedridden in late 1865, Fancher spent the rest of her life in bed. Over the following years Fancher suffered from a wide range of maladies. She experienced her first trance in 1866, and is said, in that year, to have fallen into a trance that lasted nine years – this being the period in which she became most famed for extraordinary feats. Although she was almost completely immobilized, Fancher is said to have written 6,500 letters, prepared a great deal of worsted, carried out fine embroidery, fashioned delicate wax flowers and kept a diary.

In 1875, Mollie lapsed into a coma lasting a month and upon awakening she had amnesia of all the events of the preceding nine years. Fancher now showed apparent psychic abilities, including CHANNELLING five personalities – Sunbeam, Idol, Rosebud, Pearl and Ruby. It was also reported that Fancher ate almost nothing and went for periods of three months without the need to use any toilet facilities, and that she was clairvoyant and clairaudient (see CLAIRVOYANCE; CLAIRAUDIENCE).

Mollie Fancher was investigated by spiritualists and doctors alike, and the reports polarized popular feeling. Some felt she was faking; some that she was a miracle worker. Noted showman P T Barnum attempted to pay her to appear as one of his attractions, such was her fame.

She was said to have been visited by over 100,000 people, all curious to see the famous Fasting Girl.

fetch

A form of apparitional double of a person that is said to be seen when they are close to death.

In Celtic folklore, it is believed that the phantom DOUBLE of a person may be seen when they are near to death. Such a belief is a variation of the German concept of the DOPPELGÄNGER, and some have suggested that it may have arisen from early reports of CRISIS APPARITIONS.

The antiquarian John Aubrey recorded a number of accounts of fetches in his work *Miscellanies* (1696), including cases of individuals who met their spectral doubles in the grounds of Holland House, London, shortly before their lives ended. Aubrey also recounted the case of a Sir William Napier, who experienced a vision of his own corpse lying upon a bed at an inn while he was on a journey to Berkshire. Although he was in seemingly good health, he died within a few days of arriving at his destination.

However, a fetch may not always be a harbinger of death – according to Irish tradition much depends on the time of day the fetch is seen. If it is witnessed early in the morning it is considered to foretell a long life.

flows

Paranormal manifestations in the form of mysterious flows of water and other liquids.

The idea of supernaturally induced flows of blood or water is a popular motif in folklore and fiction. It also arises in accounts of miracles associated with images of the Virgin Mary and many Christian saints, particularly in Catholic countries.

In Great Britain, many ancient houses display supposedly indelible stains purported to have arisen from murders in the past, and certain stones, grave markers and relics are said to bleed on the anniversary of heinous crimes. For example, the tombstone of Richard Smith, reputedly murdered at Hinckley, Leicestershire, in 1726, is said to become wet with blood on the anniversary of his death each year on 12 April, and the SCREAMING SKULL of BETTISCOMBE MANOR, Dorset, is said to have sweated blood before World War I. However, reliable testimony for flows of blood in haunted houses is scant – such stories seem to be confined to folklore and horror fiction.

There is better-attested evidence of the mysterious appearance of water and other liquids in POLTERGEIST cases. Flows of water and paraffin oil were reported during a poltergeist outbreak at Swanton Novers Rectory in Norfolk in 1919, where the disturbances appeared to be linked to a teenage serving-maid. In 1963, flows and pools of water appeared without explanation in a family home in Somerset during a poltergeist case that

An artist's rendition of a sighting of the ghostly *Flying Dutchman*, published in *Century* magazine (July 1894). (© Mary Evans Picture Library)

was investigated by Tony Cornell for the SOCIETY FOR PSYCHICAL RESEARCH. Pools of water were also reported during the ENFIELD POLTERGEIST case.

Flying Dutchman

A legendary ghost ship which inspired an opera by Wagner.

According to popular legend, the *Flying Dutchman* is a ship that was doomed to sail the oceans of the world for eternity because of crimes committed by its captain. Several versions of the story are known. In one version, popularized by Richard Wagner in the opera *Der Fliegende Holländer* in 1843, the vessel was captained by a man named Hendrik Vanderdecken, who cursed God and was condemned to sail the seas until doomsday.

The waters around the Cape of Good Hope have long been associated with alleged sightings of the *Flying Dutchman*, but another version of the story places the vessel in the northern seas. In this version, the captain was a nobleman by the name of Falkenburg, who murdered his brother and his bride in a fit of jealous passion. As a consequence he was condemned to sail the northern oceans in a GHOST SHIP in which evil spirits play dice for his soul. According to Sir Walter Scott, a sighting of the *Flying Dutchman* is a portent of death and disaster for those sailors who witness it. The legend of the *Flying Dutchman* was the subject of a popular stage show involving the use of magic lanterns in England in the 1820s and also inspired the story *The Phantom Ship* (1839) by Captain Marryat.

It has been claimed that as a young naval rating in 1880, the future King George V witnessed an APPARITION of the *Flying Dutchman* while aboard the flagship *Inconstant* off the coast of Australia. However, careful scrutiny of relevant diary entries reveals that the alleged experience was actually that of thirteen other seamen, who reported seeing:

> A strange red light as of a phantom ship all aglow, on the midst of which light the masts, spars and sails of a brig 200 yards distant stood out in strong relief as she came up on the port bow.

The vision may have been a mirage, an optical illusion, an effect involving phosphorescence or even an effect created by a magic lantern. Nonetheless, it was taken seriously as an omen of death, and the sailor who first sighted the phantom ship reportedly died shortly afterwards in an accident.

Fodor, Nandor (1895–1964)

Hungarian-born psychoanalyst and psychical researcher.

Born in Berengszasz, Hungary, Nandor Fodor first studied law, then worked as a journalist which took him to New York. While there he became interested in psychical research after reading *Modern Psychic Phenomena* (1919) by Hereward Carrington. Through meeting Sandor Ferenczi, an associate of Sigmund Freud, and interviewing him in 1926, he became interested in psychoanalysis. His later research reflected this interest, as Fodor applied psychoanalysis to his studies of psychical phenomena.

In 1928 Fodor moved to London and became involved in SPIRITUALISM. In 1935 he was appointed research officer of the recently formed International Institute for Psychical Research, and in that same year he became London correspondent to the American Society for Psychical Research. These positions allowed Fodor to investigate numerous MEDIUMS, POLTERGEISTS and HAUNTINGS, He was seen as somewhat controversial – psychoanalysis was not well regarded in Britain at that time, and spiritualists resented the implication that SÉANCE-room phenomena might be explainable in worldly terms – but his work eventually became influential.

Fodor's most notable investigations include the ASH MANOR ghost, the THORNTON HEATH POLTERGEIST and the BALTIMORE POLTERGEIST. At Ash Manor, Fodor concluded that suppressed sexual energies had contributed to the haunting; in the Thornton Heath case he believed that a woman's emotional problems were the cause of the phenomena; and at Baltimore, Fodor believed he 'cured' the poltergeist outbreak by increasing a teenager's feelings of self-worth.

Fodor was increasingly criticized by

the spiritualists, and in 1938 he sued the spiritualist newspaper *Psychic News*. He was dismissed from his post at the International Institute for Psychical Research, and returned to the USA, where he felt his ideas would have a more receptive audience. Fodor became a successful psychoanalyst, and editor of the *Psychoanalytic Review*. He also worked with the Irish medium EILEEN GARRETT, whom he had met in Britain, and contributed articles to her journal *Tomorrow*.

Fodor wrote widely on psychical research and poltergeists. His best-known works include *An Encyclopedia of Psychic Science* (1934), *Haunted People* (1951) and *On the Trail of the Poltergeist* (1958).

Fox sisters

Internationally famous mediums who sparked the modern spiritualism movement by claiming that they had achieved direct two-way communication with the dead.

In 1848, the Fox family were living in a small house in Hydesville, New York. The house already had a reputation for being haunted when they moved there, and in March of that year the family reported hearing strange noises and rapping sounds during the night. It was claimed by their mother that, on the night of 31 March, the two youngest daughters, Margaret (Margaretta, 1836–93) and Kate (Catherine, 1838–92), began communicating with whatever was causing these noises by use of a code – this was apparently started by Kate issuing the challenge 'Mr Splitfoot, do as I do' and clapping her hands. Margaret followed suit and over time, in front of various neighbours, the family proceeded to ask questions, which were correctly answered with rapping noises. The daughters eventually claimed that they had established that the entity was the SPIRIT of a pedlar called Charles B Rosma, who had been murdered and buried in the cellar of the house some years earlier.

The girls were sent away to Rochester. Kate went to stay with her elder sister, Leah, and Margaret was sent to her brother's home – but apparently the noises followed them. Stories of their abilities soon spread and they started to hold public demonstrations, initially at private SÉANCES but then in music halls and theatres. Leah Fox took on the job of managing her two younger sisters in their capacity as public MEDIUMS. They eventually moved in high circles on both sides of the Atlantic, greatly impressing, among others, the scientist William Crookes. While others had claimed to be able to contact the dead, the Fox sisters were the first to claim a direct two-way communication with the 'other side'. Communication with spirits took the world by storm, and the modern SPIRITUALISM movement was born as a direct result.

However, by 1888 alcoholism was taking its toll on both Kate and Margaret, leading them into difficulties in their relationships with their older sister and other members of the spiritualist community. Leah had given

The Fox sisters apparently demonstrate their powers by causing a table to levitate. From Louis Figuier, *Mystères de la Science* (c.1850). (© 2004 Fortean/TopFoto)

up managing her two younger sisters, and embarked on her own career as a medium. While the two sisters were at this low ebb, a reporter offered $1,500 to Margaret and Kate for an exposé of their methods. On the night of 21 October 1888 Margaret performed at the New York Academy of Music, with Kate in the audience. Margaret showed how a simple cracking of the joints of her toes could produce a sound loud enough to be heard throughout the whole theatre. This had been put forward as a possible explanation for the rapping sounds in 1851 but no one had been able to prove it until this admission was made. In 1889, Margaret retracted her confession and returned to the world of the séance. Kate had never stopped performing, although she had been badly affected by her sister's confession. Both Kate and Margaret died within a few years and were buried in paupers' graves.

In 1904, the house where it all began was taken down and moved from Hydesville to be reconstructed in Lily Dale, a spiritualist community in New York State. During the move a skeleton was discovered buried in the basement, apparently substantiating the sisters' original claims. However, no record of a missing person named Charles B Rosma has ever been found.

funerals, phantom *see* PHANTOM FUNERALS

G

Garrett, Eileen (1893–1970)

Celebrated Irish-born trance medium, known among other things for her association with the R101 airship disaster.

Eileen Garrett was born in County Meath in 1893. She apparently had clairvoyant experiences as a child, seeing and interacting with a deceased relative, and as an adult she attended meetings at the London Spiritualist Alliance. During one of these meetings she entered a trance, and saw the deceased relatives of other members of the group. During a visit to a hypnotist, Garrett again fell into a trance, this time revealing a CONTROL called Uvani. She returned to the London Spiritualist Alliance, and was introduced to HARRY PRICE's National Laboratory of Psychical Research. In 1930, she was famously involved in the R101 AIRSHIP DISASTER, working with Price and apparently communicating with a dead airman. Her association with the case did much to enhance her reputation as a medium.

In 1931, she travelled to the USA to participate in research being carried out by the American Society for Psychical Research, and she was later involved in experiments into extrasensory perception with influential parapsychologist J B Rhine at Duke University in North Carolina. She was in Britain again in 1936, when she joined NANDOR FODOR in his investigations of the haunting at ASH MANOR, but in the early 1940s she settled in the USA permanently, becoming a US citizen in 1947. For a time she published a journal, *Tomorrow*, and in 1951 she established the Parapsychology Foundation in New York, with the aim of supporting scientific research into PARAPSYCHOLOGY. At Garrett's death, her daughter took over her work at the Parapsychology Foundation, and the organization still exists today.

In the 1960s, Garrett spent more than 500 hours with New York psychologist Lawrence LeShan. As well as questioning Garrett, LeShan designed a number of experiments to test her psychic abilities. In one test, for psychometry – the gaining of information about an object simply by holding it – LeShan gave Garrett a series of items, including a fossilized fish, an old Greek coin and an ancient clay tablet. The objects were disguised – wrapped in tissue and placed in a box, the box then being placed first in one numbered envelope and then, by another person, in a second envelope, so that no one knew which item was in which package. On holding the package containing the clay tablet, Garrett apparently described not only the item, but also the secretary who had parcelled it up.

While Uvani remained as Garrett's principal control throughout her life, Garrett herself doubted the spirit hypothesis of mediumship. She did not see her controls as spirits, but as elements of her own subconscious, and was unusual, as a professional MEDIUM, in her desire to further the scientific study of the paranormal through parapsychology.

Gef the Talking Mongoose

Bizarre early-20th-century poltergeist case from the Isle of Man.

Possibly the strangest British POLTERGEIST case of the 20th century allegedly occurred between 1932 and 1936 at a farm called Cashen's Gap on the Isle of Man. The farm was occupied by a Mr and Mrs Irving and their teenage daughter Voirrey. What took the case far beyond a conventional poltergeist outbreak was that the family claimed the manifestations to be the work of a talking mongoose named Gef which lived on their farm. Gef was allegedly capable of conducting lengthy conversations with the family on a range of subjects but was rarely seen. The story was investigated by English ghost hunter HARRY PRICE, and a Captain MacDonald, who attended the farm on behalf of Price, heard a strange whistling sound that lasted for 20 seconds and was attributed to Gef. Predictably, such an extraordinary story caused a sensation and generated much ridicule in the media of the day. There was little independent evidence from outside the family of the phenomena and a fuzzy photograph supposedly showing Gef failed to convince.

Together with G S Lambert, Price later devoted a remarkably low-key book to the case, *The Haunting of Cashen's Gap* (1936). As well as giving an account of the alleged manifestations, Lambert and Price considered the possibility of conscious and unconscious ventriloquism or mediumship on the part of members of the family, ultimately concluding that the case involved 'a voice and little else'. Most poltergeist researchers have preferred to shut their eyes to the story altogether, an exception being Sacheverell Sitwell, who, in his book *Poltergeists* (1940), pointed to parallels with 17th- and 18th-century witchcraft cases, including the DRUMMER OF TEDWORTH. The case was also examined by the US psychoanalyst NANDOR FODOR, who put a Freudian interpretation on events, spawning even more extraordinary speculation. The most fantastic theory which emerged was that the mongoose was a phallic symbol psychically projected from the unconscious mind of Voirrey Irving in an attempt to express the sexual feelings that she had stifled in an authoritarian family environment. The Irvings later sold Cashen's Gap and moved away. In 1947, a later owner of Cashen's Gap farm claimed to have shot a real mongoose on the land.

ghost

Term given to the spirit of a human being or animal that appears after death.

The term 'ghost' has been used popularly for centuries, but defies precise definition. Broadly speaking, it encompasses alleged manifestations believed to arise from a human being or animal, once living and now deceased. Ghosts typically involve the sighting of APPARITIONS, but a range of other phenomena are taken as indications of their presence (see HAUNTINGS). Traditional beliefs regarding ghosts have invariably viewed them as manifestations of SPIRITS or DISCARNATE ENTITIES, which may occur only once or reoccur over a lengthy period of time at a particular location. Attitudes to the reality of ghosts remain ultimately governed by personal belief, such as the question of the possibility of an AFTERLIFE.

Spiritual belief has played a significant part in the interpretation of ghosts. In the Middle Ages ghosts were often described as REVENANTS, delivering requests and complex messages (particularly regarding the fate of the soul of the deceased) to the living. During the 16th and early 17th centuries the meaning and nature of ghosts was the subject of controversy between Catholic and Protestant theologians, the former seeing apparitions as evidence of souls in Purgatory, while the latter interpreted them as tricks played by the Devil. However, in later years ghost stories were recounted as a rebuttal of atheist doctrines, or for propaganda purposes – particularly in the case of dramatic AERIAL PHANTOMS.

Artist Harold Copping's portrayal of Hamlet encountering his father's ghost. There is a rich tradition of ghosts featuring in literature and drama. (© Mary Evans Picture Library)

From an evidential viewpoint, the more interesting accounts appear from around 1650 onwards in the form of direct witness testimony, rather than through a filter of preconceived religious doctrine. From the end of the 17th century, limited steps were taken to try to corroborate the authenticity of the reports of ghostly phenomena, as with Joseph Glanvill's study of the DRUMMER OF TEDWORTH. Even in such early accounts of alleged ghost experiences we can see patterns that persist to this day, particularly in cases of POLTERGEIST disturbance. The rise of SPIRITUALISM in the mid 19th century stimulated a Victorian interest in ghosts, but was largely independent of ghost experiences; spiritualism concentrated on deliberate attempts at communicating with the dead, while ghost experiences tend to involve spontaneous and uninvited appearances, generally lacking any specific message or meaning. Indeed, the last 150 years have shown that ghosts continue to be reported even by people who reject the idea of any post-mortem 'survival'.

The significance of ghosts in many forms of spiritual belief is matched by their popularity as a cultural theme. They are frequently used in literature and drama as symbols of emotional states, as representations of loss and grief occasioned through death or simply as entertaining subject matter. Shakespeare, Jonson and Dickens, to name but a few, all used ghosts as characters. Ghost fiction itself is still a popular genre, although some would say that its heyday was 100 years ago, in the era of M R JAMES. Behind the rich literature of ghosts is an even greater body of popular folklore. Generations of people have expressed a belief in ghosts in many forms – in Britain alone, this body of traditional and popular lore is so enormous that no complete catalogue of it has ever been made (or is probably even worth attempting). Folkloric apparitions tend to be dramatic but are now rarely reported, although popular examples such as a WHITE LADY, BLACK MONK and BLACK DOG do still sometimes occur in modern accounts. Others, such as PHANTOM HITCH-HIKERS, appear to have been adapted from older themes, but are now popular in urban legends. Published collections of 'true' ghost stories have been in vogue since the Victorian era, and it has been estimated that Great Britain has at least 10,000 reputedly haunted sites (see HAUNTED HOUSES).

Despite more than a hundred years of scientific study, no single theory has been advanced to adequately explain all aspects of reported ghost phenomena. After centuries of belief, and years of research and investigation, ghosts still remain a mystery – further progress is only likely to occur when the intricacies of human perception, consciousness and the operation of the brain are better understood.

ghost dogs

Spectral manifestations in the form of a dog.

Accounts of ghost dogs take three forms: apparitions of domestic animals; manifestations of symbolic canine creatures; and members of phantom hunting packs in folklore. Among apparitional reports of domestic dogs, one of the best known was the experience of British ghost hunter Andrew Green (1927–2004), who claimed to have seen a black terrier in a locked bedroom in the house of a relative in Sidmouth, Devon, in 1951. A number of previous occupants of the room had also reported seeing a similar dog over the previous twelve months. Green subsequently traced the couple who had previously lived in the property and had owned a much-loved dog which strongly resembled the apparition. When the dog was accidentally killed by a car they had been so traumatized by its loss that they had sold their home and moved away. Such instances raise the question as to whether the apparition arises from the death of the dog itself or represents a visual form created by the minds of human owners. More rarely, ghost dogs have also been reported as a form of CRISIS APPARITION. In 1904 the writer Rider Haggard apparently experienced a waking nightmare of his dog being killed, the same night as his dog was fatally wounded by a train on a Norfolk railway line, prompting extensive correspondence in *The Times* on the topic.

Symbolic ghost dogs have a supernatural significance (eg a portent of death or disaster) and frequently possess a variety of striking visual characteristics which distinguish them from domestic canines. Such dogs are often of immense size with black shaggy coats (see BLACK DOGS) but may also be white, as with the phantom dog reputedly seen at Mistley in Essex before major floods in 1953. However, reliable testimony is lacking for some of the more bizarre visual features recounted in ghost dog traditions such as large, saucer-like eyes, luminous features, discharges of fire and the dog appearing headless. More fantastic still may be the incorporation of human features or elements from other species. An oft-quoted example is the Cambridgeshire tradition of the 'Shug-Monkey', a dog with the face of an ape said to prowl the lanes of the village of West Wratting. First recorded by folklorists in the 1950s, the story is dubious even as folklore, but parallels may be drawn with stories of dog-headed men and the tales of werewolves and lycanthropy that flourished in Europe during medieval times.

The existence of the third category of ghost dogs (see HELLHOUNDS), perhaps fortunately, seems to be confined to folklore – there are virtually no reports outside established tradition.

ghost hunting

Organized investigations of alleged ghostly manifestations.

Although previous centuries saw occasional localized attempts at the investigation of GHOSTS and POLTERGEISTS, the first 'scientific' investigations of HAUNTINGS did not take place until the latter half of the 19th century. Prior to the 1870s, ghost

The 'ghost-hunting' kit used by English psychic researcher Harry Price. (© Mary Evans Picture Library)

hunting was largely indistinguishable from the efforts of the necromancer or the spiritualist (see SPIRITUALISM), whereby spirits were summoned to a specific place (for example, the SÉANCE room) rather than being the subject of an active search at a specific location, typically a HAUNTED HOUSE. Greater ease of travel and communication made practical ghost hunting an option for psychic researchers from the end of the 19th century, although many claims of success must be treated with suspicion. From the early 20th century there were increasing efforts to deploy instrumentation at allegedly haunted houses, notably by HARRY PRICE (1881–1948) at BORLEY RECTORY, where teams of observers hoped to record ghostly phenomena. However, such efforts still often degenerated into attempts to contact the dead by way of séances and scientific ghost hunting languished after Price's death.

The growth in the availability and affordability of audio and video recording equipment in the 1970s and the publication in 1973 of a popular guide to ghost hunting by Andrew Green (1927–2004) revived interest in technical approaches to investigating hauntings. However, the results of equipment-based ghost hunting have been disappointing, although some apparent success has been achieved in poltergeist cases (see ROSENHEIM POLTERGEIST). Most investigations yield little more than evidence of natural causes behind the 'ghostly' phenomena, or subjective impressions from participants; some would hold that the study of haunted sites is handicapped by a lack of any common agreement as to the nature of manifestations and whether they occur on an objective or subjective level. A further problem is that virtually all ghost hunting is conducted at an amateur level without any shared consensus as to the approach to be taken and often without any critical perspective. Although a minority of ghost hunters seek to conduct research by reference to scientific standards, they are greatly outnumbered by those who either see ghost hunting simply as fun or as an exercise in confirming existing spiritualist beliefs.

ghost lights

Unexplained lights attributed to a supernatural force or presence.

Ghost lights are a cross-cultural paranormal manifestation, with anthropological studies revealing remarkable convergences in respect of their supposed nature and behaviour. Both indigenous and developed societies provide numerous reports of their appearance. Ghost lights are often centred on particular places, especially rural, undeveloped or wild areas. In many Old and New World traditions ghost lights are the SPIRITS of the dead, while cultures ranging from the Guissi of Kenya to the Hispanic population of New Mexico in the USA explain ghost lights as manifestations of witches or non-human spirit entities. Ghost lights may be considered to be good or evil omens. They are also said to be a sign of buried treasure in widely separated traditions, ranging from Romania in Eastern Europe to Colombia in South America.

In reports, ghost lights are regularly described as resembling a torch or lantern. They are usually spherical in appearance, but can be other shapes, and may even alter their shape as they are observed. Some may be the size of basketballs and many commentators place them within the wider, general category of ufos. Ghost lights may react to sound and light and on occasion seem to respond to the presence of observers. In some cases ghost lights may only be seen from certain angles and perspectives, may appear to be highly manoeuvrable and may emit sounds.

In the USA, ghost lights are often known as 'spook lights' and are said to frequent cemeteries and lonely roads. The most celebrated examples are at Marfa, Texas, reported since 1886, and the Hornet Spook Light, near Joplin, Missouri, which was investigated by the University of Michigan in 1942 and the US Army Corps of Engineering in 1946. Neither investigation was able to find an explanation. In 1982 ghost hunter Dale Kaczmarek succeeded in photographing the Hornet Spook Light, but its cause remains a mystery.

Notable British examples of ghost lights include the 1904–5 outbreak at Barmouth in Wales, which was linked with a religious revival, and strange luminous forms seen in Norfolk in 1924–5, which were implausibly ascribed to a luminous owl – an avian wonder which has never been reported before or since. The St Brides Bay area of Wales, the Oban area in Scotland and, in England, Hexworthy on Dartmoor and Castlerigg in Cumbria have generated well-attested examples of anomalous lights over the years. Glastonbury Tor in Somerset has also apparently been a long-standing centre of light activity.

Ghost lights may also be accompanied by APPARITIONS, such as that experienced by a doctor at Broadford on the Isle of Skye in around 1950. He reported seeing a globe of light followed immediately by a vision of a cloaked woman holding an infant. At Anolaima in Colombia in July 1969 over 20 witnesses saw a strange light come close to a farm, and one witness, 54-year-old Arcesio Bermudez, reported seeing what appeared to be the figure of a small man within the light. Unfortunately, Bermudez died soon afterwards, his sudden decline and sickness being ascribed to his venturing too close to the light. However, stories of such fatalities are very much the exception.

There is little doubt as to the existence of ghost lights in at least some form, with the most convincing evidence coming from a remote valley at Hessdalen in Norway, where anomalous lights have been tracked on scientific instruments and regularly filmed since 1984. A long-standing theory to explain some ghost lights is that they are caused by the spontaneous combustion of marsh gas in swampy or low-lying areas arising from putrefying organic matter. However, very little scientific work has been done on the chemistry of the processes involved. In the 20th century, the phenomena have been linked with faultlines in the earth's crust or with anomalous weather, although the fact that some reportedly appear to interact with observers remains puzzling.

The term 'ghost lights' can also be used to refer to a seemingly separate person-centred PSYCHIC phenomenon. A number of 19th-century mediums, such as DANIEL DUNGLAS HOME and EUSAPIA PALLADINO, were reportedly able to produce strange lights; the phenomenon has also been associated with saints and mystics as well as with stories of HAUNTED HOUSES and POLTERGEISTS. Unexplained lights have also been reported as a form of death-bed apparition. What connection, if any, such reports have with those of ghost lights seen in the open remains a matter of speculation.

ghost photographs

Photographs which allegedly show images of ghosts.

Photography has often been regarded as more of a hindrance then a help in attempts to prove the existence of ghosts. In the 19th-century heyday of SPIRITUALISM, some of the images published by séance-room photographers were taken up by the enthusiastic as proof of genuine mediumistic talents. However, it is hard today to see how anyone was ever deceived by such crude pictures, including clear cases of 'spirits' that were actually all-too-physical human hoaxers wrapped in linen. Since the 1930s, the emphasis has shifted away from such SPIRIT PHOTOGRAPHY towards attempts to capture photographs of ghosts at haunted locations (particularly HAUNTED HOUSES). With few exceptions, the results have been disappointing, a large number of purported images of ghosts being identified as deliberate hoaxes, accidental double exposures, flaws on the film or simple misperceptions of natural objects. A few cases, such as the famous photograph of the BROWN LADY OF RAYNHAM HALL and a small number of images collected by the SOCIETY FOR PSYCHICAL RESEARCH, are generally held to be interesting. However, such examples are few and far between.

This famous 'ghost photograph' apparently shows an apparition on the Tulip Staircase of the Queen's House, Greenwich. The phantom was not visible to the photographer at the time. (© Mary Evans Picture Library)

Since the advent of digital photography in the 1990s the idea that strange images, particularly ORBS, represent evidence for ghosts has become widespread. However, there is ample evidence to show that identical photographic anomalies can be produced simply through the presence of dust particles or moisture droplets in the air; so their appearance in allegedly haunted locations – which are often dusty and damp buildings – is really no mystery at all. Odd effects can also be generated by mundane household electrical equipment, such as the infrared emission of television remote controls.

Nonetheless, some doubt remains about the persistent appearance of fogging and mist effects on a number of photographs taken in haunted houses. Electromagnetic anomalies are often reported at such locations and it is postulated that these may be recorded as blurry images on photographs. An alternative theory, representing something of a halfway house, is the idea that these images represent a signature effect of a haunting presence. If so, they are indicative of the presence of an apparition but do not constitute a picture of the ghost itself.

Certainly, the idea that ghosts may be recorded on film continues to have a strong emotional appeal for many, particularly the recently bereaved. The attraction is obvious since ghost photographs seemingly provide tangible proof for the existence of an AFTERLIFE. In the 21st century, the Society for Psychical Research still receives a regular supply of photographs from puzzled members of the public. It is noticeable that in nearly all such cases neither the photographer nor any other person nearby reports seeing anything unusual at the time the picture was taken – the 'ghost' only appears when the film has been developed. Frequently, the interpretation of the photographic anomaly as a ghost appears to be a subjective perception, brought to the image by a viewer who is often hoping for a confirmation of personal beliefs.

Over 140 years after the first claims that images of apparitions had been captured on film, the question of whether photography can ever provide evidence of the existence of ghosts remains unresolved.

ghosts, animal *see* ANIMAL GHOSTS

ghosts, cyclic *see* CYCLIC GHOSTS

ghost ships

Ships and sailing craft that have taken on spectral form.

Ghostly boats and ships are known in the lore of many seafaring societies, ranging from paddle-propelled canoes in tribal cultures to apparitions of much larger vessels in European societies. A number of mythologies feature phantom ships as the means by which souls of the dead are conveyed to the AFTERLIFE. Legends of phantom ships occur in the folklore of Great Britain (particularly around the Cornish coast) and many other parts of Europe, including France (particularly Brittany), Norway, Denmark, Germany and Iceland. Ghost ships have also proved a popular theme in poetry, such as Coleridge's 'The Rime of the Ancient Mariner'.

A spectre ship was said to haunt Cap d'Espoir in the Gulf of St Lawrence, off Canada. It was supposedly an English flagship wrecked in the reign of Queen Anne. Sightings of the ghost ship were described by Rev Thistleton Dyer in *The Ghost World* (1893):

> … crowded with soldiers, lights are seen, and on the bowspit stands an officer, pointing to the shore with one hand, while a woman is on the other … [The] lights suddenly go out, a scream is heard, and the ill-fated vessel sinks.

But by the time it was described in print there had been no reported sightings for many years.

In February 1998 watchers hoping to see the ghost ship *The Lady Lovibond* near Deal, Kent, were disappointed when the vessel failed to materialize. Supposedly wrecked on the Goodwin Sands on 13 February 1748, the ship was said to appear at 50-year intervals, with sightings being claimed in 1898 and 1948. However, later research failed to reveal any official record of a ship called *The Lady Lovibond*, let alone ghostly re-appearances every 50 years.

One of the few plausible sightings of a ghostly vessel was made off Cape Town in 1923, and recorded by Sir Ernest Bennett in his classic collection *Apparitions and Haunted Houses* (1938). The witnesses were four members of the crew of the SS *Barrabool*, which was en route between Australia and London. Late one night they saw a luminous but apparently derelict ship. The vessel was estimated as being around 3–5 kilometres (2–3 miles) away and was spotted through a telescope and binoculars. Travelling on a course towards the *Barrabool*, it vanished when it was less than a kilometre away. Sir Ernest Bennett received two first-hand accounts of the sighting and noted that 'many legends were current of a phantom ship in these waters', a reference to the legend of the *FLYING DUTCHMAN*.

Although in vogue in the 19th century, stories of ghost or phantom ships seem to have undergone a dramatic decline following the development of steam- and oil-powered ocean-going vessels. Although oceans are now busier than ever and vessels continue to be lost, no cases of modern ships returning as ghosts are known.

Ghosts of the Broads

Tongue-in-cheek book about ghosts allegedly haunting the waterways of Norfolk and Suffolk

In 1931, Harley Street doctor and yachting enthusiast Charles Sampson (1881–1941) penned a short book called *Ghosts of the Broads*. Nearly all of the stories featured in the book purported to be examples of CYCLIC GHOSTS manifesting on certain days and nights of the year on the waterways and lakes that make up the Norfolk and Suffolk Broads. Far removed from the shadowy forms and footsteps familiar in modern ghost stories, the apparitions were often highly dramatic and involved in wholesale re-enactments of scenes from the past, including transformations of entire landscapes. Showing a predilection for phantom skeletons, ships and manifestations of the Devil, many of the apparitions had been supposedly witnessed by people of authority and eminence and further documented in a variety of sources. Sampson also claimed to have personally encountered a number of the ghosts by either accident or design.

Despite a sardonic style and the highly improbable nature of many of the ghosts, Sampson's stories were often accepted as real reports by gullible holidaymakers and some ghost-book authors in later years. Reprinted with staged photographs in 1973, *Ghosts of the Broads* went through a number of editions in the next 15 years, ensuring an even wider circulation of the tales. Research undertaken by Mike Burgess of Lowestoft in 1982 for the magazine *Lantern* revealed that none of the alleged witnesses ever existed. Furthermore, with a couple of possible exceptions, there was not even a folkloric basis for any of the stories, since many of Sampson's source materials were pure invention too.

ghosts of the living

'Ghosts' which appear to be of living persons rather than the deceased.

One of the conclusions drawn from the *Census of Hallucinations* conducted by the SOCIETY FOR PSYCHICAL RESEARCH in 1894 (see APPARITIONS) was that many reported ghosts were actually those of living people, rather than the deceased. Numerous examples can be found in psychic literature. In 1922, Lady Troubridge reported seeing the ghost of a living acquaintance she was due to meet later the same day, and the apparitional form of Anglican envoy Terry Waite was reported by a visitor to Canterbury Cathedral in 1987, at the time he was being held as a hostage in Lebanon. One British ghost researcher, Andrew Green (1927–2004), considered that as many as 40 per cent of reported apparitions represented ghosts of the living. Ghosts of the living occur in reports of CRISIS APPARITIONS, but in many instances appear only to represent the last moments of that person's life, being seen close to the time of their death.

Sceptics would claim that reports of ghosts of the living simply represent misperceptions on the part of the observer. See also BILOCATION; DOPPELGÄNGER.

ghosts, re-enactment *see* RE-ENACTMENT GHOSTS

ghosts, theatre *see* THEATRE GHOSTS

Ghostwatch

Controversial BBC television drama that took the form of a 'live' broadcast. It was aired on 31 October 1992 and involved an investigation of a family tormented by a poltergeist. It was inspired by the case of the Enfield Poltergeist.

Broadcast on Hallowe'en 1992, the BBC drama *Ghostwatch* took the form of a 'live' televised investigation into a haunted house in north London. The play featured well-known BBC presenters appearing as themselves, seemingly reporting in real time from the haunted house and linking up to veteran chat-show host Michael Parkinson in a broadcasting studio. In reality, the programme was pre-recorded and all participants were following a fictional script. Punctuated with apparently real telephone calls from concerned viewers, the play culminated in the eruption of ghostly forces, firstly within the house and then spreading to devastate the television studio. *Ghostwatch* ended with Parkinson grunting incoherently at the camera, supposedly possessed by an entity from the house.

While many members of the audience realized that they were watching a drama, others were convinced that it was real. The BBC phone lines were jammed by angry viewers claiming that they and their children had been truly frightened by the 'irresponsible' programme. Headlines in British newspapers on the following day included 'TV Spoof Spooks Viewers' (*Sunday Mirror*) and 'Parky Panned for Halloween Fright' (*News of the World*). On 8 November the *Mail on Sunday* claimed that the programme had caused the suicide of a young man (although the programme was not mentioned by the coroner). The BBC immediately tried to distance itself from the programme.

It has been noted that the POLTERGEIST case in the programme bears many similarities to that of the ENFIELD POLTERGEIST.

Glamis Castle

The ancestral home of Queen Elizabeth, the Queen Mother, said to be haunted by several entities and to contain a secret room.

Glamis Castle, near Forfar, Scotland, is the ancestral home of the Bowes Lyon family, having been granted to Sir John Lyon by King Robert II in 1372. It is also known as one of the most haunted castles in Britain. Among the many APPARITIONS said to haunt Glamis Castle, the chapel is famous for its 'Grey Lady', said to be the ghost of Janet Douglas, the wife of the 6th Lord Glamis. She was burned at the stake on Castle Hill in Edinburgh in 1537, following a trumped-up charge of witchcraft laid against her for political reasons. Her ghost is said to pray at the altar in the chapel, and has also been reported at the clock tower. Visitors who claim to have seen her believe she is a benign presence.

A somewhat noisier ghost is said to be that of Earl Beardie, a Lord Crawford, who was staying as a guest at the castle when, after a bout of drinking, he demanded that someone should play him at cards, even if that someone be the Devil himself. According to legend, the Devil duly appeared, and Earl Beardie played against him, eventually losing his soul. Some claim that Earl Beardie's ghost wanders the castle, but it is also said that he is gambling with the Devil for all eternity, and that occasionally one can hear his stamping and loud swearing and the rattling of dice.

According to local legend, other apparitions include a woman with a bloodied mouth, said to be the ghost of a serving-woman who had her tongue cut out, and that of a young black boy, perhaps the ghost of a servant who was badly treated. Alleged POLTERGEIST phenomena include the regular opening of a door at night, no matter how well it is locked, and the plucking of bedclothes off overnight guests.

The castle is also said to contain a secret chamber, which legend has it

Glamis Castle, Scotland, is reputedly one of the most haunted castles in Britain.
(© 2004 TopFoto/Woodmasterne)

was used to incarcerate the severely malformed first-born son of the 11th Earl of Strathmore in 1821. A second son was later passed off as the rightful heir, and the secret of the hidden room and its inhabitant is said to have been passed down to each heir on his 21st birthday.

guardian spirit

A spiritual protector or guide, the idea of which features in many religious belief systems, spiritualism and some areas of New Age thought.

In numerous cultures individuals are said to be protected by guardian SPIRITS. In many cases, such as in some Native American spiritual belief systems, these take the form of an animal spirit and the person is sometimes said to be imbued with some of the powers and qualities of the animal in question. In some systems it is believed that all people are protected in this manner, whereas in others it is only the holy or wise people, or the tribal shaman. In some interpretations of Christian teaching people are believed to have a 'guardian spirit' in the form of an angel – belief in guardian angels is particularly popular in the USA. In SPIRITUALISM and many New Age belief systems a guardian spirit might be variously understood to be a spirit helper who brings messages from the spirit realm, an assistant on visits to the astral plane (see ASTRAL PROJECTION) or a guide who helps with an individual's spiritual development.

H

hairy hands

A local tradition of disembodied phantom hands being held responsible for traffic accidents on a stretch of road on Dartmoor, Devon.

In 1921 an article in the *Daily Mail* purportedly told the story of a series of bizarre incidents on a lonely road across Dartmoor, Devon. Apparently, a medical officer from Dartmoor prison was riding on a motorbike, with his two children in a sidecar, along the road between Two Bridges and Postbridge, when the motorbike suddenly went out of control. The children managed to jump clear before the machine crashed, killing the doctor. Some weeks later another motorcyclist travelling the road was involved in a crash at the same spot but survived. He claimed that seconds before the crash he felt rough, hairy hands trying to wrench away control of the handlebars of his machine and force him from the road. A third story told of a coach driver also feeling invisible hands pulling at the steering wheel of his vehicle as he passed near the spot. Three years later a self-proclaimed psychic who was staying in a caravan near to the road reputedly saw a pair of disembodied hairy hands climbing up the window pane – they apparently vanished when she uttered a prayer.

No further encounters seem to have been reported in the press, but the story was promoted in the region for many years by Graham Danton, a West Country broadcaster. As late as 1974 the author Marc Alexander heard stories in the area that the 'hairy hands' (as the phenomenon was dubbed) were still being blamed for inexplicable accidents on the road.

hallucinations, auditory *see* AUDITORY HALLUCINATIONS

Hampton Court Palace

A palace built by Henry VIII which has a century-old tradition of ghosts and hauntings.

Hampton Court is reputedly Britain's most haunted royal palace. Stories of hauntings have been in circulation since 1894, when *Cassell's Family*

In this old postcard, Hampton Court Palace shows how proud it is of its ghostly reputation. Note the image of an 'apparition' in the bottom-right corner. (© Mary Evans Picture Library)

Magazine published a letter from a resident telling of 'loud screams at dead of night' in the Long Gallery. Among those alleged to have heard the screams were a Lady Westlake and a Mrs Cavendish Boyle. The cries were attributed to the ghost of Catherine Howard running along the gallery, and were said to be most regularly heard at around the anniversary of her arrest, on 4 November.

Another alleged apparition associated with the anniversary of a death is that of Jane Seymour, who reputedly walks near the building in October. For many years a staged photograph purporting to show this ghost was sold at the palace as a souvenir. Yet another ghost associated with the palace is that of Sibell Penn, nurse to the future Edward VI. She is said to have haunted certain apartments following the disturbance of her tomb in nearby Hampton Church in 1829, making her presence felt through the sound of a spinning wheel. Other less specific ghostly occurrences that have been reported include disembodied sighs and mutterings, and the sensation of being touched.

Such stories have been endlessly repeated in popular ghost books, although it is many years since the ghost of Catherine Howard has been heard. However, there is no doubt that many staff and visitors continue to report strange experiences in the Long Gallery and elsewhere in the palace. Official interest has led to a log of phenomena being maintained by curators since 1999.

In 2003 Hampton Court Palace was selected along with EDINBURGH'S VAULTS for mass experiments in the psychology of ghost experiences conducted by Dr Richard Wiseman. In the same year it was revealed that a ghost had apparently been caught on film by CCTV cameras at the palace. Apparently, on three successive days in October, an alarm signalled that a set of fire doors had been opened. CCTV footage of the first and last occasions simply showed the doors swinging open, but on the second occasion a 'ghostly' figure was recorded closing them. Some claimed that the film showed a ghost of Henry VIII, others that the figure (apparently wearing a hood and a long cloak) looked more like the Grim Reaper. It has also been suggested that the figure was simply a (slightly oddly dressed) member of the public, helpfully shutting the doors, or a costumed guide.

In total there are believed to be legends relating to 30 separate ghosts at Hampton Court Palace.

haunted highways

A belief that man-made roads and tracks may be haunted by apparitions.

In many folk tales, GHOSTS and supernatural entities are encountered by travellers during the course of their journey, and there are many stories of haunted roads and highways throughout Europe, the USA and other parts of the world. Some researchers believe that such stories ultimately derive from even earlier traditions of sacred roads and spirit paths in the landscape, dating back to prehistory.

Whatever the background, there is no doubt as to the continuing appeal of road ghosts, with one of the most popular modern folk tales being that of the PHANTOM HITCH-HIKER – typically, a young female hitch-hiker who mysteriously vanishes part-way through a journey. Other reports of what are termed SPECTRAL PEDESTRIANS include apparitions seen crossing or standing in the road. Numerous examples have been collected since the end of the 19th century. Sometimes the figure is said to be immediately recognizable as an apparition because of its unusual movement or appearance – such as seeming to float above the level of the road – while in other cases people believe they have seen a spectral pedestrian when someone they take to be a living person suddenly vanishes. There are many cases of motorists reporting apparent collisions with such figures only to discover no physical traces of any person on the road. A strong symbolic or archetypal element attaches to many road ghosts, lonely highways frequently providing the backdrop for encounters with either a WHITE LADY, BLACK DOGS or phantom monks (see BLACK MONK). More rarely cases of auditory ghost experiences are associated with highways, particularly the sound of galloping horses when this would seem to be impossible.

Haunted highways have also been the setting for alleged encounters with apparitional vehicles. In the past, some people believed that they witnessed PHANTOM COACHES, but in more recent times tales are reported of spectral cyclists and ghostly motor vehicles.

The vast majority of apparitional experiences on haunted highways take place on quiet and empty roads, usually at night, a pattern also found with PHANTOM FUNERALS in Scottish and Celtic tradition. It may simply be that when travelling at night, the combination of darkness, isolation, tiredness and monotonous visual stimuli generates hallucinations; alternatively, some have suggested that the same factors may encourage the brain to enter into a relaxed state, making it more receptive to psychic impressions – and able to see ghosts.

haunted houses

Domestic dwellings that are allegedly subject to hauntings; haunted houses are recorded in many cultures.

Stories of haunted houses are known throughout the world and have been in circulation since ancient times. In tradition, haunted houses are properties to which the spirits of former inhabitants return; to psychical researchers they are dwellings where psychical phenomena occur spontaneously over a period of time, the precise mechanism behind this being unclear.

One of the earliest recorded stories of a haunted house is found in one of the letters of Pliny the Younger, written in around AD 90. It concerns a house in Athens abandoned by its inhabitants because of the disturbance caused there by the ghost of a filthy old man with a flowing beard and rattling chains. Following this, the house was rented by a philosopher named Athenodorus, who, on seeing the ghost for himself, followed it to a spot in a courtyard where it vanished. The ground there was subsequently dug up – revealing the bones of a man. After these bones were given a religious burial the ghost appeared no more. Stories in which the dead return to haunt their former abodes to secure proper funeral rites can be found in many cultures and countries – including China, ancient Egypt and South America – spread over many centuries. The idea that the ghostly phenomena found in haunted houses are caused by unquiet spirits remains strongly in vogue today, despite the alternative theories that have been postulated from the 19th century onwards (see HAUNTINGS).

The first attempt to study haunted houses in a 'scientific' manner was made by the 'Committee on Haunted Houses', as established by the SOCIETY FOR PSYCHICAL RESEARCH at its foundation in 1882. The committee immediately found itself overwhelmed with material, declaring, 'Our labours in this direction have been fruitful beyond our expectation.' Seeking to separate haunted houses from other types of ghostly phenomena,

The ghosts of both a lady in a green cloak and a medieval knight are said to haunt Bamburgh Castle, one of Britain's many 'haunted houses'. (© 2000 Topham Picturepoint)

another contemporary researcher, Ada Goodrich Freer, declared in 1894:

> What we have to deal with here are those houses which are, with more or less frequency, habitually visited by phantasms commonly supposed to be those of former inhabitants.

From the outset, the 'scientific' researchers of the 19th century claimed that the manifestations described in haunted houses indicated a place-centred form of haunting, with successive living occupants experiencing paranormal phenomena suggestive of the continuing presence of a deceased individual or individuals. Often these dead individuals had a habitual or emotional association with the property, but in many other cases no clear link could be established.

Classic phenomena reported by those who have either lived in or visited a house they believe to be haunted include visual APPARITIONS, the sensation of there being 'a presence', feelings of being touched, unexplained noises (particularly footsteps), temperature variations, unusual smells, and the unexplained movement of objects.

Domestic pets, such as cats and dogs, are often said to display unusual reactions inside haunted houses, and anomalous electrical activity of various sorts is also frequently reported. With the exception of the disruption of electrical devices such as televisions or tape recorders, and the fogging or misting of photographs, these patterns are consistent in reports since the 19th century. In a number of cases the reported phenomena resemble those in POLTERGEIST cases, but classically poltergeists seem to be focused on a particular person rather than a place.

The literature of haunted houses is vast and it is often claimed that Great Britain has more haunted houses than anywhere else in the world. Such assertions remain unprovable, but it seems certain that Great Britain has recorded and preserved more stories than any other nation. Classic Victorian collections include the research of Mrs Catherine Crowe in *The Night Side of Nature* (1848) and John Ingram's two-volume work *The Haunted Homes and Family Traditions of Great Britain* (1884). The latter concentrates upon stately homes, castles and manor houses and set the pattern for popular collections of 'true' ghost stories which continues to this day. Houses which are famously reputed to be haunted include Bamburgh Castle in Northumberland, BETTISCOMBE MANOR in Dorset and BURTON AGNES HALL in Yorkshire (see also SCREAMING SKULLS), Corby Castle in Cumbria, Felbrigg Hall in Norfolk, Himpton Ampner Manor House in Hampshire, NEWSTEAD ABBEY in Nottinghamshire (see also BLACK MONK), Peele Castle on the Isle of Man, SAWSTON HALL in Cambridgeshire and WOBURN ABBEY in Bedfordshire. Most royal residences are reputedly haunted, including Buckingham Palace, GLAMIS CASTLE in Scotland, HAMPTON COURT PALACE in Surrey, St James's Palace in London, Sandringham in Norfolk and Windsor Castle in Berkshire, and virtually every historic ruin in Great Britain has a ghost story associated with it, particularly monastic remains. Such locations inevitably provide a more interesting and impressive background than more humble residences, as well as fitting the dramatic demands of a popular ghost story.

However, from the end of the 19th century reports were being made of hauntings at middle- and working-class dwellings, the latter apparently being more prone to poltergeists than visual apparitions. The 19th and early 20th centuries also saw a preponderance of alleged hauntings at rural rectories and parsonages, such as BORLEY RECTORY in Essex, but this category seems to have declined in recent decades. From the mid 20th century onwards there are numerous reports of haunted council houses as well as many other types of building, and it would seem that today any house may be haunted, no matter how grand or small.

haunted people

People believed to be haunted by ghosts or other supernatural entities.

The folklore of many nations avers

that GHOSTS can attach themselves to the living. Sometimes the attachment is affectionate (for example, deceased relatives who protect children) but more often the returning presence will be the victim of a crime, a wrong or a broken promise perpetrated by the living person. A classic example is the 17th-century story of Caisho Burroughs recorded by John Aubrey in *Miscellanies* (1696). Caisho Burroughs was a handsome man who took the virginity of a passionate Italian gentlewoman who had fallen in love with him. The lady swore him to secrecy but after her death he boasted of the affair to friends at a tavern. Almost immediately, her ghost appeared before him, though she was unseen by others. Thereafter she made regular appearances to him, always preceded by a sense of chilliness, with her last appearance being on the same morning Burroughs was killed in a duel.

Many religious traditions also countenance the possibility of SPIRITS or demons possessing or harassing the living, sometimes displaying violence (see INVISIBLE ASSAILANTS). Such ideas were mostly replaced in the 20th century by theories which attributed such POLTERGEIST phenomena to an effect of the mind of a living person rather than to a DISCARNATE ENTITY. In 1928 the German researcher A F von Schrenk-Notzing wrote:

> So, we see that these phenomena take the place of neurosis. Sensations of guilt, sadistic inclinations, an attitude of enmity and malice toward the environment, all these come to a reality, through the phenomena, in other words through paranormal and unconscious channels.

The idea that poltergeist phenomena are generated by the unconscious mind of individuals, particularly those under stress, was taken up by the American psychoanalyst and psychical researcher NANDOR FODOR. It has become widely accepted among parapsychologists (see PARAPSYCHOLOGY) in the decades since. PSYCHICAL RESEARCH has thus embraced the idea of haunted individuals – but as examples of manifestations of RECURRENT SPONTANEOUS PSYCHOKINESIS rather than some form of external entity.

However, not all researchers believe that the unconscious mind is at the root of every poltergeist outbreak. The methodology for making such assessments has been severely criticized, and there are examples of cases which (if the truth of the reports is accepted) appear to stretch the theory to its limit. These include cases in which the poltergeist apparently inflicts suffering and harm on its human focus, and cases of alleged possession; although whether the claims that exorcism has been successful in some of these cases support a spiritual explanation, or simply offer evidence for the power of suggestion, is a matter of opinion.

hauntings

Place-, person- or object-centred spontaneous paranormal phenomena – the word is popularly understood to relate to cases where the events are said to be caused by discarnate, supernatural entities.

Although in some cases the phenomena may seem to be focused upon a particular individual (see HAUNTED PEOPLE) or even an object, the term 'haunting' is most often used for those that are place-centred. The popular view is that hauntings involve the GHOSTs of the dead. The phenomena may include visual apparitions, the sensation of a presence, anomalous noises (particularly footsteps), temperature variations, smells, object movements, doors opening and closing by themselves, electrical anomalies and strange reactions on the part of domestic animals. In certain cases, manifestations reported in HAUNTED HOUSES are reminiscent of POLTERGEISTS; they can also resemble certain alleged SÉANCE- room phenomena although they seemingly occur without the deliberate involvement of any identifiable MEDIUM. However, attempts to record haunting activity with automated equipment have been largely disappointing – one of the (less cynical) suggestions to explain this being that hauntings may always require the presence of living persons to occur.

Interestingly, the 20th century saw a marked expansion in the types of premises that featured in reports of hauntings. They are apparently no longer confined to ancient castles, ruined abbeys or stately homes and have now been reported in a wide variety of domestic, commercial and industrial buildings – including offices, power stations and factories – as well as in the open air.

Theories relating to the nature of hauntings have been discussed for centuries and can be divided into naturalistic and spiritual (or PSYCHIC). Naturalistic theories include explanations based around human frailties, including fraud, wishful thinking, mental illness and misperception of normal phenomena, and there is no doubt that these certainly account for many claims. More complex 'geophysical' theories, particularly those proposed by Guy Lambert (1878–1973) of the SOCIETY FOR PSYCHICAL RESEARCH in the 1950s and 1960s, suggest that hauntings arise from vibrations set up by tides and underground water. Other advanced seismic theories contend that electromagnetic energy released from tectonic plates may be responsible for some reports – an idea suggested primarily by the Canadian researchers Michael Persinger and R A Cameron. Such discharges, it is proposed, might affect the temporal lobes of the brain, causing hallucinations. Man-made electromagnetic radiation and infrasound have also been offered as potential causes.

Spiritual and psychic explanations are equally varied. Until the end of the 19th century hauntings were predominantly seen as spiritual phenomena, arising from manifestations of unquiet SPIRITS or even diabolical forces. The unquiet spirit hypothesis remains a popular theory even in the 21st century.

However, a number of other psychic theories have been proposed.

From the 1890s onwards, it was accepted by many psychical researchers (see PSYCHICAL RESEARCH) that visual APPARITIONS were essentially hallucinatory in nature and a number of theories about hauntings reflect this. G N M Tyrrell was one of a number of researchers who proposed that telepathy plays a major part in their creation. Such theories maintain that apparitions are perceptual ideas, transmitted through telepathy from living minds, and perhaps also from those of the deceased who may survive as DISCARNATE ENTITIES. Other theories see thoughts as capable of independent existence and capable of leaving traces or imprinting themselves either upon the environment (see STONE TAPE THEORY) or upon a postulated 'psychic ether' which permeates all matter. Other psychic theories include those based around interactions with other dimensions, or a 'level of reality' beyond the material world – however, on our present understanding of the nature of the universe such ideas can at best only be described as speculative.

Currently, no one theory is adequately able to account for all of the phenomena reported in connection with hauntings, particularly those involving object movements and the disturbance of the physical environment. Certainly, the psychic theories will require further understanding (and of course indisputable proof) of PSYCHOKINESIS, poltergeist phenomena and mediumship before they can be developed to provide a satisfactory explanation of the mechanism by which hauntings occur.

One final common claim in relation to hauntings is the observation that they appear to become milder and fade away with time – suggesting that whatever energy sustains them may gradually dissipate. It has even been postulated by some researchers that ghosts may have a 'life' of about 400 years; relatively few visible apparitions seem to date from before this period, in so far as any historical origin can be identified – although phantom monks and nuns seem to be an exception to this rule. Reports of Roman ghosts are exceedingly rare, and the ghostly horseman allegedly witnessed by Dr R C C Clay (who, conveniently, was an archaeologist) at Bottlebush Down in Dorset in 1927 is the only known example of a Bronze Age ghost in the British Isles. Whatever lies behind hauntings, it would seem that even ghosts are not immortal.

headless horseman

A decapitated phantom known in folklore and common in popular ghost fiction.

The ghostly motif of a headless rider upon a phantom horse is a popular and widespread one. Early instances arise in German and Scandinavian folklore and are linked with the Norse legend of the WILD HUNT. Although examples of headless horsemen are also known in British and Irish folklore, such as the Headless Rider of Castle Sheela,

Ireland, there are fewer examples in folklore (taken to refer to oral tradition rather than imaginative literature) than might be supposed.

Accounts of apparently real-life sightings of headless horsemen are certainly few and far between, although apparitions of a ghostly decapitated horseman are occasionally linked with a historic incident. Legends of a headless horseman at Temple Bridge, Icklingham, Suffolk, were linked to the Peasants' Revolt of 1381, when the clergyman John de Cambridge was beheaded there by Wat Tyler's mob.

Headless horsemen are most often found in fiction, with perhaps the best known appearing in Washington Irving's story 'The Legend of Sleepy Hollow' (1820) and the novel *The Headless Horseman* (1869) by Captain Mayne Reid.

Latin American ghost tradition also contains an archetypal horse-riding phantom who is sometimes considered to be headless, the 'jinete negro' or 'black rider'.

hellhounds

Ghostly dogs that hunt in a pack, often linked with the Devil.

Stories of packs of hellhounds feature particularly in the folklore of the west and north of England. Some commentators have linked these stories with Norse legends of Odin and the WILD HUNT; these were later Christianized, with the huntsman becoming the Devil on a quest to snatch up the souls of sinners and unbaptized children. Later traditions replace the Devil with the spirit of a human being of ill repute and transform the dogs into a supernatural menace to the life of anyone unfortunate enough to encounter them. In many stories their barks and howls alone are considered fatal or at the very least an omen of impending death.

Hellhounds are known as the Devil's Dandy Dogs in Cornwall, as the Wish or Yeth Hounds in Devon, Cwn Annwn in Wales, the Hooters in Warwickshire and the Gabriel Ratchetts in Lancashire. On Dartmoor, the leader of the hellhounds is said to be Sir Francis Drake – it is locally rumoured that he dabbled in black magic. In other local traditions the pack-master is identified as an unpopular member of the local aristocracy or judiciary, as with Colonel Sidney, an 18th-century squire at Ranworth, Norfolk, or Judge Sir John Popham (1531–1607) at Wellington, Somerset.

Herne the Hunter

In folklore, a spectral huntsman wearing a pair of stag's antlers who is said to haunt Windsor Great Park. According to legend, he appears when the monarch is about to die or at other times of national crisis.

The first recorded reference to Herne the Hunter, a ghostly figure wearing a pair of stag's horns who is said to haunt Windsor Great Park, is from around 1597, in Shakespeare's play *The Merry Wives of Windsor*:

There is an old tale goes that Herne the Hunter
Sometime a keeper here in Windsor Forest,
Doth all the winter-time, at still midnight,
Walk round about an oak, with great ragg'd horns …
You have heard of such a spirit, and well you know
The superstitious idle-headed eld
Receiv'd, and did deliver to our age,
This tale of Herne the Hunter for a truth.

There are several versions of the legend of Herne the Hunter, but the traditional story is that he was one of many huntsmen employed by King Richard II on the Windsor Castle estate. During a hunting party, Herne saved the King's life when he was attacked by a wounded stag, but in doing so was mortally injured himself. A local wizard called Philip Urwick appeared from nowhere and offered to help, and he ordered that the dead stag's antlers should be removed and placed on Herne's head. He then took Herne to his hut and tended him for a month, and when he was restored to health, Herne returned to court and the King made him his favourite, giving him magnificent gifts such as a gold chain. But Herne's fellow foresters, jealous at his rise, went to Urwick and persuaded him to use his powers to remove Herne's hunting skills. He did so, and the King was forced to dismiss Herne from his service. In one version of the story, Herne's rivals also framed him for poaching. In shame and despair, Herne hanged himself from an oak tree in the forest, and the tree was blasted by lightning during a terrible thunderstorm.

Herne's rivals were at first delighted, but soon they too lost their hunting abilities, and consulting Urwick, they were told that they would have to appeal to Herne's spirit for mercy. They went to the oak and called on him, and he appeared, wearing his antlers, and ordered them to bring the royal horses and hounds to him and ride out to hunt with him the next night and every night following. They obeyed, and soon the deer herds were depleted and the King demanded to know the cause. The huntsmen confessed their story. That night, Richard walked through the park, and Herne's spirit appeared and told him that the huntsmen who had brought about his death must be hanged from his oak. After this was done, the deer returned to the park as if by magic, and Herne never appeared again during Richard's reign until the King's murder. Every winter he is said to ride out at midnight on a black horse, accompanied by fierce hunting dogs and a horned owl, carrying a hunting horn and his golden chain, and still wearing his antlers. The hanged huntsmen are compelled to ride with him for all eternity, and he leads a WILD HUNT through the forest at the midwinter solstice, collecting damned souls to join with him. He is said to appear at the tree now known as

Herne's Oak whenever the monarch behaves unjustly, or is about to die, or when the nation is in danger, and is said to have been sighted before such historic events as the execution of Charles I in 1649, the eve of both World Wars in 1914 and 1939, the abdication of Edward VIII in 1936, and George VI's death in 1952. It is generally believed that the Herne's Oak of Shakespeare's time was felled by accident in 1796, and that replacements have been planted on or around the original site since then.

hidden memory *see* CRYPTOMNESIA

hitch-hikers, phantom *see* PHANTOM HITCH-HIKERS

Home, Daniel Dunglas (1833–86)

Renowned Scottish-born medium whose famous feats included levitation.

Daniel Dunglas Home (pronounced 'Hume') is renowned as possibly the greatest ever MEDIUM, and was the first person to whom the word PSYCHIC was applied. He is said to have exhibited a wide range of extraordinary powers – as well as simply conducting SÉANCES (apparently displaying the abilities of a DIRECT VOICE MEDIUM, a TRANCE MEDIUM, a PHYSICAL MEDIUM as well as CLAIRVOYANCE) Home could reputedly levitate (once allegedly flying out of one window and into another on the third floor), handle hot coals with impunity and elongate at will.

Born in what is now part of Edinburgh, Home claimed to be the illegitimate son of the 10th Earl of Home. Early documents list his name as 'Hume' and they also indicate that his middle name (sometimes quoted as being 'Douglas') was probably a later addition. By the age of 17 he was living with an aunt in the USA when their house was beset by the kind of noises and POLTERGEIST events that also apparently infested the home of the FOX SISTERS. Fearing that he had called the Devil upon them, Home's aunt threw him out of the house, and he spent the next 20 years travelling the USA and Europe, earning money (in the form of gifts) by performing at séances. Hume moved in exceedingly well-to-do circles, and could count many famous people among his acquaintances – William Makepeace Thackeray defended him and Mark Twain praised him, while Michael Faraday denounced him and George Eliot described him as 'an object of moral disgust'. In London the famous chemist SIR WILLIAM CROOKES (who also investigated FLORENCE COOK) declared that he was a genuine medium, and attested to his other paranormal skills.

One of the most famous effects in a Home séance was the apparent spirit-playing of an accordion sealed in a metal framework. It was claimed many years after his death that a number of mini one-octave mouth organs had been discovered among his personal effects – the suggestion being that these

A hand-coloured wood engraving showing an artist's impression of Daniel Dunglas Home levitating to the ceiling – a feat he apparently performed before a number of witnesses. (© 2003 Charles Walker/TopFoto)

had been employed as a means of faking the performance. Sceptics have also pointed out that he sported a rather large moustache, which they suggest could potentially have been used to hide small objects to be produced later as APPORTS. However, no mouth organs have ever been produced in support of the former claim, and the latter, somewhat bizarre suggestion remains equally unproven.

In 1866 a Mrs Lyon adopted Home and gave him a very considerable sum of money. This money was eventually returned as the result of a court case in which it was successfully argued that he had obtained the money by adverse influence. It was alleged that Home had conducted a number of séances in which the spirits had told Mrs Lyon to adopt him and give him the money.

In 1871, shortly after his second marriage, Home retired from the public séance circuit, claiming that his powers were leaving him. In truth he had suffered from tuberculosis for most of his life and the disease was taking its toll. In 1877 he wrote a book called *Lights and Shadows of Spiritualism*, in which he exposed the techniques of fraudulent mediums – he apparently had little time for many of his contemporaries.

Although Home exercised a great deal of control over the conditions in which he demonstrated his alleged abilities and, as such, is open to the challenge that he may well have employed misdirection, sleight of hand and a number of other stage magic techniques, in an age characterized by charlatans and fraudulent mediums he is notable for the fact that he was never convincingly exposed as a fake. See also SPIRITUALISM.

Houdini, Harry (1874–1926)

US magician and escape artist who set out to expose mediums as frauds.

Harry Houdini was born as Erich Weiss in Budapest, Hungary. His family emigrated to the USA and he became a trapeze artist, magician and, most notably, an escapologist, taking his stage name in honour of the French conjurer Robert Houdin (1805–71), whom he greatly admired.

Houdini became interested in SPIRITUALISM, especially after the death of his mother, but, incensed at the frauds being perpetrated on a public eager to believe, he spent much of his time exposing the tricks used by fake MEDIUMS. This made him enemies, including the Scottish writer SIR ARTHUR CONAN DOYLE, a convinced spiritualist with whom he had previously been on friendly terms. According to Houdini's wife, he told her that when he was dead, if there was an AFTERLIFE, he would find a way to communicate with her. After ten years without receiving any message from the beyond she apparently gave up waiting.

household spirits

In folklore, benign spirits that are attached to a domestic dwelling; stories of household spirits are found in many cultures.

Although the idea of a HAUNTED HOUSE is a source of dread in many cultures, there also exist a number of folkloric beliefs in which the haunting entity is considered to be a benign presence. Such household spirits perform positive or protective functions for the occupants of the dwelling and help to bring them prosperity and wellbeing. In some instances such traditions are linked with a belief that the spirits of ancestors remain in a house to help future generations.

Indications from archaeology and folklore suggest that belief in household spirits was once widespread in Europe, including many parts of the British Isles. Household spirits often manifest as a benign type of POLTERGEIST, their presence detected by occasional noises, object movements, the performance of domestic chores and the delivery of gifts. When visible they are often said to resemble diminutive human figures – examples include Spanish and Latin American traditions of *duende* and the brownies of British folklore.

Cultures as widely spread as Europe, the Far East, Africa and the Pacific stress that household spirits can be temperamental on occasion and demand respect. Many household spirits are said to be obsessed by cleanliness, and houses must be kept tidy if friendly terms are to be maintained. Often household spirits may be kept happy with offerings or token payments (particularly food and tobacco), by the performance of special rituals or by the maintenance of domestic shrines.

A belief in benign household spirits has an undoubted appeal, and some people have suggested that modern HAUNTINGS that are attributed to the loving presence of a deceased relative represent a continuation of the tradition.

Paul Cropper, one of the researchers who investigated the Humpty Doo Poltergeist, holds a handful of pebbles which had apparently fallen from the ceiling. (© TopFoto/Fortean)

Humpty Doo Poltergeist

A remarkable stone-throwing poltergeist case from Australia.

What became known as the 'Humpty Doo Poltergeist' afflicted a house at Humpty Doo in the Northern Territory of Australia early in 1998. Occupied by two adult couples, a friend and a child, the house apparently suffered repeated bombardment by stones, a classic feature of many POLTERGEIST cases, as well as other missiles. As with many similar outbreaks, pebbles were reported falling both outside and inside the property, often seeming to materialize out of thin air or teleport into the room. The stones matched those from a gravel driveway at the house, but even in the monsoon season those that fell were said to be completely dry when picked up. The whole household was also disturbed by strange messages that appeared on the walls and floors of the house, purporting to come from a friend who had been killed in a road accident.

These messages were either scrawled in pen or carefully spelled out with Scrabble tiles or lines of pebbles.

At the request of the occupants, a series of blessings and exorcisms were conducted by religious ministers of different denominations. However, these seemed to exacerbate rather than reduce the phenomena. The case came to the attention of the local press, and Humpty Doo became famous. The 'hauntees' signed an exclusive contract with the television network Channel 7, which sent a film crew that set up camp in the house for 24 days. The film crew were apparently convinced by the poltergeist phenomena that they witnessed, but in their time at the house they only succeeded in recording three object movements on film, the poltergeist seemingly being adept at avoiding their cameras. The final broadcast actually suggested that the poltergeist was a hoax.

Two psychic researchers, Paul Cropper and Tony Healy, who also stayed at the property were convinced that the case was genuine, having observed a number of inexplicable phenomena for themselves. While the Humpty Doo Poltergeist resembled many other similar cases recorded around the world, one observation was considered unique. This was a strange black object seen flying up a driveway. Described as smaller than a fist, it left a trail of gravel behind it and was interpreted as 'a poltergeist reloading' by Cropper and Healy.

I

illusion

A false appearance or deceptive impression of reality, especially one performed for entertainment in conjuring or stage magic.

Illusion, or the deceptive impression of reality, may be caused in a number of ways. Optical illusions created by means such as the use of false perspective exploit the assumptions made by the visual system, and mirages are natural illusions caused by distortions in the atmosphere. But the best-known type of illusions are those which have been performed for centuries to entertain and amaze as part of the art of conjuring or stage magic. The illusionist uses various techniques to give the audience the impression that they have seen something which is apparently impossible, although it is generally understood by all that the 'magic' has been accomplished by sleight of hand and trickery and not by any occult or supernatural means; the performer seeks to present an effect so skilfully that the audience cannot believe the evidence of their own eyes and cannot think how the illusion has been achieved.

Modern magicians do not usually claim to possess genuine spiritual or occult powers, but the techniques used by illusionists have, in the past, been exploited by those making such claims. In the late 19th century, at the height of the vogue for SPIRITUALISM, many fraudulent MEDIUMS used the methods of conjuring and stage magic to perform illusions designed to convince those present at their SÉANCES that genuine supernatural events were taking place – such as apparitions of spirits, ghostly music, and objects moving without being touched. Since the séances were invariably held in darkened rooms, it was not difficult for a fake medium, often aided by an accomplice, to fool the participants, and in the last century or so, several professional magicians, most notably HARRY HOUDINI, Joseph Dunninger and, in modern times, James Randi, have devoted themselves to exposing phoney mediums and fraudulent paranormal claims.

This technique – named 'Pepper's ghost' after its inventor, John Pepper – uses a mirror and a hidden room to create the illusion of an apparition appearing on stage. It was especially popular in the 19th century. (© 2006 TopFoto/Fortean)

invisible assailant

An invisible entity that can apparently inflict physical force or violence upon a victim.

Stories exist around the world of invisible assailants that can inflict physical harm on human beings. The lives of medieval saints often feature torments and temptations inflicted by demons and evil spirits and even in more recent periods certain religious figures, such as St John Vianney, the Curé of Ars, claimed to be the victim of supernatural attacks.

However, stories of religious figures being persecuted by invisible assailants have declined, and in the 20th century were almost wholly replaced by examples featuring secular individuals. According to the popular mystery writer Frank Edwards, in August 1960 a South African police chief and three constables watched helplessly as 20-year-old Jimmy de Bruin was cut deeply on the legs by 'an invisible assailant with an equally insubstantial scalpel'. Other cases are found in the literature of POLTERGEIST phenomena: cuts and bites appeared on the skin of the young girls at the centre of the LAMB INN poltergeist case, and ELEONORE ZUGUN displayed scratches and weals on her face and body. In 1928 in Poona, India, a young boy apparently suffered poltergeist assaults in a case examined by the AMERICAN SOCIETY FOR PSYCHICAL RESEARCH. More recently, mysterious bruises, cuts and scratches have been claimed among parties of tourists and sightseers visiting a vault in the Greyfriars Churchyard in Edinburgh (see EDINBURGH'S VAULTS). And in Colombia in 1999, scratched messages threatening death were said to have appeared on the skin of a young woman as she was being interviewed by journalists from the newspaper *El Tiempo*.

While such instances may be labelled assault by an invisible assailant, it is by no means certain that an external agency is involved. Firstly, such claims of physical injury must be treated carefully, given the tendency of some psychologically vulnerable people towards self-harm, consciously or subconsciously, or the possibility that such 'paranormal' injuries are simply hoaxed. It has also been suggested that in some instances, marks have apparently been induced on the skin by suggestion alone. Cases of apparently spontaneous bodily damage are often comparable to examples of stigmata on the bodies of saints and mystics in the Christian tradition.

J

James, M(ontague) R(hodes) (1862–1936)

English writer and scholar.

The son of a clergyman, M R James spent much of his adult life at Cambridge – as a fellow, dean, tutor and ultimately provost of King's College. Later he became provost at Eton. James was a distinguished medieval scholar and author of what remains the leading study of the apocryphal books of the Bible. However, it is for his 30 short stories about ghosts that his name endures.

Most of the stories were written between 1893 and 1911 and published as *Ghost Stories of an Antiquary* (1904) and *A Warning to the Curious* (1911). Their success results from the skilful creation of atmosphere, with James adopting a restrained, antiquarian tone reflecting the scholarly world in which he spent his adult life. Many of his human characters are scholars and academics into whose dry, bookish lives James progressively introduces manifestations of malevolent and physically dangerous ghosts, with the reader being terrified by the use of suggestion rather than explicit horror. Classic stories include 'Oh, Whistle, and I'll Come to You, My Lad', 'Count Magnus', 'Lost Hearts', 'The Treasure of Abbot Thomas' and 'Number 13'. These stories have remained in print for over a century, either as collections or in anthologies, and have frequently been adapted for radio, television and the theatre.

James stated openly that he sought to make his fictional ghosts consistent with the spectres of supernatural folklore and declared that he was prepared to accept the evidence for ghosts if it convinced him. He was willing to explain what he considered to be the rules of the genre to a wider audience and for his own part considered the 19th-century Irish writer Sheridan Le Fanu as the greatest exponent of the literary ghost story. James also took a scholarly interest in historic ghost stories, translating a number from medieval Latin manuscripts.

Although he denied that his stories were based upon personal

An illustration from the classic ghost story 'Oh, Whistle, and I'll Come to You, My Lad' by M R James. (© Mary Evans Picture Library)

experience, it later emerged that the village of Great Livermere, Suffolk, in which James grew up, enjoyed a local reputation for being very haunted. This stimulated speculation that his interest in ghosts and his last story, 'A Vignette', had arisen from a childhood experience or nightmare.

kachina

Spirit being who acts as an intermediary between humans and the gods among the Pueblo people of the south-western USA.

The Hopi word ‘kachina’ refers to a SPIRIT being capable of influencing the natural world. Kachinas are associated with the ancestral dead and with duties such as bringing rain. In Hopi mythology they live in the San Francisco Mountains (which is also the location of the world of the dead) and their return from there to the people is symbolized in dances, in which male dancers dress in masks and costumes, each designed to represent an individual kachina. The masked dancers take on the powers of the kachinas during the dance, and the masks must not be worn outside the ceremony. The kachinas are also represented by dolls, which, unlike the masks, do not have any powers or sacred significance.

Another Pueblo people, the Zuñi, have a similar tradition. They refer to the kachinas as koko, and the otherworld in which they reside is at the bottom of the Lake of the Dead (Listening Spring Lake at the junction of the Little Colorado and Zuñi rivers).

knockers

Cornish mine spirits.

Mine spirits are often thought to be the ghosts of miners who have died underground, and may either help or hinder miners, who therefore treat them with the utmost respect, frequently leaving them gifts of food and drink. They are described as being small in stature, between 45 and 90 centimetres (1.5–3 feet) tall, and are usually dressed as miners themselves in leather aprons, and carry small picks, lamps and hammers.

The knockers who inhabit the tin mines of Cornwall are perhaps the best known of the mine spirits. Benign in nature, they are also known by a variety of other names, including ‘knackers’, ‘nickers’ and ‘spriggans’, and ‘blue caps’ in the north of Cornwall. Their name reflects their penchant for making knocking sounds, signalling when miners approach rich seams.

Some Cornish miners maintain that they have also guided rescuers to the location of cave-ins by their tapping. Knockers are said to enjoy singing, particularly Christmas carols. They have a reputation for frightening miners by appearing suddenly and pulling faces, but miners are careful not to show anger if they do so, for fear of upsetting them. And no Cornish miner will ever whistle or swear while underground, because the knockers find both highly offensive. The tradition of knockers appears to have crossed the Atlantic to the USA, where they have gained the prefix 'Tommy' to become 'Tommy-knockers'. Tommy-knockers are said to be volatile in temperament, and sometimes malicious, and do not like to be seen by humans; one story tells of a coal miner whose co-workers wondered how he managed to produce so much more coal than they did every night without ever getting tired. They followed him one night and found him sitting smoking in a shaft while a large team of Tommy-knockers did the work for him. On seeing his companions, the Tommy-knockers, thinking he had betrayed them to his fellow-miners, were furious, and in their rage they caused the entire mine to burst into flames.

Mine spirits are known throughout European folklore, particularly in Wales, Scotland, Germany, Poland, Romania and Austria, as well as Cornwall. The German Kobolde are mischievous and enjoy frustrating the miners' work, and the Cutty Soams of the Scottish Borders are said to enjoy cutting the ropes that pull the coal trucks. If insulted, all mine spirits may, like the Polish Karzelek, cause rock showers or cave-ins. But they are in general disposed to be helpful to miners, as long as they are treated well. In south Germany, the Wichtlein warns of miners' deaths by tapping three times, and his presence indicates the proximity of rich seams of coal or ore. In Scotland, the Black Dwarfs perform a similar service, as do the Welsh Coblynau. The Coblynau are occasionally spotted on rock faces, apparently hard at work, but never actually achieving anything because they only pretend to mine.

L

Lamb Inn

The location of an 18th-century case of a biting poltergeist in Bristol.

The alleged POLTERGEIST activity at the Lamb Inn, Lawfords Gate, Bristol, started in November 1761 and lasted until December 1762, making it contemporaneous with the COCK LANE GHOST. Affecting a family named Giles, the phenomena were said to focus particularly on two young sisters, 13-year-old Molly and 8-year-old Dobby. The first incidents involved strange scratching and rapping sounds from the girls' bedrooms, followed by the mysterious movement of various objects. Many of the events described were what came to be thought of as 'routine' poltergeist disturbances, but a remarkable feature was a series of assaults upon the two girls. Both Molly and Dobby were said to suffer severely from pinches and bites from an unseen assailant. More seriously, pins were thrust into the girls by some undetected agency and they were repeatedly cut; on one occasion Molly received more than 40 cuts described as:

> ... all about two inches and a half long, and about the thickness of a shilling deep; the skin not jagged, but smooth, as if cut with a penknife.

Events were investigated by a Mr Henry Durbin, who later wrote a pamphlet on the case which was posthumously published in 1800. Durbin and other investigators made efforts to observe the phenomena under conditions which excluded fraud. On 30 January 1761, he witnessed a bite mark appear on Dobby's shoulder:

> I saw Dobby wiping her hands in a towel, while I was talking to her, she cried out [and] was bitten in the neck. I looked and saw the mark of teeth, about eighteen, and wet with spittle.

As with the Cock Lane ghost and the later ENFIELD POLTERGEIST, the poltergeist appeared to show signs of intelligence and was said to engage in communication with the family and investigators by means of scratching noises. The messages declared that the disturbances were the work of a witch. Eventually the family resorted to sympathetic magic, and after they followed the advice of a 'cunning woman' the disturbances ceased. Although nearly 250 years old, the Lamb Inn case is considered by many modern researchers to be evidential because of the detail set down in the account by Durbin and the resemblance to other cases involving biting poltergeists, both historic and modern.

Lemp Mansion

A mansion in St Louis, Missouri, reputed to be one of the USA's most haunted houses.

The Lemp Mansion, now a popular restaurant and inn, was built in the 1860s for William Lemp, son of the founder of the Lemp Brewery. The Lemp family became one of the richest in St Louis, the brewery having been established by the German immigrant Johann Adam Lemp and built up to massive commercial success. William Lemp inherited the business in 1862, and he and his wife and seven children enjoyed an opulent lifestyle. His eldest son, Frederick, was seen as the future head of the brewery, but died of a heart attack when he was only 28 years old. His father, William, took the blow badly, and a few years later he shot himself in the office he had built into his home. William Lemp Jnr inherited the brewery, but it did not flourish under his management as it had done previously. With the passing of the Prohibition law in 1919, the family's wealth declined, as the brewery was forced to close. In 1920 William Jnr's sister, Elsa, shot herself as her father had done. In 1922 the business was sold, but for a fraction of its pre-Prohibition value. Some months later, William Jnr also shot himself.

The Lemp Mansion was then lived in by Charles Lemp, another of William Jnr's siblings. Said to have been an eccentric, with a fear of germs, he shot himself there in 1949. Another brother, Edwin, sold the house. He went on to live a long life, dying of natural causes at the age of 90, although he was again said to be eccentric, having a dreadful fear of being alone. For a time the Lemp Mansion became a boarding house, but it was later said that the boarding house did not thrive because of the ghosts that boarders shared their residence with. However, the house's haunted reputation became truly established in the mid 1970s, when it was bought by the Pointer family.

The Pointers employed a number of workmen to renovate the house and develop it into a restaurant and inn. Immediately, these workers began to report strange incidents. It was said that they had a feeling of being watched, and that they could often hear strange noises, such as the sound of a horse's hooves on cobblestones, and they reported that their tools regularly disappeared. When the restaurant opened, the haunting phenomena continued – glasses have been known to fly off the bar, doors lock and unlock themselves and occasional APPARITIONS are reportedly glimpsed.

No doubt directly linked to the tragic history of the Lemp family, the reputation of the Lemp Mansion as one of the USA's most HAUNTED HOUSES is firmly established, and visitors are now able to stay there, eat in the restaurant, and take a guided ghost tour.

Leonard, Gladys Osborne (1882–1968)

English trance medium.

Gladys Osborne Leonard was born in Lancashire in 1882. Sometimes referred to as the English LEONORA PIPER, she too apparently had an early experience which presaged her mediumship, seeing heavenly visions as a child. Leonard hoped for a career as a singer, but after an illness which affected her throat she became an actress with a touring company. She began TABLE-TURNING with some colleagues in the dressing-room, and after a number of attempts apparently communicated with 'Feda', the spirit of a young Indian girl, who became Leonard's CONTROL. Leonard claimed that it was Feda who instructed her to become a professional MEDIUM.

Leonard's main claim to fame came from her sittings for Sir Oliver Lodge, a prominent member of the SOCIETY FOR PSYCHICAL RESEARCH (SPR). Lodge lost a son, Raymond, in 1915, and was convinced, from the description she gave to him of a photograph taken of Raymond shortly before he died, that Leonard had established contact with his spirit. Leonard became famous, and Lodge had regular sittings with her for several years. In 1918, for a period of three months, Leonard exclusively gave séances arranged by the SPR. The sitters were generally impressed with her abilities.

Leonard worked successfully until the 1950s, when 'Feda' instructed her to cut down on the amount of work she did. While she was never proved to be a fraud, critics contend that her reputation was based solely on the word of the rather credulous Sir Oliver Lodge.

levitation

The lifting into the air of people or objects without any visible physical means.

Levitation is the lifting of people or objects into the air without any visible physical means being present. Some believe that it is a form of PSYCHOKINESIS, and it has been claimed as a power by spiritualists, fakirs and stage magicians.

Reports of instances of demonic possession often include details of the possessed person levitating or of objects being invisibly, and often violently, hurled around. Similar effects have been attributed to the activities of POLTERGEISTS.

Spiritualist MEDIUMS have often claimed the power of levitating themselves or objects, whether in a state of trance or fully conscious. The Scottish spiritualist DAVID DUNGLAS HOME was said to have levitated himself out of a building by one window and back in by another, although witnesses to this act appear to disagree over what it was they actually saw.

Does levitation really exist? As far as SPIRITUALISM is concerned, sceptics believe that it is always an illusion, relying on the suggestibility of the audience, or even a crude deception involving wires, powerful magnets and other hidden devices.

Nowadays, unlike in the past, conjurers are often persuaded to reveal the secrets behind levitation and other well-known feats of 'magic'. Street magicians are known to achieve an illusion of levitating themselves a few inches into the air simply by carefully choosing the angle at which they are seen, which allows them to disguise the fact that the toes of one foot are still in contact with the ground.

life after death *see* AFTERLIFE; REINCARNATION

life review *see* NEAR-DEATH EXPERIENCE

London Underground ghosts

Ghostly apparitions reportedly seen on the London Underground.

A number of hauntings are associated with stations on the underground railway in London. Sightings have generally been reported by employees rather than passengers, and some are associated with stations that have long been closed, such as the British Museum station. These unused stations are often referred to as ghost stations.

The British Museum station, which was closed in 1933, was reputedly haunted by the ghost of an ancient Egyptian – sometimes described as complete with headdress and loincloth, and in other tales described as a mummy from the collection at the museum. It has also been claimed that when the station closed, a newspaper offered a reward to anyone willing to spend a night in the station – although as this newspaper is never apparently named, it may be that this part of the

The actor William Terriss, who was murdered in 1897. His ghost is said to haunt both the Adelphi Theatre and the London Underground. (© Mary Evans Picture Library)

story, and the ghost itself, are entirely fictional.

Aldwych is no longer a working station (although it is hired out as a party venue and for filming) and it too has a ghost legend associated with it. In this case, the ghost of an actress is said to appear on the tracks at night, startling engineers.

At Covent Garden station the ghost of a tall man wearing a frock coat and a top hat was reputedly seen in the 1950s and 1970s. The ghost has been identified as actor William Terriss, murdered by a rival in 1897 (see ADELPHI THEATRE).

The ghost of a woman was reported at Aldgate in 1951, and the apparition was apparently accompanied by strange whistling sounds. Apparitions were also reported at Victoria during construction work in 1968.

However, in proportion to the size of the Underground network and the number of staff and passengers who use the Underground each day, the number of actual reports is tiny, and some have wondered why these dark and often ominous places do not actually generate more 'ghost' experiences.

Maskelyne, John Nevil (1839–1917)

A 19th-century English stage magician who famously exposed a number of fake psychics and mediums.

John Nevil Maskelyne, a descendant of the one-time Astronomer Royal Nevil Maskelyne (1732–1811), was a renowned Victorian magician and member of the Magic Circle. Born in Cheltenham, he originally worked as a watchmaker, and later went on to design and manufacture many of his own mechanical magical effects. He is also credited with inventing a lock, activated by a penny, which was placed on the first pay toilets in London.

In 1865, he watched a performance by the famous 'MEDIUMS' Ira and William Davenport in his home town of Cheltenham. At the time, the DAVENPORT BROTHERS, from the USA, were performing at SÉANCES all over the world, and many believed that they were genuine mediums. A typical Davenport séance would be carried out in a theatre and would see the two brothers placed inside a cabinet, bound hand and foot. Then a number of items, such as musical instruments and tools, were placed in the cabinet with them. When the stage was plunged into darkness the instruments would be heard playing, and the sound of hammering would emanate from the cabinet – all apparently due to the actions of SPIRITS. When the lights came back up the brothers would be found to be still bound, exactly as they had been. Maskelyne quickly spotted how the trick was performed – in one version of the story, a small gap in the blackout curtains allowed him to actually see the Davenports escape from their ropes and perform the feats themselves, before retying their bonds and accepting the applause. He decided to set out on his own career as a professional magician and publicly exposed the Davenports by demonstrating their methods.

As a stage magician, Maskelyne was well placed to expose the tricks and sleight of hand employed by fraudulent mediums. On the back of his public exposure of the Davenports he toured the country for eight years with his

A poster dating from c.1885 advertising Maskelyne's performances at the Egyptian Hall, London. (© The British Library/HIP/TopFoto)

partner, often performing some of the tricks fraudulent spiritualists employed at séances. As part of his act Maskelyne included an escape from a box in which he was tied with ropes, similar to that of the Davenports. In 1873, he and his partner took a permanent residency in a London theatre, the Egyptian Hall, Piccadilly.

Maskelyne was an eternal self-publicist and he engaged in constant exposures of mediums to gain publicity for his stage act, in which he replicated the effects that mediums attributed to spirits. He billed himself as an 'anti-spiritualist', and in 1914 he founded the Occult Committee, which aimed to 'investigate claims to supernatural power and to expose fraud'.

materialization

The manifestation of material objects apparently from nowhere.

Materializations are often claimed to have occurred during SÉANCES and also often feature in POLTERGEIST cases. Materializations take one of two forms: either they can involve something mysteriously transported from elsewhere within the real, physical world (usually referred to as an APPORT), or they can involve the apparent spontaneous creation of an object (by spirits or other supernatural means). ECTOPLASM is the name given to the hypothetical material from which such objects are said to be created.

Materializations that were claimed to have been produced by MEDIUMS include a vast range of (often bizarre) inanimate objects, as well as human figures – for example the materializations of Katie King by the medium FLORENCE COOK. In the stories of poltergeist cases the materializations are usually more mundane and include such things as stones, coins and water.

Although materializations were extremely fashionable during the heyday of Victorian SPIRITUALISM, the production of an apport or the manifestation of ectoplasm was never successfully demonstrated under laboratory conditions. Claims to have produced a materialization are now uncommon, although they do still occasionally appear.

The medium and spiritualist Doris Stokes, photographed in 1986. (© TopFoto/UPP)

medium

Someone who is allegedly able to communicate directly with the spirits of the dead or is able to allow such communication to take place through them.

The idea of the 'medium', or 'spirit medium', was popularized during the rise of the spiritualist movement in the 19th century (see SPIRITUALISM), although the concept of direct communication with SPIRITS has formed part of many religious and spiritual belief systems throughout history. Spirit mediums are attributed with the ability to be able to sense, hear or even see spirits (see CLAIRSENTIENCE, CLAIRAUDIENCE and CLAIRVOYANCE), and some are said to be able to bring about MATERIALIZATIONS of ECTOPLASM or APPORTS (see MEDIUM, PHYSICAL) – including on occasion physical manifestations of the spirits themselves. Such alleged abilities are usually demonstrated during a SÉANCE and may involve the medium having to go into a 'trance' (see MEDIUM, TRANCE and TRANCE, MEDIUMISTIC).

Some mediums claim to be able to manifest voices (see MEDIUM, DIRECT VOICE), while others apparently allow the spirits to possess them so they can speak through them, and a few even claim that they can effectively be transformed into the spirit (MEDIUM, TRANSFIGURATION). Processes such as this, where the spirit apparently communicates through the medium, are often described as forms of CHANNELLING. Channelling is also associated with the production of AUTOMATIC ART, AUTOMATIC SPEECH and AUTOMATIC WRITING. Other mediums claim that they experience the communication with the spirits themselves, and then pass on the messages to the other séance sitters (see MEDIUM, MENTAL).

Famous 19th-century mediums include the FOX SISTERS, DANIEL DUNGLAS HOME, EUSAPIA PALLADINO and HÉLÈNE SMITH, and those from the 20th century include STANISLAWA TOMCZYK, RUTH MONTGOMERY and DORIS STOKES. The activities of those who claim to be mediums have always been highly controversial, and the efforts on the part of such people as JOHN NEVIL MASKELYNE, HARRY HOUDINI and, more recently, members of organizations such as the Committee for the Scientific Investigation of Claims of the Paranormal have resulted in many mediums being exposed as frauds. Indeed, many of the feats originally associated with mediums are now standard features of stage magic acts, making it increasingly difficult for those who claim such powers to be taken seriously by the world at large.

medium, direct voice

A medium who can produce a voice which appears to have no physical source.

The voices produced by direct voice mediums appear to come out of 'thin air' and are supposedly those of SPIRITS.

One explanation offered by spiritualists for the mechanism by which this takes place is that ECTOPLASM is withdrawn from the medium and coalesces into a voice box which is used by the spirit. If only a small amount of 'energy' is available then amplification (usually by means of a trumpet or loudhailer) is required. If a large amount of 'energy' is available (such as that which apparently comes from an accomplished medium) then the voice can be heard without assistance. Direct voice mediums were particularly popular during the late 19th and early 20th centuries, although the phenomenon has undergone something of a resurgence in recent years in the UK.

Some direct voice mediums have been shown to fake their abilities through the use of ventriloquism techniques or concealed tape recorders and record players.

medium, mental

A medium who apparently experiences contact with the spirits in his or her mind only.

Mental mediums claim that they effectively act as an interpreter for the other participants in a SÉANCE.

They themselves apparently have a direct experience of contact with SPIRITS through processes described as CLAIRVOYANCE, CLAIRSENTIENCE or CLAIRAUDIENCE rather than producing direct, external communications from the spirits, or allowing the other séance participants to communicate with the spirits through them (see CHANNELLING). Modern PSYCHICS who claim to work in this way include the British mediums Derek Acorah and Gordon Smith – watching them perform can be likened to listening to a conversation take place while only being able to hear one of the people involved.

medium, physical

A medium who apparently manifests physical evidence of the existence of spirits.

Physical mediums claim to be able to produce (with the assistance of SPIRITS) MATERIALIZATIONS such as APPORTS or ECTOPLASM, or physical effects such as TABLE-TURNING or LEVITATION. During the heyday of SPIRITUALISM it was even claimed that some mediums were able to materialize spirits in full human form – and photographs of such 'materializations' were very popular during the 19th century (see SPIRIT PHOTOGRAPHY). Performances involving physical effects and manifestations usually required darkness, or at least semi-darkness, leading to the obvious suggestion that this was a cover for trickery.

medium, trance

A medium who claims that he or she must enter a trance to contact the spirits of the dead.

The trance (see TRANCE, MEDIUMISTIC) entered into by a trance medium is described as being similar to that which can sometimes be induced by hypnosis. Some would argue that it is an example of an altered state of consciousness.

Trance mediums will apparently enter a trance during a SÉANCE and, while they are in this state,

This photograph taken in 1928 shows a medium in a trance. Note the table in the foreground, which is apparently levitating to the extent that the image is blurred. (2005 Charles Walker/TopFoto)

communication with the spirits occurs. When they return from the trance at the end of the séance they are supposedly unaware of the details of what has taken place. A number of such mediums were involved in the investigation into life after death (see AFTERLIFE) undertaken by the SCOLE GROUP. The technique employed by trance mediums is sometimes described as mentally 'stepping aside' to allow the spirit to enter them. It can apparently be carried out only with the willing co-operation of both parties and requires a significant amount of training. However, those that claim that mediums are nothing more than stage magicians would argue that the apparent entry into a trance is simply showmanship.

medium, transfiguration

A medium who supposedly takes on the physical characteristics of the dead person with whom he or she is in contact.

Transfiguration mediums claim that they can be possessed by the SPIRIT of a dead person to the point that they will (usually very fleetingly) take on aspects of that person's appearance when they were alive. Such a change is an example of physical mediumship (see MEDIUM, PHYSICAL). Generally, it is said that no communication with the spirit is possible while the medium is taking on their appearance – this is supposedly due to the large amount of 'energy' required to achieve the change. It is claimed that the most advanced transfiguration mediums can even manifest the appearance of such things as facial hair – however, the few photographs in existence that allegedly show a transfiguration medium in action are remarkably similar to pictures of people simply pulling faces.

mediumistic trance *see* TRANCE, MEDIUMISTIC

mentalism

A performing art whereby mental acuity and principles of stage magic are used to present the illusion of such supernatural abilities as mind-reading, psychokinesis and precognition.

Mentalism is generally used as a form of entertainment and is often considered to be a branch of stage magic – it uses many of the same skills and principles in its performance, although some mentalists prefer to distance themselves from the theatrical trickery of stage magicians.

While some performers who call themselves mentalists claim that they have PSYCHIC powers, others profess that they reproduce the supernatural abilities of a psychic, including CLAIRVOYANCE, mind-reading, PSYCHOKINESIS and precognition, by natural means. This has brought some mentalists into conflict with spiritualists and MEDIUMS, as sceptical mentalists such as DERREN BROWN show that they can replicate the SÉANCE room without recourse to the supernatural.

Through misdirection, suggestion, psychology, the reading of body language, and not least showmanship, successful mentalists can convince an audience that they can read minds or predict the future, when in fact they are cleverly gaining the information they need from the audience members without them realizing it, and manipulating events towards a conclusion which they are then thought to have 'magically' predicted.

mental medium *see* MEDIUM, MENTAL

Miami Poltergeist

A poltergeist case that centred around a teenage worker at a Miami warehouse.

On 14 January 1967 a Miami warehouse manager phoned the police. He reported that a ghost was in the warehouse, breaking things. When the police arrived they witnessed objects mysteriously falling from the warehouse shelves, but could offer no help or explanation.

The POLTERGEIST activity continued, causing serious problems in a warehouse that was owned by Tropication Arts, a novelty item wholesaler – it contained thousands of small breakable items. The case came to the attention of various parapsychologists (see PARAPSYCHOLOGY), including William Roll, who coined the term RECURRENT SPONTANEOUS PSYCHOKINESIS (RSPK), and J G Pratt. From an early point in the investigation, Roll believed that the phenomena centred around one young warehouse worker – a 19-year-old Cuban shipping clerk called Julio. The mysterious movement of objects and subsequent breakages generally happened when Julio was nearby, and it is said that the intensity of the phenomena increased when Julio was irritated or upset.

In total, over 224 incidents of poltergeist activity were recorded at the warehouse, and there were numerous reputable witnesses – including the police officers who had been called on 14 January. Roll and Pratt carried out on-site investigations for two weeks, both of them seeing and carefully recording a number of incidents. However, no activity was recorded on film, as the poltergeist failed to co-operate at the times when video cameras were produced. Roll and Pratt also checked the warehouse shelves, pushing the stock back to eliminate the possibility that the objects were falling naturally through the action of vibrations. By placing notebooks in front of a row of glass items on a shelf, and subsequently finding broken glass on the floor and the notebooks undisturbed, Roll suggested that the objects lifted up into the air before dropping to the ground. The investigators kept certain objects under constant surveillance, and also measured the distances that displaced objects moved. They discovered that while the closer they were to Julio the more objects moved, objects that were further away from him actually travelled further. Roll and Pratt found no evidence of trickery in their investigations, although some have claimed that the effects were carefully staged using thread to pull objects from their places. At times, activity was observed while Julio himself was being closely watched.

At the request of the researchers, Julio agreed to undergo a series of psychological tests. It seemed he was a troubled young man who did not like his boss, whose home life was not happy, and who suffered from nightmares. On 30 January the warehouse was broken into and some petty cash stolen. Julio was suspected, and admitted to the crime, but no charges were pressed. Julio then stole from a jeweller's, and was given a six-month prison sentence, after which the incidents at the warehouse ceased.

The Miami Poltergeist is one of the best-documented poltergeist cases, and some people hold it up as an example of evidence that poltergeist activity can be caused through RSPK, in this case with Julio acting as the AGENCY, unwittingly causing the disturbances because of his own anger and repressed emotions.

mine spirits *see* KNOCKERS

Montgomery, Ruth (1913–2001)

A US journalist who after investigating mediumistic abilities apparently found that she had them herself.

Ruth Montgomery was a journalist whose career in the world of PSYCHIC phenomena began in 1965 when she was working on her book about the famous psychic Jeane Dixon (*A Gift of Prophecy: The Phenomenal Jeane Dixon*, 1965). Montgomery investigated the world of mediums further and apparently discovered she was able to produce AUTOMATIC WRITING, and soon found herself CHANNELLING information from her CONTROLS or spirit guides. She wrote down the revelations she claimed to receive and published them in a series of eleven books (the first being *A World Beyond* in 1973). Among other things, the SPIRITS who communicated with Montgomery gave details of a karmic 'other life' involving REINCARNATION, existence on 'higher planes of being' and punishment for those who have committed wrong in the physical world (although with the potential eventually to earn redemption). Such spiritual notions were popular with many New Age thinkers at the time. However, the books also contained a number of predictions, the accuracy of which has since proved to be somewhat disappointing.

Morton ghost

An apparition that was apparently witnessed repeatedly in a house in Cheltenham in the final quarter of the 19th century.

Often considered the best-attested example of an apparitional haunting, the Morton ghost was the apparition of a woman which members of a family named Despard claimed they saw repeatedly between 1882 and 1889 in their house in Pittville Circus Road, Cheltenham, England. The family was given the pseudonym Morton in a report on the haunting published by the SOCIETY FOR PSYCHICAL RESEARCH in its *Proceedings* under the title 'Record of a Haunted House'. It was claimed that the apparition was seen by 17 people and heard by 20. Rosina Despard described the figure as:

> … that of a tall lady, dressed in black of a soft woollen material, judging from the slight sound in moving. The face was hidden in a handkerchief held in the right hand … a portion of a widow's cuff was visible on both wrists, so that the whole impression was that of a lady in widow's weeds. There was no cap on the head, but the general effect of blackness suggests a bonnet with long veil or hood.

Some witnesses spoke of a cold wind that accompanied the figure, and said that dogs seemed to react adversely to its presence. The ghost was seen mostly at night but never when the family watched for it or when they were talking about it. Suggestions that the figure was that of a living woman secretly residing in the house do not seem sustainable on account of its ability to pass through strings placed in its path, reports that it could simply vanish and its success in eluding pursuers trying to touch or catch it. The apparition was said to be that of Imogen Swinhoe, second wife of Henry Swinhoe, a former resident who had died in 1878 and was buried at the Holy Trinity Church, close to the house. Apart from footsteps that were sometimes heard, the haunting seemed to cease in 1890. B Abdy Collins, who reviewed the evidence of the haunting in his book *The Cheltenham Ghost* (1948), considered the haunting as evidence of survival after death, but other researchers have been more cautious.

While some simply do not accept that the ghost ever appeared, later 20th-century reports suggest that the haunting did not cease as initially believed, and indicate that a similar figure continued to be seen in the area until the 1960s. Ghost researcher Andrew MacKenzie collected an account of a figure of a woman in black seen in Pittville Circus Road in 1985.

Murphy, Bridey

The name supposedly given by a 19th-century Irishwoman who it was claimed had either been reincarnated as, or whose spirit had possessed, a 20th-century woman from the USA.

Bridey Murphy supposedly lived in Cork, Ireland, roughly in the period between 1798 and 1864. In 1952, it was claimed that she paid a rather unexpected visit to Pueblo in Colorado, USA. When placed under hypnosis by the amateur hypnotist Morey Bernstein, Virginia Tighe (1923–95) started to recount details of Murphy's life, in an Irish accent, complete with colourful tales of 19th-century Irish life and a few Irish songs for good measure. More hypnosis sessions followed, recordings were made, and after each session Tighe and Bernstein

An issue of *Fate Magazine*, from November 1956, which included an investigation of Bridey Murphy. (© Mary Evans Picture Library)

would listen to the tapes together. It was claimed that this case provided conclusive proof of the reality of either REINCARNATION or possession.

In 1956, Bernstein published a book, *The Search for Bridey Murphy*; a film version of the story was released and recordings from the original hypnosis sessions were made available to an eager public. Tighe was renamed Ruth Simmons in an attempt to protect her identity, but journalists rapidly tracked her down. Some researchers claimed that, as a child in Wisconsin, Tighe had lived opposite an emigrant from Ireland called Bridey Murphy Corkell. Corkell had entertained the young Tighe with stories of her early life in Ireland. It was suggested that Tighe was just recounting stories she had heard in her youth, a claim perhaps borne out by the fact that she had used slang that would not have been current during the early 19th century. However, none of this prevented a number of other people from coming forward with similar claims in the years that followed. See also BLOXHAM TAPES.

Myrtles Plantation

An 18th-century house in St Francisville, Louisiana, reputedly one of the most haunted houses in the USA.

Now run as a bed and breakfast and restaurant, Myrtles Plantation advertises itself as 'one of America's most haunted homes'. The house was built in around 1796, and a number of families have owned it. Its haunted reputation seems to date from the second half of the 20th century.

The most famous ghost legend associated with the house is that of Chloe, a servant or slave, said to have belonged to the house in the early 1800s. Tradition has it that Chloe's master, Clark Woodruff, forced his sexual attentions on her, and that he had one of her ears cut off to teach her a lesson for eavesdropping. Whether for revenge, or to put herself in a better position by saving the family from their sickness, Chloe is said to have baked a cake with poison in it. The poisoned cake killed Woodruff's wife and two daughters (perhaps because Chloe had used more poison than she realized), but Woodruff did not eat any, and remained well. The other slaves are then said to have hanged Chloe and thrown her weighted body into the river, perhaps because they feared that Woodruff would punish them too for her actions.

The ghost of Chloe, in the green turban she wore to hide the scar of her ear having been removed, is said to regularly appear at the house. One past owner apparently captured her on camera, and postcards have been sold showing a blurry figure between two of the buildings – allegedly the ghost of Chloe. However, many question the story of Chloe, claiming that the legend is entirely fictional; Chloe never existed, and the murders never took place – Mrs Woodruff died of yellow fever.

Other murderous legends have been associated with Myrtles Plantation. It is said that during the Civil War three Union soldiers were shot dead when they broke into the house, leaving indelible bloodstains on the floor, and, on at least one occasion, leaving a body-shaped space on the floor which a maid simply could not clean, as though it had a force field around it. Again, there is no historical evidence to support the story, and it is not known that any soldiers were shot there.

A mirror in the house is said to show the handprints of some of the spirits of those who have died there, and is a popular point on the tours that are regularly given around the property. The APPARITION of a young girl is said to manifest in the room in which it is said she died, and the ghost of William Winter, who was actually murdered at the house in 1871, is also said to appear. His spectre ascends the stairs to the seventeenth step, either by walking or crawling. The story goes that after he was shot, he managed to climb the stairs to the seventeenth step, where he died in the arms of his wife, although his ability to do so has been disputed.

While many of the background stories associated with the hauntings at Myrtles Plantation have been shown to be false, there are those who believe that the house might still be the home of a number of ghosts, the true histories of which are simply not known.

Naseby, Battle of

A major battle of the English Civil War, fought in Northamptonshire; legend has it that the battle was re-enacted in the sky above the battlefield for many years after the event.

At the Battle of Naseby, fought on 14 June 1645, the Royalist forces of Charles I, outnumbered by two to one, were defeated by Parliament's New Model Army. As with the BATTLE OF EDGEHILL, a legend soon arose that AERIAL PHANTOMS re-enacted the battle in the sky, apparently witnessed by many people.

In the past, stories regularly circulated telling how the whole of the battle was re-enacted on the anniversary of the event – some claim that for a hundred years after it villagers would come specially to watch the ghostly parade, picnicking on nearby hills – or that a column of soldiers could be seen, sombrely pushing carts along an old drovers' road. More recent reports suggest that only the shouts of the soldiers and the clash of weaponry are still heard. See also SOUTHER FELL; SPECTRAL ARMIES.

near-death experience

A dream-like narrative supposedly experienced by some people when their physical body is at the point of death – successful resuscitation then allows them to relate the details. Such experiences are often interpreted as a journey of the self, or spirit, towards the afterlife.

Near-death experiences (often abbreviated to NDEs) are regularly reported by people who recover from being very close to death, or in some cases from being clinically dead for a short period. NDEs became a popular area of study after 1975, when the originator of the term, Dr Raymond Moody, published a book called *Life After Life*, listing a number of cases he had recorded. However, records exist of earlier reports of what would later be described as NDEs, such as, famously, that of the psychologist Carl Jung after he suffered a heart attack in 1944.

The stories related by those who report NDEs vary, but there are a number of commonly occurring elements.

An artist's impression of the Battle of Naseby, featured in *Pictures of English History* (c. 1892). (© Print Collector/HIP/TopFoto)

Typically, the experience may begin with a buzzing or ringing sound followed by a sense of peace and the sensation of 'leaving the body' – some even report being aware of floating around the room in which the physical body is lying (see OUT-OF-BODY EXPERIENCE). This is often followed by the impression of moving through a tunnel towards a light, and as they approach the light they may 'meet' dead relatives, friends or other spiritual beings. Another commonly reported feature is that of the 'life review'. Essentially, this means the person has a vision of the whole of their life or of the key events in it; this may include being 'shown' things that they did that they can identify as being morally good or bad, and the consequences of these actions. While the 'review' covers the person's whole life, they feel that it passes very quickly. The NDE usually ends with the person being told to return to their body because their time for death has not yet come.

A 1992 Gallup poll reported that nearly eight million Americans claimed to have had an NDE, and a Dutch report published in *The Lancet* in 2001 stated that in a sample of 344 patients who had been successfully resuscitated after a heart attack, 18 per cent reported a classic NDE. When questioned about their NDE many people say they believe that they have seen a glimpse of the AFTERLIFE. Most report that it was a positive experience, although approximately 15 per cent report a negative experience of a 'hellish' place. A large number even say that they were disappointed when they 'returned', because there was such a feeling of calm and love around them during the NDE.

Some people regard NDEs as positive proof of life after death, while others argue that there is a fundamental philosophical (or even theological) problem with this, in that the patient was not really dying during the experience, as they did 'come back'. Some researchers have offered non-supernatural explanations for the experience. They believe that the NDEs result from normal, chemical processes in the brain which may occur as a natural result of the brain 'closing down', releasing endorphin-like chemicals to reduce pain and preparing to die. The images may well be akin to hallucinations resulting from the expectations many people have relating to what will happen when they die – it has, for example, been observed that certain drugs produce hallucinations which bear all the hallmarks of a classic NDE.

It has been claimed that some surgeons have placed a card bearing a message in such a way that the message can only be read from the top of the operating theatre. They have then asked patients who have reported an NDE to tell them what the message was. Apparently this has not produced any success.

Spiritual interpretations of NDEs remain extremely popular, and a fictional depiction of attempts to induce them deliberately formed the central theme of the 1990 film *Flatliners*.

Newstead Abbey

A historic house in Nottinghamshire, England; it was once the home of the poet Lord Byron, and is associated with a number of ghostly legends.

Newstead Abbey was originally an Augustinian priory, founded in the latter part of the twelfth century. The abbey was closed in 1539, and the buildings and land were bought for use as a private estate by Sir John Byron of Colwick in the following year. The property later came to the poet Lord Byron, and while it is said that he was very fond of the (by then near ruinous) property, he sold it in 1818.

Byron's father, known as the 'Devil Byron', lived and died at Newstead Abbey. One legend states that he was haunted during his life by the ghost of his sister, whom he had shunned for many years following a family scandal. The ghost was said to call to him, begging him to speak to her again. In a ballad by Ebenezer Elliott (1781–1849), the ghosts of both Devil Byron and his sister go forth on stormy nights:

> On mighty winds, in spectre coach,
>
> Fast speeds the Heart of iron;

On spectre-steed, the spectre-dame—
Side by side with Byron …

On winds, on clouds, they ride, they drive—
Oh, hark, thou Heart of iron!
The thunder whispers mournfully,
'Speak to her, Lord Byron!'

Another ghost associated with Newstead is that of Sir John Byron. Although apparently seen less often in recent years, it is said that at one time he would regularly appear sitting beside the fire, reading. Another story tells that Sir John's ghost would step down from his portrait and walk around the state apartments.

The apparition of a WHITE LADY has been reported at Newstead, and some claim that the ghost of Lord Byron's Newfoundland dog, Boatswain, also haunts the house. Apparently, Lord Byron asked that his body be interred there, next to that of his dog, but the request was ignored. Some say that the ghost of Boatswain is vainly searching for its master.

Perhaps the most famous ghost at Newstead is a BLACK MONK known as the 'Goblin Friar'. Some claim that this apparition acts as a harbinger of disaster to any member of the Byron family – Lord Byron is said to have seen it before his ill-fated marriage to Anne Millbanke in 1815 – but others claim that the apparition existed only in Byron's imagination, and in the cantos of *Don Juan*:

It was no mouse, but lo! a monk, array'd
In cowl and beads and dusky garb, appear'd,
Now in the moonlight, and now lapsed in shade,
With steps that trod as heavy, yet unheard.

Those who believe the 'Goblin Friar' legend to be genuine link it to a 17th-century tradition that to live in a previously monastic building which became secular with the Dissolution of the Monasteries is sacrilegious, and carries with it a curse.

O

OBE *see* OUT-OF-BODY EXPERIENCE

Okehampton Castle

A ruined 11th-century castle in Okehampton, Devon, associated with the legend of the ghost of Lady Howard.

Legend has it that Okehampton Castle is haunted by the ghost of Lady Mary Howard, condemned to travel each night from her home, Fitzford House in the town of Tavistock, to the castle riding in a coach made from the bones of her murdered husbands. Headless black horses drive the coach, with a black dog running in front of them, and a headless coachman steers the way. In his *Devonshire Characters and Strange Events* (1908), Rev Sabine Baring-Gould includes a version of the legend in ballad form:

> My Ladye hath a sable coach
> With horses two and four
> My Ladye hath a gaunt blood-hound
> That goeth on before.
> My Ladye's coach hath nodding plumes
> The driver hath no head.
> My Ladye is an ashen white
> As one that long is dead.

The much-maligned Lady Howard is said to have married four times (which seems to be true) and to have murdered at least two of her husbands and possibly two of her children (which seems not to be true). Her nocturnal coach ride, setting out at midnight every night, is punishment for her wickedness. When the grisly coach reaches Okehampton Castle, Lady Howard must pluck a single blade of grass (although in some versions the black hound performs this task) before returning to Tavistock. The punishment will not end until all the grass has been removed from the very grassy mound on which Okehampton Castle sits – which it never can be, as it grows faster than it can be plucked. The legend is well known in the area, and as Baring-Gould recalled:

> I frequently heard of the coach going from Okehampton to Tavistock when I was a boy … I remember the deadly fear I felt lest I should be on the road

The ruins of Okehampton Castle. (© Mary Evans Picture Library)

at night, and my nurse was wont to comfort me by saying there was no fear of the 'Lady's Coach' except after midnight.

orbs

'Ghostly' spheres which have appeared on photographs taken by many digital and compact cameras since the 1990s.

Since the advent of digital photography in the 1990s, and the changing design of compact cameras at this time, many photographs have been taken which show small globular luminous patches or smudges, apparently not visible to observers at the time the picture was taken. Such blemishes have been dubbed 'orbs' and were virtually unknown before this time. Various extraordinary claims have been made for orbs – some have said that they represent packages of psychic energy invisible to the naked eye, while others have suggested that they are the spirits or souls of the deceased. Some even claim to see structures, faces or messages within orbs. The orb phenomenon became a hugely popular topic on the Internet, and in the USA the first orb photography courses have been offered.

However, the perception of orbs is very much in the eye of the beholder; it appears that only individuals predisposed to a belief in the supernatural are convinced of the reality of orbs as a psychic phenomenon. The major objection to a paranormal explanation for orbs is that the air is constantly filled with minute specks of moisture, smoke or dust and these may be recorded on sensitive cameras, particularly where the flash is situated close to the lens, as with most modern cameras. Research conducted by British photographer Philip Carr and incorporated into a short film, *The Riddle of the Orbs* (2004), demonstrates that such photographs can be easily obtained or created anywhere by taking flash photographs of mundane airborne particles, the resultant images being indistinguishable from alleged orb pictures. Certainly, the frequent appearance of orbs in photographs obtained using flash photography in dusty and damp environments such as ruined castles and ancient manor houses – sites often selected for ghost hunting – is consistent with them being nothing more than mundane airborne particles. Nonetheless, advocates of a paranormal explanation for orbs often stridently reject this solution. As with other GHOST PHOTOGRAPHS, the will to believe sometimes overrides a more rational assessment of the images.

ouija board

An item of equipment employed during séances through which messages can allegedly be received from spirits of the dead.

A ouija board (also known as a 'talking board' or 'spirit board') consists of a board upon which the letters of the alphabet and the words 'yes' and 'no' are written. Some boards also have a few additional words, or numbers, on them. A PLANCHETTE sits on top of the board. The participants in a SÉANCE each place a finger on the planchette. Questions are then asked and the planchette moves over the board, supposedly under the guidance of the SPIRITS, spelling out their answers.

The ouija board was invented in the 1890s and originally sold in the USA. The final version employing the planchette (which had previously been used as a system for producing AUTOMATIC WRITING) developed from an early version which used letters placed on a table over which a pendulum would be swung to spell out the message. The name was originally claimed to be the Egyptian for 'good luck', but when this was rapidly discredited it was then said that it was in fact derived from a combination of the French and German words for 'yes'. The use of ouija boards went on to become a very popular parlour game during the early 20th century, and many examples are still available today – some are sold as games by well-known manufacturers, while others are marketed as specialist items specifically for séances.

Although believers hold that the movement of the planchette is wholly down to the actions of the spirits, sceptics argue it is unconscious (or even conscious) movement by the participants that causes the messages to be spelt out – pointing to observations which indicate that when the participants are blindfolded the result is usually nonsense.

out-of-body experience

An experience in which an individual allegedly has the sensation of the self leaving the body – usually claimed

A simple ouija system in operation, using a table rather than a board. (© 2004 Charles Walker/TopFoto)

to involve being able to observe the physical body from elsewhere.

Out-of-body experiences (OBEs) are commonly reported to occur as part of NEAR-DEATH EXPERIENCES (NDEs). They can also apparently be brought on by a traumatic experience, and are sometimes said to occur to people while they are in comas, under anaesthetic or under the influence of certain drugs. Some even claim to be able consciously to induce them – for example, the supposed ability to engage in ASTRAL PROJECTION allegedly involves a form of out-of-body experience; in this instance it is interpreted as being due to the SPIRIT being deliberately allowed to leave the physical body.

A common feature of OBEs is the apparent sensation of looking down on one's own body. The period during which the experience is said to have occurred is often very short (typically only minutes); however, the subject often reports feeling that a longer period of time has elapsed. At the end of the OBE the subject may report the sensation of 'snapping back into' their body. Some research carried out in the area has indicated that as many as one in ten people report experiencing an OBE at some point in their lives. Proposed explanations include the suggestion that they are experiences manufactured within the brain when it is cut off from external stimuli, and that they resemble dreams or hallucinations, although a significant number of people accept the objective reality of OBEs and offer spiritual explanations involving the soul leaving the body. The very nature of the experiences ensures that evidence for their existence is mostly anecdotal, and those who claim to be able to induce them at will have so far failed to demonstrate satisfactorily that they can use OBEs to obtain information which could not have been gained by other means.

Palladino, Eusapia (1854–1918)

Widely regarded as one of the most remarkable mediums in history.

Born in a small Italian village, Eusapia Palladino was orphaned at an early age, and moved to Naples. Her PSYCHIC abilities apparently manifested when she was still very young, and she became a successful MEDIUM. She came to the attention of Dr Ercole Chiaia, who had an interest in the occult, and in 1888 he wrote to the eminent Italian psychiatrist and criminologist Cesare Lombroso to alert him to her amazing abilities:

> The case I allude to is that of an invalid woman who belongs to the humblest class of society. She is … very ignorant; her appearance is neither fascinating nor endowed with the power which modern criminologists call irresistible; but when she wishes, be it by day or by night, she can divert a curious group for an hour or so with the most surprising phenomena. Either bound to a seat, or firmly held by the hands of the curious, she attracts to her the articles of furniture which surround her, lifts them up, holds them suspended in the air … and makes them come down again with undulatory movements, as if they were obeying her will … If you place in the corner of the room a vessel containing a layer of soft clay, you find after some moments the imprint in it of a small or a large hand, the image of a face (front view or profile) from which a plaster cast can be taken … This woman rises in the air, no matter what bands tie her down … she plays on musical instruments – organs, bells, tambourines – as if they had been touched by her hands or moved by the breath of invisible gnomes.

When Lombroso attended one of Palladino's SÉANCEs some two years later, he too was impressed by her apparent gift of PSYCHOKINESIS:

> Eusapia's feet and hands were held by Professor Tamburini and by Lombroso. A handbell placed on a small table more than a yard distant from Eusapia sounded in the air above the heads of the sitters and

Eusapia Palladino apparently materializing disembodied arms during a séance in the 1880s. (© Mary Evans Picture Library)

> then descended on the table, thence going two yards to a bed. While the bell was ringing we struck a match and saw the bell up in the air.

Members of the SOCIETY FOR PSYCHICAL RESEARCH (SPR) took Palladino to Cambridge in 1895 to test her abilities for themselves. In a series of 20 sittings, the researchers deliberately allowed Palladino to cheat – which she did, constantly. The SPR concluded that she was nothing but a fraud, but this did not deter her supporters, who claimed that she only cheated when her powers were weak or when the SPIRITS were not communicating, and this was done merely to prevent disappointment. Others said that her deception was the result of a mischievous temperament. She toured widely and successfully, despite further exposures for fraud at her séances, and while many dismissed her she retained some supporters until the end. While there is absolutely no doubt that Palladino frequently employed trickery, there are some who still claim that this was mixed with genuine psychic ability.

parapsychology

Parapsychology is concerned with paranormal phenomena, such as telepathy and clairvoyance, which seem to be inexplicable in terms of current scientific understanding, and often encompass hauntings and poltergeists.

Parapsychology might be defined as the scientific study of 'anomalous cognition' (normally referred to as extrasensory perception, or ESP) and 'anomalous influence' (PSYCHOKINESIS, or PK). ESP typically includes CLAIRVOYANCE (discerning information that is beyond the normal range of sense or perception), telepathy (sharing thoughts and images with another individual through mind-to-mind contact) and precognition (gaining prior knowledge of future events). PK is typically divided into macro-PK (large-scale, observable demonstrations of PK, such as the movement of objects using the power of the mind) and micro-PK (small-scale demonstrations of PK, unobservable but measurable via statistical analysis, such as influencing a random number generator). The term psi (the Greek letter ψ) is a blanket term used to refer to any paranormal phenomenon or process. Thus, the psi hypothesis in parapsychology is that some of these experiences at least are indeed paranormal, the result of ESP or PK. However, research in parapsychology has always included the pseudo-psi hypothesis, ie that most, perhaps all, such experiences are misattributed 'normal' experiences, the result of self-deception and deception. Research into ostensibly paranormal experiences and paranormal belief, therefore, overlaps with the interests of 'normal' or mainstream psychology.

The origins of parapsychology can be found in Victorian SPIRITUALISM, when many scientifically minded individuals took an interest in the phenomena of the SÉANCE room. The first serious experiments were those of SIR WILLIAM CROOKES in 1870–1, when he began testing the 'physical phenomena' (similar to what is now called PK) of the medium DANIEL DUNGLAS HOME. The following year, in the *Quarterly Journal of Science*, Crookes announced that, as a result of these experiments, he had discovered the existence of a new 'PSYCHIC' force. The response of the scientific community was largely negative, however, and subsequent exposures of fraudulent mediums did not help. In 1882, the SOCIETY FOR PSYCHICAL RESEARCH (SPR) was founded, and focused less on physical phenomena than on mental phenomena (similar to what is now called ESP), the word 'telepathy' being coined in 1892, though the SPR retained a significant interest in the question of survival after death. Thus, in Britain at least, psychical research has tended to be broader than parapsychology, including non-experimental research into case studies of, for example, REINCARNATION. Such an approach is unavoidable with spontaneous phenomena (such as POLTERGEISTS), but invariably relies upon eyewitness testimony, the problems of which make strong conclusions difficult.

While there remains widespread scepticism within the scientific community about the existence of psi, parapsychological research is being carried out in several universities in the UK and elsewhere, with chairs having been established at Edinburgh, Northampton and Lund. Given that ostensibly paranormal experiences are common, and belief in the paranormal is widespread, a better understanding of what is going on would seem to be highly desirable, even if the scientific community is unconvinced that such experiences might be explained in terms of psi. Meanwhile, regardless of what happens in academia, the media and the public will no doubt continue to be fascinated by the possibility, and the inevitable mixture of enthusiastic investigators, sincere believers and outright frauds will ensure that the mystery never entirely goes away.

passing caller

The term used to refer to a discarnate entity that manifests only once to deliver a message.

Those who consider GHOSTS to be a

spiritual manifestation indicative of survival after death may embrace the idea of the 'passing caller' – a DISCARNATE ENTITY that appears only once to deliver a message, typically a warning or a farewell. Many CRISIS APPARITIONS might fall into the category of passing callers, although psychical researchers since the 1880s have preferred to account for them in terms of telepathy rather than visitation of a spirit. Spiritualists link the idea of passing callers with 'drop-in communicators' at SÉANCES who appear in place of invited or regular communicators.

past-life regression

The apparent recovery under hypnosis of details relating to individuals' 'previous lives', taken by some to be evidence of reincarnation.

The use of past-life regression became popular following the BRIDEY MURPHY case in 1952, and the subsequent publication of Morey Bernstein's book, *The Search for Bridey Murphy*, in 1956. The procedure involves the use of hypnosis, under the effect of which a suitable subject will appear to recall details of a former life (or lives). Some have even claimed that the process can be used for therapeutic purposes – the suggestion being that problems in our current life may result from events in our past lives.

Hypnosis itself is a notoriously controversial process, and it is widely known that a number of bizarre effects can apparently be produced through its application. Indeed, it has been shown that subjects (whether it is through a desire to please the hypnotist, the use of leading questions or suggestion or for other reasons) can be made to apparently recall all sorts of strange information. In practice, it can often be demonstrated that the past-life regression subject has, or certainly could have, previously encountered most of the information in books or through other 'ordinary' sources. The difficulty for the believer lies in demonstrating that the subject is not simply consciously, or unconsciously, recalling this. See also the BLOXHAM TAPES.

pedestrians, spectral *see*

SPECTRAL PEDESTRIANS

Petit Trianon, ghosts of *see*

VERSAILLES GHOSTS

phantasm

The term used by early psychical researchers for visual apparitions, or ghosts.

During the early years of the Committee on Haunted Houses – organized by the SOCIETY FOR PSYCHICAL RESEARCH – it was felt that the traditional word 'GHOST' was an inappropriate term to describe the phenomena which the society was engaged in studying. Noting that many apparitions appeared to be hallucinatory in nature and showed little or no awareness of observers and that the forms of living people were as frequently encountered as those of the dead, it was felt an alternative terminology was needed. Furthermore, the word 'ghost' was felt to have spiritual and superstitious connotations which the fledgling society was keen to be dissociated from, considering itself to be engaged upon a scientific exercise. As a result, a number of leading members of the society adopted the term 'phantasm' to describe an apparitional appearance. Phantasm was used by Edmund Gurney, Frederic Myers and Frank Podmore in the title of their monumental two-volume work *Phantasms of the Living* (1886), which detailed hundreds of contemporary reports of CRISIS APPARITIONS. However, while psychical researchers and parapsychologists still remain wary of the term 'ghost', the word 'phantasm' failed to catch on outside a limited circle.

phantom aeroplanes

The manifestation of ghost aeroplanes, either seen or heard.

Reports of phantom aeroplanes have emerged sporadically since the 1930s in different parts of the world. In some cases they have come in waves, as with reports of unidentified ghost planes in the skies over Scandinavia during the 1930s, and have been considered as an aspect of wider UFO phenomena. In other reports the phantom is identifiable as a specific aircraft which is known to have crashed or a military aircraft dating from World War II.

The first British case appears to have been a ghostly biplane seen by local residents over Shepperton, Surrey, during 1931. It was believed to be the spectral form of a Vickers Vanguard test aircraft which had crashed in the area two years earlier, killing its pilot. Former World War II aerodromes have also produced reports of phantom aeroplanes, including an account of a phantom plane seen landing at Barkston Heath, Lincolnshire, witnessed by a 17-year-old girl in the late 1960s. There are also reports of a phantom bomber plane seen in the 1990s over Bleaklow Hill in Derbyshire, in the vicinity of a number of known bomber crash sites.

In other cases the phantom aeroplane may be heard rather than seen; a ghostly Spitfire is said to have been heard over Biggin Hill in Kent, and the sound of a World War II phantom plane was allegedly captured on tape at the former Bircham Newton Aerodrome in Norfolk in 1972.

phantom armies *see* SPECTRAL ARMIES

phantom coaches

Apparitions of horse-drawn carriages.

Stories of phantom coaches are common in English folklore, but some consider that there are a small number of reports that suggest that they may also constitute a genuine apparitional experience. With most examples the phantom coach is a horse-drawn private carriage, but in other cases the vehicle may be a funeral hearse. In many traditional tales both

An 18th-century depiction of a phantom coach being driven over the sea. (© Mary Evans Picture Library)

the occupants of the coach and the horses pulling it appear headless, but no reliable first-hand sightings are known.

Tales of phantom coaches were particularly common in the English county of Norfolk in the 19th century. Tradition frequently links phantom coaches with the aristocracy (who were among the few who could afford the luxury of a private coach), with particular landed families or with executed criminals (usually noblemen, rarely commoners). In some folk tales, driving a phantom coach is a form of punishment for the soul of someone who has committed heinous sins in life, such as Tobias Gill at Blythburgh, Suffolk, who was hanged for murder in 1750 and who is said to be seen thundering past in a phantom coach pulled by four black chargers (see also OKEHAMPTON CASTLE). Similarly, a phantom coach is said to carry Sir Thomas Boleyn, father of Anne Boleyn (the second wife of Henry VIII), from his home of BLICKLING HALL around a circuit of twelve Norfolk bridges. The story goes that Sir Thomas is atoning for his part in his daughter's execution, and that if anyone speaks to him they will be carried away.

Some phantom coaches are said to have a prophetic function, acting as an omen of death for particular families, while others are said to be dangerous to encounter and capable of causing injury or of stealing the lives or souls of witnesses (as with that of Sir Thomas Boleyn). Folklorists have detected within this tradition both echoes of the belief in the WILD HUNT of Odin and also the abduction motif common in supernatural folklore and UFO mythology.

Sightings of phantom coaches that some researchers believe may be more than simple tradition include examples reported at Enfield, London, in December 1961; a phantom coach seen to plunge into the moat at the Old Court House, Shelsey Wash in Worcestershire, on Christmas Eve 1965; and a coach and horses reputedly seen by a motorist at Lion's Grave near Ditchingham, Norfolk, in the early 1970s.

phantom dogs *see* GHOST DOGS

phantom funerals

Apparitions of funerals, thought to herald the death of a local person.

In Celtic tradition, apparitions are often considered to be warnings of future events, particularly an impending death in the locality. In many such stories the warning takes the form of a sensory perception of a funeral some days or weeks before the real burial ceremony occurs. In Scotland such impressions are taken as examples of second sight. An extensive tradition of phantom funerals as a warning was also known in Wales, examples having been documented since the 18th century. It is often thought that the experience is limited to a vision of a funeral cortege or procession, almost invariably encountered on an empty highway at night. However, analysis of traditional and contemporary reports suggests that the predictive vision may in fact be conveyed by a much wider range of visual or auditory hallucinations. The vision may be of acts preparatory to the funeral (such as sounds of coffins being made) or forming part of the ceremony itself (the sound of psalms being sung). A study conducted into modern Scottish second-sight experiences by Edinburgh-based researcher Dr Shari Cohn in the mid 1990s showed a decline in sightings of phantom funeral processions, but this might be accounted for by the fact that people no longer travel long distances on foot at night. Nonetheless, the survey of 140 women and 68 men who claimed second-sight experiences indicated phantom funeral processions were reported by 10 per cent of the women and 4.8 per cent of the men. The study also confirmed the continuing role of auditory hallucinations, with accounts of noises variously interpreted as symbolizing a forthcoming funeral, such as the clink of glasses used at a wake. Fragmentary accounts of ghostly funeral processions in other parts of the UK may suggest that the belief was once more widespread.

phantom hitch-hikers

Ghostly hitch-hikers, the subject of ubiquitous folktales in which a hitch-hiker is picked up by a driver only to vanish during the journey.

One of the most widespread of ghost motifs is the story of the phantom hitch-hiker (or vanishing hitch-hiker, as they are known in the USA). The basic story involves a motorist picking up a hitch-hiker, usually a young woman, at night. The hitch-hiker travels some distance only to vanish inexplicably from the vehicle. On reporting the disappearance to the authorities (or going to an address mentioned by the hitch-hiker in the course of the journey), the motorist often learns that she was killed in a road accident in the recent past. In some accounts the driver lends the phantom hitch-hiker an item of clothing which is later found on top of the girl's grave; in other versions it is the hitch-hiker who leaves an item, such as a book or a purse, that is apparently later identified as belonging to the deceased person. Versions of the story have been recorded in every state of the USA and in many British counties. Examples are also known from other countries, including Italy, Pakistan and Colombia. Alternative versions of the story from the late 1960s have the phantom hitch-hiker as a hippy who utters prophecies to the driver of disasters or the Second Coming. A study of over 100 different variants of the story, carried out in 1984 by the folklorist Michael Goss, concluded that such stories have been in circulation for many years and long pre-date the motor car: in a Swedish case from 1602 the vehicle was a sleigh.

Although tales of phantom hitch-hikers are widespread, the stories invariably lack any hard facts capable of corroboration. Also, reliable first-hand accounts for any such phenomena are virtually non-existent, as most tales seem to relate to 'a friend of a friend who picked up a hitch-hiker', giving them the status of urban legend. One of the few British cases in which a named witness is cited is the story of Roy Fulton. Fulton claimed that he picked up a silent male hitch-hiker on 12 October 1979, along a road at Standbridge, near Dunstable, Bedfordshire. The passenger then vanished without explanation during the journey; subsequent investigation revealed that Fulton had reported the case to the police, but no similar encounters were known in the area. Reviewing such stories, Goss concluded that the phantom hitch-hiker is a 'classic fabrication', though some would argue that it is likely that occasional genuine apparitional encounters, particularly with SPECTRAL PEDESTRIANS, may have contributed to its propagation and survival as a story. See also RESURRECTION MARY.

phantom pedestrians *see* SPECTRAL PEDESTRIANS

phantom phone calls

Telephone calls purportedly made by discarnate entities.

The first account of a phantom

telephone call was detailed in the spiritualist journal *Borderland* in the autumn of 1896. A correspondent claimed that the psychic message 'Go to your father's house poor Nellie is dead' was heard over the telephone at the moment of his sister's death. Since then, occasional reports of telephone calls purportedly from discarnate entities (see DISCARNATE ENTITY) have appeared in the literature of SPIRITUALISM, and phantom phone calls are also a feature of many popular ghost stories, but research in this area reveals that the testimony relating to allegedly true cases rarely reaches evidential significance.

Telephone interference has been reported in a number of POLTERGEIST cases, most notably in the ROSENHEIM POLTERGEIST case in Germany in 1968. Alleged UFO witnesses in the USA have also claimed that they have received mysterious phone calls – typically menacing voices – but if such incidents are true, human pranksters cannot be eliminated.

Some believe that phantom phone calls represent a form of ELECTRONIC VOICE PHENOMENA, and that they are essentially messages from the spirit world. Indeed, the US journalist and parapsychologist D Scott Rogo published a number of claims of phone calls from deceased persons in his 1979 book, *Phone Calls from the Dead*. However, the claims were met with widespread scepticism and were ridiculed by Robert A Baker (a sceptical psychologist) in a chapter entitled 'Calling All Corpses: Dial D for Dead' in his book *Hidden Voices* (1990), and little has been heard of the phenomenon since.

phantoms, aerial *see* AERIAL PHANTOMS

phantom ships *see* GHOST SHIPS

phantom trains

In British folklore, apparitions of trains, particularly associated with the sites of earlier rail accidents.

While stories of apparitional vehicles such as PHANTOM COACHES are occasionally reported as fact, ghost researchers suggest that there appear to be only folkloric accounts of phantom trains. A phantom train is said to be heard running along the route of the former mineral line near Washford in Somerset that closed in 1917, and is associated with a train collision of 1857. A ghostly train is said to cross the River Tay at Wormit, near Dundee, on the anniversary of the Tay Bridge disaster – when the rail bridge collapsed on 28 December 1879 and 75 lives were lost. A phantom train is also said to run along the old Highland line at Dunphail, Grampian, appearing a few feet above the ground. At Soham, Cambridgeshire, a ghostly train is said to appear at the site of the now-closed station on the anniversary of the destruction of an ammunition train in 1942, when two people were killed. First-hand accounts of these phantom trains are largely lacking (hence they are labelled as folklore), but phantom trains still regularly feature in fiction, and 'ghost trains' are a popular entertainment at fairgrounds and theme parks.

Philip experiment

A parapsychological experiment in Toronto in the 1970s in which a 'ghost' was created.

In September 1972 members of the Toronto Society for Psychical Research, led by Iris Owen, engaged in an experiment to create an artificial ghost. Known as the Philip experiment, it drew inspiration from 19th-century accounts of TABLE-TURNING and the work of Kenneth Batcheldor who tried to create physical manifestations of ghosts on demand in Great Britain in the 1960s. Members of the group invented an imaginary 17th-century character named Philip. They created a wholly fictitious biography for Philip: born in 1624, he was an aristocrat, married to a beautiful woman called Dorothea, but he kept a mistress named Margo in a gatehouse on his estate – when Dorothea discovered his infidelity she had Margo burnt as a witch, and the broken-hearted Philip committed suicide in 1654.

Initially the group tried to make an apparition of their imaginary ghost materialize through meditation and visualization, but for some months little happened at their weekly meetings. Eventually they took a different approach, and they attempted to communicate with Philip through verbal questions while the members of the group were seated around a card table. Within a few sessions the group were rewarded by rapping sounds in response to these questions – answers which sometimes confirmed, but sometimes contradicted elements of Philip's fictitious biography. 'Philip' was also apparently able to apply force to the table, causing it to levitate, and the group also claimed he could produce cool breezes. The story of Philip was first published in *New Horizons* magazine in 1974 and a short factual film, *Philip, The Imaginary Ghost*, was made the same year; on one occasion the table movement was captured on film by a local television station. Further experiments by the Philip group were also conducted at Kent State University in March 1975, allowing physicists to test the processes involved. Iris Owen also wrote a book, *Conjuring Up Philip: An Adventure in Psychokinesis* (1976), describing the experiment.

As Philip was wholly invented, it appears that the phenomena attributed to the ghost were the product of PSYCHOKINESIS (coming from the unconscious minds of the sitters) rather than from any form of DISCARNATE ENTITY. However, a limited range of phenomena having been established, interest in the project waned and the group ceased their sittings in 1978.

Despite its success, there have been few attempts to recreate the Philip experiment, although a number of other

Canadian groups have produced similar results with other fictional 'ghosts'.

phone calls from the dead *see* PHANTOM PHONE CALLS

photographs, ghost *see* GHOST PHOTOGRAPHS

photography, spirit *see* SPIRIT PHOTOGRAPHY

physical medium *see* MEDIUM, PHYSICAL

Piper, Leonora (1857–1950)

Famous American trance medium.

Leonora Piper, known professionally as Mrs Piper, was born in Nashua, New Hampshire. The first sign that she would develop apparently mediumistic qualities came when she was eight years old. It is said that she was playing in the garden when she felt a blow to her ear, then heard the words 'Aunt Sara, not dead, but with you still'. It was discovered several days later that Aunt Sara had indeed died, at the time and on the day that the child had 'received' the message. Apart from occasional incidents, her childhood was normal, and her abilities did not receive any further attention until, in 1884, she visited a clairvoyant's circle. While there, Piper fell into a trance, and wrote a message for one of the other people in the group. The message was for a Judge Frost, and apparently came from his dead son. Frost was greatly impressed by the experience.

Piper went on to hold a private sitting for a Mrs Gibbins, mother-in-law of Professor James, who was involved in establishing the AMERICAN SOCIETY FOR PSYCHICAL RESEARCH. Then James himself attended one of her SÉANCES, and became convinced that she revealed family knowledge that she could not have had through normal means. He managed her sittings for the next 18 months. Piper used a CONTROL named as Phinuit, apparently a French doctor, although he seemed to know little of his own language, and only a small amount

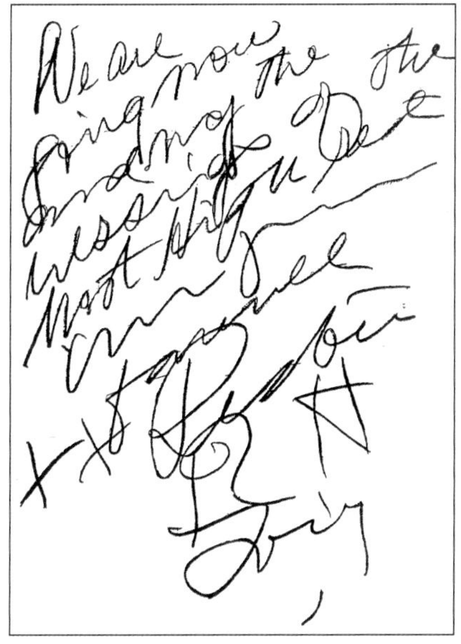

An example of automatic writing produced by Leonora Piper. (© 2004 Topham Picturepoint)

about medicine. However, Piper's talent was considered extraordinary, and in 1889 she travelled to England, where she held 83 further séances, observed by members of the SOCIETY FOR PSYCHICAL RESEARCH (SPR). Her fame grew – even when closely watched she seemed to perform without resorting to fraud.

Back in the USA, in 1901 the *New York Herald* published a statement by Mrs Piper, which it advertised as being her 'confession'. While some believe that in this she confessed to fraud, it is more accurate to say that she simply discussed the possibility that she received information through extrasensory perception rather than through communication with the spirits. However, she still accepted the possibility that spirits might be involved – she simply did not know for sure. In 1906 she returned to England to take part in the continuing work on CROSS CORRESPONDENCE. Her results were impressive, her accuracy apparently exceeding that which would be expected by chance. Following what have been described as 'badly managed' sittings on her return to the USA, Piper's mediumistic abilities seemed to fail, until her final trip to England in 1909. Her trance did not return, but from this time she used AUTOMATIC WRITING to pass messages on. However, she held very few sittings after her return to the USA in 1912.

Piper was much studied during her lifetime, and was never caught out as a fraud. She convinced many people of the possibility of life after death, although sceptics would claim that her accuracy came from the clever questioning of her subjects, essentially 'fishing' for what they wanted to hear, and through watching their reactions to what she said.

planchette

A device purported to assist the user to communicate with the spirits of the dead.

The name 'planchette' is sometimes said to be derived from the name of its inventor. However, it is equally possible that it is simply taken from the French for 'small board'. Planchettes, or 'automatic writers', first appeared in the early 19th century. They originally took the form of a small, flat, vaguely oval-shaped piece of wood supported on two or three wheels, with a pencil held in the centre. This device would be used (usually during a SÉANCE) for the production of AUTOMATIC WRITING – the planchette is placed on a piece of paper and (if the process has been successful) it will begin to write, apparently without the conscious control of the person holding it. When it is used by MEDIUMS, the messages produced by the planchette are said to come from the spirits of the dead.

Planchettes are now more commonly encountered in combination with a OUIJA BOARD, where they are still used as a means for alleged spirit communication. A writing implement is not required when the planchette is used in this way – participants in

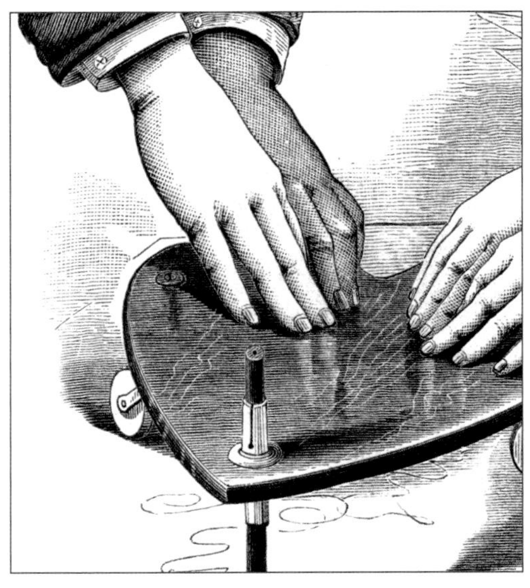

A picture of a planchette in use during a séance, from an 1885 issue of *Scientific American*. (© Topfoto/HIP)

the séance place their fingers on the planchette, which moves across the board (supposedly under the guidance of the spirits) to point at letters and spell out words.

Pollock twins

A pair of British twins who appeared to show a number of signs that they were the reincarnations of their two dead sisters.

The British twins Gillian and Jennifer Pollock were born in 1958. Two years earlier their elder sisters, Jacqueline (aged 6) and Joanna (aged 11), had been killed in a car accident. Jennifer was born with similar birthmarks to Jacqueline and when the twins began to speak they seemed to be able to recall events that had happened to their dead sisters. They were also apparently able to identify toys previously owned by their sisters, and it was even claimed that they had identified a house that the family had previously lived in. Gillian seemed to remember the life of Joanna and Jennifer that of Jacqueline.

The case received a great deal of publicity at the time and was offered as evidence for REINCARNATION. However, sceptics pointed out that although the twins' mother, Florence, was not a strong believer in reincarnation, their father, John, was – this, it is suggested, is likely to have led to even the slightest correspondences being noted, and to have shaped his interpretation.

Conversely, believers argued that there were a number of specific recognitions of places and objects that proved that the twins remembered their past lives, and that the twins were overheard discussing the accident on at least one occasion – and these are possibly difficult to dismiss as simple 'wishful thinking' or 'cognitive bias'. Ultimately, it seems likely that the tragic events surrounding the crash, and the lives of the elder sisters, would have been talked about in front of the twins – making it very difficult to establish that this case offers conclusive proof of anything out of the ordinary.

poltergeist

A mysterious invisible force asserted to cause a number of phenomena, most commonly noises (bangs, thuds and rappings) and object movements (from the hurling of smaller items to the lifting and upsetting of large pieces of furniture).

The word 'poltergeist' comes from the German *poltern*, to make a racket, and *Geist*, ghost. However, alleged poltergeist activity includes a broad spectrum of phenomena, not necessarily covered by the literal translation of the word, 'noisy spirit'. Poltergeist-related phenomena can involve objects seeming to move with no cause, including heavy items such as furniture as well as smaller items; bangs, knocking and rapping noises; thrown objects, which sometimes follow an unusual trajectory, or seem to be aimed at a specific person; rains of small objects such as stones or coins, sometimes falling inside a house or building; foul smells; spontaneous fires, sometimes breaking out on walls or ceilings; electrical disturbances, including the switching on and off of lights and appliances; telephone disruption; the levitation of either objects or people; and the manifestation of liquids such as blood, water or oil. Some poltergeists are said to physically assault their victims, although this is usually in the form of pinching and scratching rather than serious physical harm. Apparitions are only rarely reported in poltergeist cases.

Poltergeist incidents have been reported around the world since ancient times, and have exhibited many commonalities, with object movements the most consistent feature. It has been suggested that these commonalities lend weight to the existence of the phenomena, as reports were independent of each other. The activity usually starts and stops very abruptly, and occurs over anything from several hours to several months, although disturbances over longer periods have been reported. Generally, one individual seems to be at the focus of the activity. Until the 19th century poltergeist events were attributed to the Devil, witchcraft or the GHOSTS of the dead. After this time, and with the development of psychical research in the late 19th century, a more scientific explanation was sought. In the 1930s the psychologist NANDOR FODOR brought psychoanalytical analysis to his research of poltergeist cases and developed a theory that some poltergeist occurrences were caused by living individuals who were suffering from intense repression, anger or sexual tension. More recently William Roll of the Psychical Research Foundation in Durham, North Carolina, identified in his research what he termed RECURRENT SPONTANEOUS PSYCHOKINESIS (RSPK). His work suggested that the poltergeist focus (or poltergeist agent) was most commonly a child or teenager who was unknowingly using PSYCHOKINESIS (PK) to express their hostility or unhappiness. Further, the focus was usually unaware that they were causing the chaos of poltergeist activity but was pleased with the disturbances.

Most parapsychologists have adopted the explanation of the psychokinetic abilities of a living person as the source of poltergeist activity. Many of the recorded cases (both historical and modern) revolve around one individual (frequently female and under the age of 20) to the extent that phenomena only occur when that individual is present. There have also been recorded incidents of the poltergeist phenomena 'following' the focus to another location.

During some of the high-profile investigations of poltergeist activity, the focus has been seen (and sometimes recorded on film) deliberately causing the movement of objects. Some cases are revealed to be entirely hoaxed, whereas in other instances – for example, the TINA RESCH case and the ENFIELD POLTERGEIST – an example of hoaxing has been observed which does not necessarily invalidate all of the phenomena, but can be attributed to the effect of the pressure to perform during the intense and disruptive involvement of investigators and particularly the media. See also BALTIMORE POLTERGEIST; BELL WITCH; DRUMMER OF TEDWORTH; EPWORTH PARSONAGE POLTERGEIST; GEF THE TALKING MONGOOSE; HUMPTY DOO POLTERGEIST; LAMB INN; MIAMI POLTERGEIST; ROSENHEIM POLTERGEIST; THORNTON HEATH POLTERGEIST.

Price, Harry (1881–1948)

Flamboyant English psychical researcher and author.

Harry Price was born in London in 1881. An amateur magician, he joined both the Magic Circle and the SOCIETY FOR PSYCHICAL RESEARCH (SPR) in 1920. He initially used his knowledge of the techniques of conjuring and stage magic to expose fraud among those who claimed PSYCHIC ability.

In 1922, he famously exposed Billy Hope, a 'spirit photographer', as a fake. This caused something of a sensation, and made Price unpopular with such supporters of Hope as SIR ARTHUR CONAN DOYLE. However, Price became convinced that some genuine psychic phenomena exist, and should be scientifically examined, on a visit to Munich later that year, when he witnessed the feats of Austrian medium Willi Schneider. It then became Price's aim to obtain evidence of PSYCHOKINESIS.

This photograph of Harry Price, with an unidentified ghostly companion, was taken by spirit photographer Billy Hope. (© 2003 Charles Walker/TopFoto)

In 1926, Price formally opened his own organization, the National Laboratory of Psychical Research. He went on to conduct experiments on such MEDIUMS as Rudi Schneider, the brother of Willi, and ELEONORE ZUGUN, the Romanian 'poltergeist girl'. But to many people, Price is best known as the ghost hunter who investigated the notorious BORLEY RECTORY case. Price was involved in that investigation for nearly 20 years, and wrote two bestselling books on the subject – *The Most Haunted House in England* (1940) and *The End of Borley Rectory* (1946).

Price's conduct during the investigation has been greatly criticized – for example, he passed off as genuine a photograph of a brick apparently hovering in midair, when it had been set up deliberately when the house was being demolished – but the case remains one of the most fully documented examples of a HAUNTED HOUSE. Price also investigated the alleged POLTERGEIST case of GEF THE TALKING MONGOOSE.

Price's other books include *Rudi Schneider: A Scientific Examination of His Mediumship* (1930) and *Confessions of a Ghost Hunter* (1936). His autobiography, *Search for Truth*, appeared in 1942. While his reputation suffered in the years after his death, when he was criticized for a lack of integrity – he has been described as 'fame-obsessed' – and for the manner in which he conducted his investigations, Price is seen by many as the 'father of modern ghost hunting' and a popularizer of the study of paranormal phenomena.

projection *see* ASTRAL PROJECTION

psychic

A term describing both paranormal powers and the possessor of such powers.

When someone claims to be a psychic, they are now normally understood to be claiming that they possess certain powers above and beyond the normal physical abilities and senses of the human body – these would include such things as extrasensory perception, PSYCHOKINESIS and precognition.

Many people also use the word 'psychic' interchangeably with 'MEDIUM' or 'clairvoyant' (see CLAIRVOYANCE). However, while it is true that some self-proclaimed mediums or clairvoyants do also say that they have psychic powers, it is usually the case that they are actually making a separate and distinct claim to be communicating with SPIRITS, rather than exercising any innate power of their own. Equally, however, it might be argued that the ability to communicate with spirits could be understood to be a psychic power in itself – indeed, the term was first used by the scientist William Crookes in 1870, in reference to the medium DANIEL DUNGLAS HOME.

psychical research

The scientific investigation of claims of psychic powers and paranormal events.

Interest in PSYCHIC phenomena was stimulated during the 19th century, particularly by the rise of the SPIRITUALISM movement. This coincided with the development of 'scientism' and a growing belief that science could provide the answers to questions about the nature of the world around us. Although many people of a scientific bent began to dismiss the idea of the supernatural and paranormal, others felt that a scientific approach could be applied in these areas for the purposes of proving (or disproving) the multitude of claims that were being made. In the UK the SOCIETY FOR PSYCHICAL RESEARCH was founded in 1882 and very soon an American offshoot, the AMERICAN SOCIETY FOR PSYCHICAL RESEARCH, was formed. During this time many fraudulent MEDIUMS were exposed as the result of research, much GHOST HUNTING was carried out and there were investigations into the emerging areas of SPIRIT PHOTOGRAPHY and GHOST PHOTOGRAPHS. Unfortunately, a lack of conclusive evidence, and some high-profile mistakes made by some of the more credulous 'researchers', led to psychical research attracting something of a 'crackpot' image among much of the general public. However, research continued.

In the 1920s and 1930s extrasensory perception (ESP) became a popular area of psychical research and a new laboratory-based approach developed. The term 'PARAPSYCHOLOGY' was introduced in an attempt to move away from some of the negative connotations associated with the original name for the discipline. Prominent among the new investigators was Dr J B Rhine who set up a research unit at Duke University in North Carolina and provided a means of statistically analysing the results of experiments into telepathy with the introduction of card-guessing experiments. Since then, research and investigation has continued into a wide range of phenomena, from GHOSTS, POLTERGEISTS and HAUNTINGS through to CLAIRVOYANCE, remote viewing, metal bending and other examples of alleged PSYCHOKINESIS.

The whole area of psychical research remains highly controversial. In 1976 a group of sceptics in the USA set up the Committee for the Scientific Investigation of Claims of the Paranormal (CSICOP) in response to what they perceived to be poor experimental procedure and biased consideration of data resulting from research being carried out by 'believers'. Many with an interest in the area countered that CSICOP's own approach was equally flawed – they argued that its members had already dismissed the possibility that any paranormal phenomena exist and so brought their own bias to the interpretation of evidence.

The terms 'psychical research' and 'parapsychology' are now generally used interchangeably. However, it is important to note that the word 'psychical' is preferred in this context to 'psychic' – the latter implying the existence and use of psychic powers for research purposes rather than the impartial and unbiased investigation of claims of the paranormal.

psychokinesis

The movement of material objects, or the influencing of mechanical systems, using only the power of the mind.

Psychokinesis (constructed from the Greek *psyche*, meaning 'soul', and *kinesis*, meaning 'movement'), often abbreviated to 'PK', is the term given by parapsychologists to the range of effects previously known as mind over matter or telekinesis. It is one of the main areas of research in modern PARAPSYCHOLOGY, where the phenomena are now usually sub-divided into the two categories of macro-PK and micro-PK depending upon the scale of the effect under consideration. Metal bending is one of the most widely known supposed manifestations of the former. The latter would include attempts to influence the output of an electronic random number generator (a device which is used to produce a series of random numbers in tests for psychic abilities).

Russian psychic Nina Kulagina attempting to raise objects from a table using psychokinesis, c.1970. (© Mary Evans Picture Library)

The idea of psychokinesis first appeared during the 19th century (although the term was not coined until the 20th century) as a suggested explanation for a number of SÉANCE phenomena – this was in opposition to the popular belief at the time that spirits were interacting with the physical world (possibly by the production of ECTOPLASM). The concept that many phenomena previously attributed to ghosts or spirits of the dead actually have their roots in a (currently unproven) capability of the human mind has since been developed further – a prime example being the RECURRENT SPONTANEOUS PSYCHOKINESIS theory of the origin of POLTERGEIST phenomena.

Over the years, many individuals have claimed to be able to use the power of psychokinesis. Among the most famous are Uri Geller and Nina Kulagina.

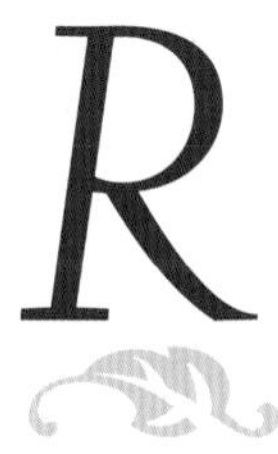

recurrent apparitions

Ghosts that are seen or experienced on a series of different occasions.

'Recurrent apparition' is the term used to refer to a ghost that is seen or experienced repeatedly, on a number of different occasions. Such apparitions are often reported in HAUNTED HOUSE cases, and a classic example of a recurrent apparition is the MORTON GHOST. Many recurrent apparitions are reported always to appear in the same location and always to perform the same actions with no awareness of the observers and little or no variation in routine (see RE-ENACTMENT GHOSTS), which has led some ghost investigators to suggest that they may be a form of recording (see STONE TAPE THEORY). It has been put forward that such phenomena represent an emotional imprint left on a place or building, arising from a tragedy (such as a suicide or murder). It has also been suggested that a routine pattern of life by a living person might leave a trace on a building which can be picked up on after their death.

recurrent spontaneous psychokinesis

The production of repeated physical effects over a period of time by psychic means, without conscious control. It forms the basis of a theory for the cause of poltergeist phenomena.

The term 'recurrent spontaneous psychokinesis' (RSPK) was coined by the parapsychologist William Roll of the Psychical Research Foundation in Durham, North Carolina. Roll studied 116 POLTERGEIST cases from around the world (including the MIAMI POLTERGEIST and TINA RESCH) and observed that there were patterns in the phenomena exhibited – particularly noting that the activity often appeared to be centred upon a single child or teenager within the household. He developed the idea that the effects might be being unknowingly produced by the human 'focus' (as opposed to an external supernatural entity) and that they might be outward physical manifestations of their internal psychological state through a process of PSYCHOKINESIS.

The idea that RSPK lies behind

the majority of poltergeist cases has all but replaced supernatural SPIRIT theories among researchers into the paranormal. The argument now tends to be between supporters of RSPK and sceptics who feel that no paranormal explanation is required.

re-enactment ghosts

Ghostly apparitions that appear to be re-enactments of events from the past.

Certain apparitions appear to be re-enactments of events from the historic past. Ghosts of this type are often referred to as 'place memories', the idea being that certain locations seem to retain images which can be re-activated and replayed in the present. The ghosts described do not recognize or react to the presence of observers, and simply perform some action. Some have suggested that such re-enactment ghosts are a form of recording, like video clips being replayed (see STONE TAPE THEORY). Should this be true, re-enactment ghosts may be established as a result of one emotional incident (for example, a suicide or a murder) or a pattern of life where the sight or sounds of a once regularly performed activity have been imprinted on the environment. See also RECURRENT APPARITIONS.

reincarnation

The rebirth of a spirit, or soul, to live a new life within a new physical body.

Reincarnation (literally 'being made flesh again') is a central tenet of many religions and philosophical systems, including Hinduism, Spiritism, Theosophy and Scientology. It has appeared among the religious beliefs of human societies throughout history – certainly as far back as the ancient Egyptians – and is a popular theme in much New Age philosophy.

During the 20th century a number of people claimed that they had recovered memories of previous lives while undergoing hypnosis (see PAST-LIFE REGRESSION). Famous examples include BRIDEY MURPHY and the BLOXHAM TAPES. In the case of the POLLOCK TWINS the apparent recall appeared to be spontaneous, and the occultist Aleister Crowley claimed that he was the reincarnation of Éliphas Lévi (among others) without recourse to any form of memory recovery.

It is sometimes claimed that apparent examples of CHANNELLING by MEDIUMS are, in fact, remembrances of past lives. See also AFTERLIFE.

Resch, Tina

A US teenager who was the focus for apparent poltergeist activity in 1984, one of the most widely known cases of modern times.

In 1984, Tina Resch was a 14-year-old girl living with her adoptive parents in Columbus, Ohio, when she became the centre of one of the most famous modern POLTERGEIST cases. Apparently, electrical items would malfunction, and objects would fly through the air (sometimes directed at Resch herself) whenever she was present. Following

A telephone flies past Tina Resch, apparently without human intervention. (© TopFoto/Fortean)

coverage of the phenomena in the local press, parapsychologist William Roll, who had spent a number of years at Duke University working under leading parapsychologist Dr J B Rhine, became one of the chief investigators of the case, studying Resch for the next eight years.

Numerous incidents of the apparently paranormal movement of objects in the house were noted, including cups that flew through the air, and lights that switched themselves on. One of the most spectacular pieces of evidence in the case is a set of photographs captured by a local newspaper photographer. The photographs show the extended cord and handset of a telephone in flight past Tina Resch as she is seated in a chair. Roll believed that the various phenomena constituted a genuine case of PSYCHOKINESIS, and Resch was tested in the laboratory for such powers. Although the case was criticized by sceptics (who claimed that Resch was simply a disturbed teenager who knowingly and deliberately caused the disturbances), Roll strongly believed that paranormal forces were at work, and that Resch had the ability to affect the physical world through the power of her mind. Opportunities for further research with Resch were curtailed in 1992, when she was convicted of the murder of her three-year-old daughter, and she was subsequently sentenced to life imprisonment with no prospect of parole.

Resurrection Mary

A phantom hitch-hiker associated with the Resurrection Cemetery in Chicago, USA.

It is rare in stories of PHANTOM HITCH-HIKERS for the ghost to have any recognizable identity, but one that has achieved at least recognition by nickname is 'Resurrection Mary', or 'Rez Mary', associated with the area around the Roman Catholic Resurrection Cemetery in Chicago.

Stories concerning Resurrection Mary seem to date back to the 1930s. One frequently related tale tells of a young man named Jerry Palus who allegedly met a woman in a white dress at the now-demolished Liberty Grove Hall Ballroom. Her skin was said to be cold and clammy when he kissed her. After a night of dancing, she asked for a lift home and to be dropped by the Resurrection Cemetery. Palus obliged and she ran to the gates of the cemetery and vanished. Stories have circulated ever since of motorists picking up a young blonde woman near the cemetery late at night (or alternatively from a dance hall) who later vanishes without explanation during the journey or when getting out of the vehicle. Such reports continued through to the 1980s but seemed to dwindle during the 1990s.

Various candidates have been put forward for the identity of the 'ghost' known as Resurrection Mary, including a number of teenage girls or young women killed in road accidents in the area between 1927 and 1936. However, in many respects she fits an archetypal WHITE LADY ghost as much as a phantom hitch-hiker.

revenant

A person who returns from the dead; a ghost.

The word 'revenant' (from the French *revenir*, meaning 'to come back') is generally used to refer to a person who returns from the dead to visit the living, particularly those who were known or loved in life. Not surprisingly, the theme of revenants has been a popular one in folklore and literature, where the deceased may manifest at their own initiative or as a result of being summoned by a sorcerer.

Revenants rarely seem to convey messages of much overt significance, seemingly being motivated more by a desire to glimpse their loved ones or revisit the scenes of their earthly activities. In cases documented since 1700, little ever happens beyond an exchange of recognition and tacit greetings between the living and the dead. However, prior to 1700 revenants often returned to deliver important personal messages or to confirm or rebuke complex theological and doctrinal beliefs. They also returned to exact revenge or right a wrong they committed in life.

The term 'revenant' is also often used to describe malign forms of ghosts from medieval folklore. These were frequently more physically solid in nature than apparitions in later historical accounts. Capable of inflicting physical harm and even jousting or fighting with the living, medieval revenants are more reminiscent of zombies than ghosts proper. Changes in theology, burial practice and attitudes to the spiritual status of the corpse in popular culture seem to have put paid to physical revenants in Western Europe, but the traditions continued in parts of Eastern Europe until well into the 20th century.

road ghosts *see* HAUNTED HIGHWAYS

Roff, Mary *see* WATSEKA WONDER

R101 airship disaster

The R101 was an airship that crashed in 1930 with the loss of 46 lives. A few days after the incident, it was claimed that the spirit of the deceased airship captain appeared at a séance, through a medium some believe had also had a premonition of the disaster.

Irish (later US) MEDIUM EILEEN GARRETT (1893–1970) is perhaps most famous for her work following the R101 airship disaster. However, some claim that her first experience of the R101 came in the years prior to the accident, when she apparently had visions of a large airship crashing in flames.

On 4 October 1930 the British dirigible R101 took off for India. Among the passengers for the flight was the then head of civil aviation, Sir Sefton Brancker. The airship crashed in the early hours of the following day, having travelled no further than France, and killing 46 people on board, including Brancker and the airship's commander, Flight Lieutenant H Carmichael Irwin.

On 7 October a SÉANCE was held at psychical researcher HARRY PRICE's National Laboratory of Psychical Research in London. Attendant at this séance was self-professed trance medium (see MEDIUM, TRANCE) Eileen Garrett. Garrett had been asked to attend at the behest of one of Price's friends, a Mr Coster, who wished to know if it would be possible for her to communicate with SIR ARTHUR CONAN DOYLE, who had died some months previously. It has been claimed that Garrett was not aware of this request.

As soon as Garret fell into her usual trance, her spirit guide or 'CONTROL', 'Uvani', apparently spoke through her and, after some standard greetings, said:

> I see for the moment I-R-V-I-N-G or I-R-W-I-N. He say he must do something about it ... apologizes for coming ... for interfering ... speaks of Dora, Dorothy, Gladys ... for heaven's sake, give this to them ... the whole bulk of the dirigible was entirely and absolutely too much for her engine capacity.

The medium's voice then changed, and this 'different' voice claimed to be that of Flight Lieutenant Irwin. This voice went on to describe, in an agitated and broken manner, the apparent details of the crash, including

The wreck of the R101 airship which crashed in 1930. (© 2000 Topham Picturepoint)

a great deal of technical information relating to problems with the airship. The 'testimony' was recorded by Ethel Bennham, secretary at the laboratory, and included such fragments as:

> … not sufficient feed – leakage. Pressure and heat produced explosion … Weather bad for long flight. Fabric all water-logged and ship's nose is down. Impossible to rise. Cannot trim. You will understand that I had to tell you … At inquiry to be held later it will be found that the superstructure of the envelope contained no resilience and had far too much weight in envelope. This was not so until March of this year, when no security was made by adding of super-steel structure. I knew then that this was not a dream but a nightmare. The added middle section was entirely wrong – it made strong but took resilience away and entirely impossible too heavy and too much over-weighted for the capacity of engines. From beginning of trouble I knew we had not a chance – knew it to be the feed, and we could never rise.

Was it possible that Irwin was communicating from the grave, giving evidence as to why the R101 had crashed? Garrett's supporters claimed that it was. They believed that Garrett simply did not have enough technical knowledge of flight and airships to have made the statements fraudulently. However, sceptics would point out that she had had two days to prepare, and although some of the suggestions made at the séance were borne out by the later crash investigation, this was down to little more than chance or educated guesswork.

Following 'Irwin's' communication at the séance, the medium lapsed into silence until an entity called 'Doyle' appeared.

Rosenheim Poltergeist

A well-attested German poltergeist case from 1967.

In November 1967 a law office in the Bavarian town of Rosenheim, Germany, was the scene of an outbreak of POLTERGEIST disturbances. Light bulbs on hanging fittings would swing wildly before exploding, fluorescent lights went out repeatedly for no apparent reason and the office's electrical fuses would blow again and again. The telephone lines were particularly badly affected – sometimes the four office telephones would all ring when there were no callers on the line, and at other times phone calls would be interrupted or cut off. The telephone bills also revealed hundreds of calls that were never made, particularly numerous calls to the speaking clock, sometimes as many as six calls a minute. Initially, the lawyer Sigmund Adam suspected that the electrical supply was to blame for the alarming disturbances, and engineers were called in. They set up monitoring equipment to detect unusual fluctuations in the power supply, and these were duly recorded, often coinciding with physical disturbances in the office. However, when the office was equipped with its own power unit, which should have been immune to such fluctuations, they continued, as did the other phenomena.

Following press coverage of the unexplained events at the office, a research team, led by Professor Hans Bender of the University of Freiburg, began an investigation of the phenomena. This team was later joined by members of the Max Planck Institute for Plasma Physics. Bender's team noted that the phenomena only occurred during office hours, and further, they concluded that the phenomena were linked to the presence of Annemarie Schneider, an employee in her late teens. Lights were observed and filmed swinging above her head as she walked down a corridor, and often the first power fluctuation of the day coincided with her arrival at the office. The investigations seemed to stimulate new phenomena, as pictures fell from the walls or rotated, and drawers opened and filing cabinets moved without physical intervention.

When Schneider left the office to find employment elsewhere, the phenomena ceased, leaving many to conclude that the disturbances had been caused by RECURRENT SPONTANEOUS PSYCHOKINESIS, with Schneider as the focus. The case remains one of the most highly attested poltergeist incidents, with around 40 witnesses, including members of the research teams, police officers, engineers and journalists.

Sawston Hall

A manor house in Cambridgeshire, England, said to be haunted by the ghosts of Mary Tudor and a grey lady.

The Tudor mansion of Sawston Hall was the home of the Huddlestons, a Catholic family known for their association with Mary Tudor, later Mary I. In 1553, following the death of Mary's younger half-brother, Edward VI, Lady Jane Grey was proclaimed queen by her father-in-law, the Duke of Northumberland, supplanting Mary. Northumberland attempted to take Mary into custody, but the Huddlestons hid her at Sawston. In retaliation against their actions the Huddleston home was burnt down, but after Mary ascended the throne, John Huddleston was knighted, and the hall was rebuilt.

The ghost of Mary Tudor has long been said to appear in the house, apparently a benign spectre with a serene appearance. Ghostly footsteps have also been reported, and it has been claimed that music has been heard – the ghostly playing of a spinet, or small harpsichord, also attributed to the queen. Those that have spent the night in 'Mary's room' have also reported hearing the bedroom door being rattled at night.

Sawston's other APPARITION is said to be that of an unknown lady in grey. She is reported to knock three times at the

The ghost of Mary Tudor, later Mary I, is reputed to haunt Sawston Hall. (© 2004 TopFoto)

door before floating across a certain room.

Scole group, the

A five-year research programme to find evidence for life after death through communication with spirits.

The Scole group set out to investigate evidence for life after death in an experiment which ran from 1993 to 1998. They took their name from the Norfolk village of Scole, where their SÉANCEs took place. Initially the project was run with seven members, two of whom were TRANCE MEDIUMS – however, the last three years of the project were carried out with the two mediums and only two others (although at various times there were outside visitors in attendance). It was claimed that the group produced over 200 different physical effects during the 500 or so séances, including APPORTS, LEVITATIONS, spirit lights, ELECTRONIC VOICE PHENOMENA, AUTOMATIC WRITING and 'psychic photographs'.

During the later years of the project, the SOCIETY FOR PSYCHICAL RESEARCH carried out an investigation of it and sent members to attend the séances as impartial observers. In a 300-page report, they confirmed that none of their investigators could find any evidence of fraud in the sessions they observed. However, as had been the problem with such investigations during the heyday of SPIRITUALISM, the séances took place in the dark and the MEDIUMS had the final say on the conditions and controls in place – the results, as far as sceptics are concerned, were therefore inconclusive.

Scratching Fanny *see* COCK LANE GHOST

screaming skulls

Ancient skulls that are said to scream or generate psychic manifestations if removed from their dwelling-place.

Screaming skull superstitions are associated with at least 20 different buildings in England, including BURTON AGNES HALL, Yorkshire; Calgarth Hall, Cumbria; Chilton Cantelo, Somerset; TUNSTEAD FARM, Derbyshire; Warbleton Priory, Sussex; and WARDLEY HALL near Manchester. In each case the skull has been preserved in the dwelling for hundreds of years and its origin is often uncertain – although screaming skulls are traditionally linked to former residents from between the 15th and 17th centuries. The skull must not under any circumstances be removed – otherwise psychic disturbances including screams, POLTERGEIST phenomena and bad luck are said to follow.

Most famous of all screaming skulls is the specimen still preserved at BETTISCOMBE MANOR in Dorset; according to tradition, attempts to disturb or dispose of this skull have had unfortunate consequences. An examination of the Bettiscombe skull carried out in 1963 indicated that it might be 2,000 or more years old, leading some to believe that the

The Chilton Cantelo skull allegedly causes poltergeist activity if it is removed from the house. (© TopFoto)

skull was originally venerated at a Celtic shrine. In a number of ancient traditions skulls had a protective function, and were said to preserve the fertility and prosperity of farmland. In 1995, researchers David Clarke and Andy Roberts undertook a study of screaming skulls, and speculated that the majority of surviving skulls could have similarly ancient origins. Others have suggested that most date to the 16th and 17th centuries and are either Catholic relics or examples of the Elizabethan and Jacobean cult of memento mori. Whatever their origins, legends relating to screaming skulls remain popular.

séance

A meeting of psychical researchers or spiritualists for the purpose of trying to communicate with the spirits of the dead.

The word 'séance' (from the French for a 'sitting' or a 'meeting') was first recorded in English in 1845 – however, the activity itself had been taking place long before that date. Early séances often took the form of social gatherings (see TABLE-TURNING) and, later in the 19th century, they even became something of a parlour game – the OUIJA BOARD allowing people to conduct their own séances (often as nothing more than light-hearted entertainment) without the help of an established MEDIUM.

Séances were the cornerstone of the SPIRITUALISM movement and were particularly popular from the middle of the 19th century. There was a massive boom in attendance at private séances or public demonstrations at theatres, fuelled by the fantastic claims of the supporters of famous mediums such as the FOX SISTERS and DANIEL DUNGLAS HOME. A wide variety of phenomena were claimed to occur during sittings, including APPORTS, SPIRIT RAPPING, table-turning, LEVITATION, MATERIALIZATIONS (such as the production of ECTOPLASM), AUTOMATIC WRITING, AUTOMATIC ART and disembodied voices.

Séances still take place today, although the range of phenomena manifested is much reduced. They are still usually held in complete darkness, or low light conditions, and often involve a group of people sitting around a table, their hands in contact. However, the exact approach to setting up, and the form that the following events take, vary depending on the type of medium involved (see TRANCE MEDIUM, DIRECT

A 19th-century newspaper illustration of a séance. The drawing includes a spirit hand writing a message and the apport of a guitar. (© Mary Evans Picture Library)

VOICE MEDIUM, PHYSICAL MEDIUM, MENTAL MEDIUM and TRANSFIGURATION MEDIUM). In most instances it is held that the medium is CHANNELLING some form of communication from the spirit world.

Sceptics argue that the conditions under which séances normally take place make fraud all the more easy, and people such as HARRY HOUDINI and JOHN NEVIL MASKELYNE spent many years exposing the mediums' tricks. Likewise, since the 19th century, organizations such as the SOCIETY FOR PSYCHICAL RESEARCH have been involved in attempts to investigate and possibly validate the claims made.

ships, ghost *see* GHOST SHIPS

Slade, Henry (1840–1905)

American medium, famously associated with slate-writing.

Little is known of Henry Slade's early life, but in around 1860 he first began giving public SÉANCES in New York. In July 1876, en route for Russia, where he had agreed to undergo investigation at the Imperial University of St Petersburg, Slade arrived in Britain. He took rooms in Russell Square, London, and held séances there, amazing those who attended with SLATE-WRITING, TABLE-TURNING, materialized hands, LEVITATION, and musical instruments played by the spirits.

For several weeks, Slade was a great success. One London journalist reported on a séance at Russell Square, saying he had been pinched by spirits, seen ghostly hands, read a number of messages from the spirits that had appeared on slates, and had heard violent rappings at the table. A number of people were greatly impressed by Slade's apparent mediumistic abilities, including the naturalist Alfred Russel Wallace, who believed in their genuineness. *The Spiritual Magazine* proclaimed that Slade was taking the place of DANIEL DUNGLAS HOME, and was 'the most remarkable medium of modern times'. However, Slade was soon to be charged with obtaining money under false pretences.

In September 1876, Professor Lankester of University College London and Dr Donkin of Westminster Hospital paid to attend one of Slade's sittings. Lankester grabbed the slate before the message was supposed to be written on it by the spirits, and discovered that the message was in fact already there. The exposé featured in *The Times*, and Slade appeared in court.

The magician JOHN NEVIL MASKELYNE appeared for the prosecution, demonstrating to the court how slate-writing could be replicated, while Alfred Russel Wallace appeared for the defence. Slade was sentenced to three months' imprisonment, although on appeal the conviction was overturned on a technicality.

Some spiritualists continued to defend Slade, but he left Britain and spent some time in Europe before touring Australia and eventually returning to the USA. He appeared before the Seybert Commission in Philadelphia in 1885, and was found guilty of fraud – again it was shown that the slate-writing had been prepared in advance, and he had been seen using his foot to move a table. In 1886 both Slade and his business manager were arrested, but were later released without prosecution. Slade died penniless in a sanatorium in Michigan.

slate-writing

A technique employed for the alleged production of written messages from the spirit world.

Slate-writing, a variation on AUTOMATIC WRITING, was a staple of many 19th-century MEDIUMS. It was first used by HENRY SLADE (1840–1905), who travelled the world demonstrating his messages. However, although a number of prominent people, including respected scientists, attested to his genuine abilities, he was eventually found guilty of fraud. The magician JOHN NEVIL MASKELYNE exposed his trickery and demonstrated in court how slate-writing could be easily replicated. But although Slade disappeared from the SPIRITUALISM circuit, slate-writing did not.

To produce the effect, a medium would take a piece of slate, wash it and seal it in a container (or wrap it up) with a slate pencil. The slate would then be left alone and writing would appear on it, apparently without human intervention. Variations included wrapping two slates together with a pencil sealed between them, laying a single slate face down over the pencil or holding a slate under a table at a SÉANCE.

Those of a more sceptical bent pointed out that it would be expected that a spirit's writing should match the writing of that individual in life – strangely, in practice, it usually bore no resemblance to it at all.

Smith, Hélène (c.1861–1929)

Swiss medium who apparently channelled messages from Mars.

Born Catherine Elise Muller in Geneva, Switzerland, the MEDIUM Hélène Smith specialized in AUTOMATIC WRITING, although she was also said to display CLAIRVOYANCE and CLAIRAUDIENCE. She believed herself to be the REINCARNATION of both Marie Antoinette and an Indian princess.

Smith became interested in SPIRITUALISM in the early 1890s, and began attending SÉANCES at which her mediumistic abilities were revealed. She claimed that two of her early 'controls' (spirits through whom she communicated with the spirit world – see CONTROL) were the French poet and writer Victor Hugo (1802–85) and 'Leopold' (alias the Italian adventurer and founder of Egyptian Rite Freemasonry, Count Alessandro di Cagliostro). Perhaps inspired by a comment from fellow spiritualist Auguste Lemaître that humans might soon make contact with life forms from other planets, Smith soon fell into a trance and reported on life on the

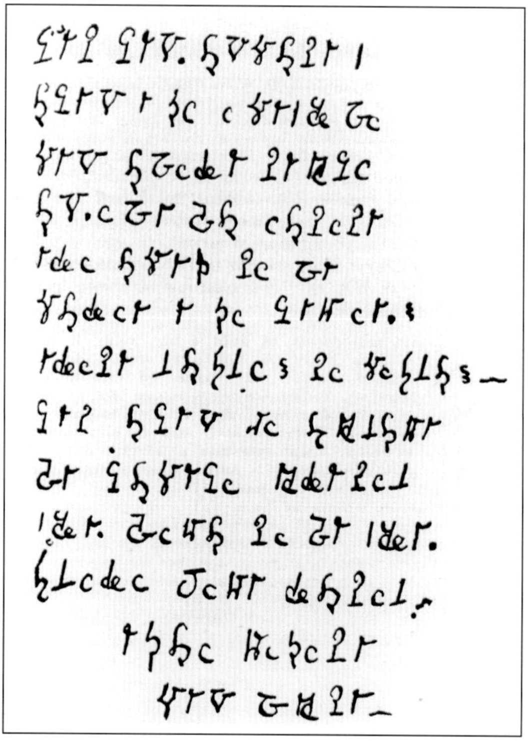

An example of Hélène Smith's 'Martian' writing.
(© TopFoto/Fortean)

planet Mars. She went on to produce a large body of work on the subject, apparently able to both speak and write in the Martian language. Her 'Martian' revelations included detailed descriptions of the landscape of Mars and its inhabitants.

Smith's apparent paranormal abilities were studied by the Swiss psychologist Théodore Flournoy (1854–1920), and his book *From India to the Planet Mars* (1900) popularized her claims. Flournoy believed that Smith's amazing Martian experiences resulted from a highly developed imagination and 'repressed' but familiar memories (see CRYPTOMNESIA). He did not accept her mediumistic abilities, although he did conclude that she may have been able to use telepathy. As to the Martian language that Smith used in her automatic writing, while it was apparently written in unknown characters, the translations provided by Smith led language experts to find remarkable similarities to Smith's native French.

Society for Psychical Research

The oldest organization still in existence that is dedicated to the scientific investigation of claims of the paranormal.

The Society for Psychical Research (SPR) was founded in 1882 with the aim of investigating, in a scientific and unbiased manner, claims of the paranormal. It was initiated by three researchers at Trinity College, Cambridge – Edmund Gurney, Frederic Myers and Henry Sidgwick – all of whom had an interest in SPIRITUALISM. They set up headquarters in London shortly afterwards but still continued to maintain library facilities in Cambridge. In its early years there was some conflict between the spiritualist members and those (led by Sidgwick) who wished to pursue a more rigorous, academic line of investigation. A large number of spiritualists left the organization before the end of its first decade. In 1885 an American branch of the SPR was formed (the AMERICAN SOCIETY FOR PSYCHICAL RESEARCH) and it eventually became an affiliate organization in 1890.

Throughout its history the SPR has produced many reports into cases that it has investigated; in some instances it debunks and in others it supports, depending upon the evidence it finds. The society takes an interest in all areas of PSYCHICAL RESEARCH such as spiritualism and mediumship, GHOSTS and APPARITIONS, PSYCHOKINESIS and extrasensory perception. Famous investigations of HAUNTINGS have included those of the ENFIELD POLTERGEIST, BALLECHIN HOUSE, the BROWN LADY OF RAYNHAM HALL and the MORTON GHOST.

The SPR currently publishes the quarterly *Journal of the Society for Psychical Research* and an infrequent *Proceedings of the Society for Psychical Research*. It continues to hold an annual conference and its stated aim is:

> ... understanding events and abilities commonly described as 'psychic' or 'paranormal' by promoting and supporting important research in this area.

Society for Research in Rapport and Telekinesis

A society which aims to investigate parapsychology and spirit communication as they were experienced during the Victorian era of séances.

The Society for Research in Rapport and Telekinesis (SORRAT) was founded in Missouri in 1961 by John G Neihardt. The intention was to conduct PSYCHICAL RESEARCH by attempting to employ many of the techniques used in the SÉANCE rooms during the heyday of SPIRITUALISM. Members believed that the key to telekinesis taking place was an initial rapport with the SPIRITS or other external 'communicators'. John Thomas Richards wrote a history of SORRAT in 1982 and eventually took over the leadership of the organization.

From the earliest sittings SORRAT recorded a range of phenomena from TABLE-TURNING and 'spirit' messages, through to whole rooms shaking. Sittings of the group resembled the traditional séance, with members seated in a circle with their hands loosely placed on a table. Messages were said to be spelt out using a system of raps. The organization became particularly well known for an experimental process which involves placing objects in a glass container with a lockable lid, where they can be observed but apparently not touched. This arrangement is called a 'minilab' and is now used extensively in PARAPSYCHOLOGY research elsewhere. SORRAT reported successes with this set-up, including such effects as rings linking and unlinking, balloons inflating and metal bending. However, the process often involved the somewhat dubious technique of leaving the box alone and unobserved for a period, and the results have never been independently verified.

The organization now keeps largely to itself after being the subject of much criticism from members of the mainstream parapsychology community. As a consequence, there is little external appraisal of their investigations.

SORRAT *see* SOCIETY FOR RESEARCH IN RAPPORT AND TELEKINESIS

Souther Fell

A fell in the English Lake District, known for its legendary association with a spectral army.

While battlefields such as those of EDGEHILL and NASEBY have long been famously associated with SPECTRAL ARMIES, this form of AERIAL PHANTOM is also said to occur at Souther Fell in Cumbria. The Souther Fell apparition was apparently first witnessed on Midsummer Eve in 1735, and was described as a ghostly army travelling along the summit ridge of the fell. The spectral army was again witnessed on Midsummer Eve in 1737, and an account of the haunting was published in the *Gentleman's Magazine* in 1747, including the tale of William Lancaster, witness to the 1737 appearance:

> Two years after on Midsummer eve also, betwixt the hours of eight and nine, Wm Lancaster himself imagined that several gentlemen were following their horses at a distance, as if they had been hunting, and taking them for such, pay'd no regard to it, till about ten minutes after, again turning his head towards the place, they appeared to be mounted, and a vast army following, five in rank, crowding over at the same place, where the servant said he saw them two years before. He then call'd his family, who all agreed in the same opinion.

When the army appeared again in 1745, 26 witnesses were said to have been present, and to have been so certain of having seen it that they climbed the fell on the following morning to check for the hoofprints of the horses, but found none there. It has also been claimed that these 26 signed an oath to what they had seen in front

A 17th-century depiction of a spectral army.
(© TopFoto)

of a magistrate. While local villagers came to believe that the apparition predicted the Jacobite Rebellion of 1745, others searched for a scientific explanation, and claimed that it was an optical illusion. One person suggested that the witnesses of 1745 had seen a mirage or reflection of the rebel army training in Scotland, although this theory does not explain the earlier sightings.

spectral armies

Apparitions of armies, generally either appearing in the sky or re-enacting previous battles.

The earliest report of a spectral army dates from c.160 AD, in an account from Pausanias's *Description of Greece* describing ghostly sounds heard on the site of the Battle of Marathon. Later, stories of spectral armies appearing in the sky were a common theme in 17th-century pamphlet literature (see AERIAL PHANTOMS). Unfortunately, the best-known British cases (including stories of phantom Civil War armies at EDGEHILL and NASEBY, and spectral soldiers seen at SOUTHER FELL, Cumbria, in the mid-18th century) seem to be merely ghost stories which collapse under critical scrutiny of the historical sources.

Nonetheless, some investigators feel that there are a small number of plausible first-hand accounts of spectral armies collected by psychical researchers. Generally, witnesses believe that they have experienced the sights or sounds of a battle from the historic past. Shortly after the end of World War I, for example, author James Wentworth Day claimed to have seen a spectral skirmish between phantom French and German cavalry in woods near Neuve Église, Flanders, at a site known for cavalry battles in 1870 and 1914. Researcher Peter McCue also considered that there was some evidence of a spectral battle being witnessed near Loch Ashie, Scotland, at various times during the 20th century.

For an example of phantom Roman soldiers, see TREASURER'S HOUSE.

spectral pedestrians

Ghostly human figures that appear on highways in the path of oncoming traffic.

One of the frequently reported forms of modern apparitional experience is the spectral pedestrian. Unlike the lore of PHANTOM HITCH-HIKERS, there are many well-attested examples of spectral pedestrians as a type of road ghost. Realistic human apparitions are seen crossing or standing in a road in the path of oncoming motorists. Frequently drivers believe they have struck or killed a living person until an immediate search of the area reveals no trace of a body.

It is surely no coincidence that spectral pedestrians have emerged in parallel with the growth of motorized traffic. Persons travelling by foot have become a rarer sight on modern roads and are more likely to be noticed by a driver. Furthermore, reports come largely from quiet, rural roads, where an individual pedestrian stands out more than on a crowded highway in more populous and urban areas. Certain country locations seem particularly prone to reports, such as the A23 near Brighton, Sussex, and most notably BLUE BELL HILL in Kent – where the ghost of Blue Bell Hill is said to be the phantasm of a young woman killed in an accident there in the 1960s.

Spectral pedestrians are usually solitary figures and may appear in modern dress or clothing from another era; some appear to be manifestations of a WHITE LADY. Occasionally a more complex apparition will appear – in 1972, a lorry driver on a road near Blythburgh, Suffolk, reported seeing the phantoms of a man and woman leading a horse. Notably, spectral pedestrians always appear to be adults;

Blue Bell Hill, Kent, is said to be haunted by the ghost of a young woman killed in an accident there. (© 2004 Trottman/Fortean/TopFoto)

phantom children do not seem to be reported in these incidents, although fatalities among children on roads are far from uncommon.

spectre

An apparition, ghost or phantom; also used of a naturally occurring phenomenon known as the Brocken spectre.

The word 'spectre' (from the Latin *spectrum*, meaning 'an appearance') is generally used to refer to any apparition or ghost of the dead, and to various classes of supernatural being. It is also famously used to refer to a type of illusory ghost, known as a Brocken spectre, that can be explained as a natural phenomenon.

Named after the Brocken, the highest peak in the Harz Mountains in Germany, where it is said to occur frequently, a Brocken spectre is the shadow cast on clouds or fog by an observer standing on a high mountain ridge or peak. The effect is caused when a low sun is shining from behind a climber who is looking down on clouds or fog, and can range from a simple shadow pattern to figures resembling vast, distorted giants moving across the clouds while surrounded by rings of light.

SPIRICOM

A series of machines designed to enable direct and immediate communication with the spirits of the dead.

During the 1970s, while carrying out research into ELECTRONIC VOICE PHENOMENA, George W Meek and William J O'Neil (of the Metascience Organisation) claimed to have invented a machine which allowed direct, real-time conversations to take place with the spirits of the dead.

Unlike the processes used until then, SPIRICOM (short for 'spirit communication') machines apparently removed the necessity to wait and play back tape recordings to hear replies. From 1972 to 1982 five different versions of the SPIRICOM machine were made; all were based around the idea that spirits would be able to manipulate an electromagnetic field, ultimately producing a voice through a loudspeaker. Various shielding was employed to eliminate extraneous interference and a number of other modifications were made, supposedly in response to a range of suggestions made (via SPIRICOM) by Dr George Jeffries Mueller, a physicist who had died in 1967.

Voices produced by SPIRICOM had a monotonal electronic sound to them, with no pauses for breathing. In addition to Mueller, it was alleged that a number of other entities (representatives of a research group composed of dead scientists) communicated via the machine. Among other things, they predicted the ultimate demise of the project in 1982. The machine was never patented (to encourage others to take the principles of SPIRICOM and expand and improve them), and a number of similar devices have been subsequently produced, including Otto Koenig's 'Generator' and Klaus Schrieber's 'Vidicom'.

spirit

Discarnate portion of a human being, animal or natural object or of 'nature' itself which is capable of independent existence.

The word 'spirit', used to describe a discarnate being, essence or supernatural 'force', comes from the Latin *spiritus*, meaning 'breath'. Within the major monotheistic faiths the spirit is understood to be the non-physical component of a human being (the word is sometimes used interchangeably with soul), and many other religions also recognize the existence of spirits in animals, plants and the natural world in general. Certain cultures and occult belief systems also admit the idea of spirits of non-human entities such as elementals, fairies and demons and do not necessarily draw hard-and-fast boundaries between the material and spirit worlds.

Belief in spirits in various forms is still strong even within urbanized, developed societies, although now it is often separated from the framework of organized religious practice. Human spirits are considered by many to be capable of surviving death – GHOSTS and HAUNTINGS are often attributed to their presence. Many psychical researchers have also been prepared to consider the existence of spirits as a possible explanation for many other PSYCHIC phenomena. In his book *Human Personality and Its Survival of Bodily Death* (1901), Frederic Myers described the spirit as 'that unknown fraction of a man's personality ... which we discern as operating before or after death in the metetherial environment', and the spirit hypothesis has been variously proposed as the explanation for mediumistic communications (see MEDIUMS and SPIRITUALISM), the apparent evidence for past lives (see REINCARNATION and PAST-LIFE REGRESSION), OUT-OF-BODY EXPERIENCES, NEAR-DEATH EXPERIENCES and apparent instances of possession.

spirit cabinet *see* DAVENPORT BROTHERS

spirit drawing

The sketching of images of spirits by a medium.

A number of MENTAL MEDIUMS who claim that they can see SPIRITS attempt to communicate their impressions to others. Usually, this takes the form of a verbal description – however, a small number choose to draw the spirit they say that they are able to see. Rita Berkowitz of Boston is one of the best-known mediums currently using this technique.

As well as producing drawings of spirits from a SÉANCE, such mediums sometimes also claim to be able to draw people's GUARDIAN SPIRITS or GHOSTS that are responsible for HAUNTINGS.

The term 'spirit drawing' is also sometimes used to refer to AUTOMATIC ART, although in these cases the drawing is supposedly produced by a medium under the direct control of a spirit.

spirit guide *see* CONTROL

spiritism

The belief that the human spirit or soul survives the death of the physical body and may communicate with the world of the living.

Spiritism – essentially the belief that the spirits of the dead survive and are able to communicate with the living – is a feature of many religious and spiritual belief systems throughout the world, although the word is now often used more specifically as a collective term for a wide variety of syncretist religious practices found in Brazil. Followers of such religions, or holders of the basic belief, are called spiritists.

Spiritism is also the name of a movement founded in France in the mid 19th century (sometimes described as Kardecist Spiritism for the sake of clarity). The set of beliefs and ideals held by its members were similar to those of SPIRITUALISM, but there were some differences, particularly in the prominence given to the idea of progressive REINCARNATION. The movement was founded by Hippolyte Léon Denizard Rivail, working under the pseudonym of Allan Kardec. In the mid 1850s Kardec apparently felt that religion was an ineffective guide for humanity, although from his spiritual research he was convinced of the continued existence of the human soul after death. Spiritism was to offer a way for people to commune with the world of the dead, and to come to terms with it and the process of reincarnation, without the need to turn to the traditional organized religions. The official books of Spiritism were allegedly CHANNELLED by Kardec. He claimed that they included the words of Jesus Christ and that Spiritism was the successor to Christianity.

This particular brand of Spiritism fell out of favour in Europe in the first half of the 20th century. However, the group of Brazilian religions collectively referred to as Spiritism, within which SÉANCES, mediumship and spirit possession are central, continues to draw millions of followers.

spirit medium *see* MEDIUM

spirit photography

A once-popular pastime involving the alleged photographing of spirits.

In 1861 in Boston, William H Mumler was developing some glass-plate photographs he had taken when he found something strange. There were images of people on the photograph – but they had not been present when it was taken. The images were semi-transparent, looking like the classic description of a GHOST. Recognizing an opportunity, he went into business as a spirit photographer. This worked well – until someone recognized some of his 'ghosts' as living people from the area around his Boston studio. Mumler moved to New York and continued in business until he was finally convicted of fraud in 1869.

Prior to Mumler, GHOST PHOTOGRAPHS had been sold as novelties, but he was the first to claim they were the real thing. The growing interest in SPIRITUALISM proved to be fertile ground for the new art of 'spirit photography'. Photographs were produced at SÉANCES allegedly depicting the SPIRITS materialized by the MEDIUM. Interest increased during and after World War I when photographs were produced claiming to show soldiers who had died – SIR ARTHUR CONAN DOYLE famously attempted to obtain such a photograph of his deceased son. In the case of these séance photographs, it was usually stated that ECTOPLASM had come together to produce the spirit form. However, many of the early photographs are now regarded as laughable – they often clearly involve very crude attempts at deception, such as a 'spirit' that can be clearly seen to be a piece of cloth with a cardboard cut-out face attached.

Other spirit photographs (such as Mumler's) were produced using the standard photographic technique of double exposure. Glass plates would be pre-exposed, with a slightly underexposed image of a person

One of William H Mumler's spirit photographs.
(© Mary Evans Picture Library)

posing as the 'ghost', before being used to photograph the customer. When the plate was developed, both images would be present.

As early as 1875, even the medium William Stainton Moses declared in an article in *Human Nature* that:

> Some people would recognise anything [as a ghost]. A broom and a sheet are quite enough for some wild enthusiasts who go with the figure in their eye and see what they wish to see … I have had pictures that might be anything in this or any other world sent to me and gravely claimed as recognised portraits.

Part of the explanation lies in the fact that such photographs reached a less visually sophisticated audience. However, a more powerful factor was the will to believe, even in cases of explicit fraud. This was illustrated during the prosecution in Paris, in June 1875, of an infamous spirit photographer, Jean Buguet. Despite his confession, and the discovery by the police of his large stock of fake heads, there remained bereaved relatives who were prepared to testify for the defence at his trial and to insist his pictures were genuine. Buguet was fined and jailed for a year but continued to have his supporters.

In the 20th century the introduction of infrared photography into the séance room, and the increasing sophistication of the public, led to a marked decline in the popularity of spirit photographs.

spirit rapping

Apparent communication from spirits in the form of tapping, knocking and banging noises – supposedly produced by the interaction of spirits with physical objects.

Since the Victorian heyday of the SPIRITUALISM movement, spirit rapping has been an important ingredient of many SÉANCES. Rapping is supposedly a spirit communicating by hitting a solid object to make a sharp noise – sometimes explained as occurring through the means of a brief MATERIALIZATION of ECTOPLASM, allowing the spirit to affect the physical world.

The spirit-rapping craze began with the FOX SISTERS in 1848, after they allegedly used this method to establish communication with a spirit for the first time. Initially, a method was used in which the number of raps corresponded with the position of the appropriate letter in the alphabet, so that communications could be spelt out. Eventually, this gave way to the much less cumbersome (and now much parodied) 'once for yes, twice for no' system.

This form of spirit communication became very popular and still continues, to a lesser extent, today – despite the Fox sisters' admission that they obtained their results fraudulently by cracking their toe joints.

spirits of the dead *see* SPIRIT

spiritualism

Spiritualism started as a 19th-century religious movement centred on the belief that the spirits of the dead could be contacted directly by the living.

Contact with the spirit world was usually accomplished through a MEDIUM during a SÉANCE. The spirits were believed to exist on a different 'plane' and it was thought that they could offer help and advice to overcome earth-bound problems.

Modern spiritualism is often said to have begun on 31 March 1848 with the FOX SISTERS of Hydesville, New York. From 1849, they gave demonstrations of their table-rapping communications with spirits; it was from this that the traditional code of 'one knock for yes and two for no' arose. In 1852, the first public demonstrations were carried out in the United Kingdom. From 1856 to 1869, French scholar Allan Kardec wrote a series of books which looked at the philosophy and practice of spiritualism, and these became the basis of another religious movement called SPIRITISM.

A key year for spiritualism was 1861 – it brought the first recorded instance of SPIRIT PHOTOGRAPHY. William H Mumler took photographs in his studio which, upon development, appeared to show spirits next to the sitters. Frequently the sitters would claim to recognize the individuals. Photographs of spirits had been produced prior to this but they had been deliberately faked and sold as such. Mumler was the first to claim his apparitions were genuine, although he was convicted of fraud in New York in 1869. Despite this apparent setback, spirit photography thrived, and it was not until the 1920s that it ultimately fell out of fashion.

Almost as soon as public performances by mediums started to be given, people began exposing the methods they used. One of the most

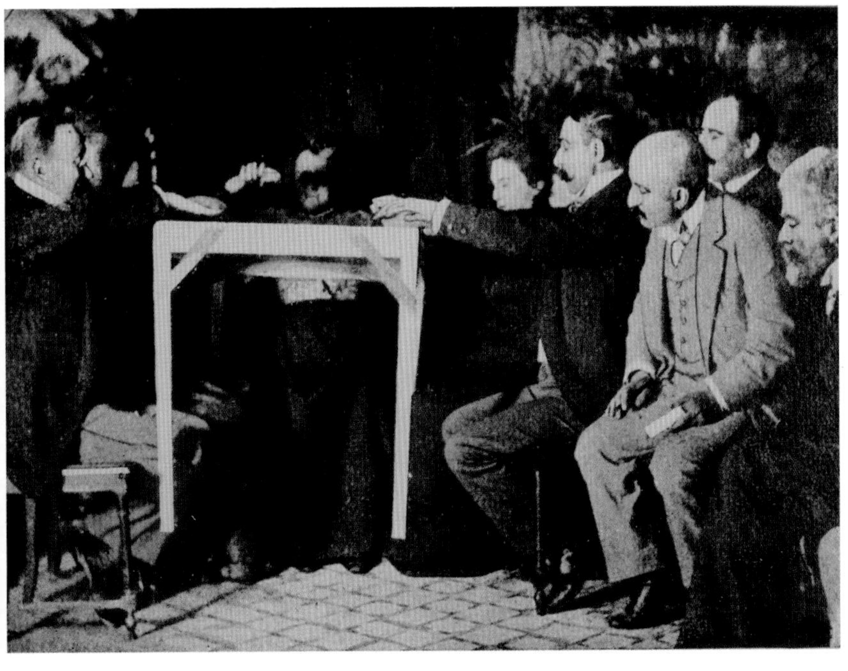

A table levitating during a séance conducted by Eusapia Palladino. This type of movement, known as table-turning, was a popular feature of séances in 19th-century spiritualism. (© 2003 Charles Walker/TopFoto)

famous debunkers was JOHN NEVIL MASKELYNE, who saw a performance by the US mediums the DAVENPORT BROTHERS in 1865. Due to a chance opening of a curtain, Maskelyne was able to see how they produced their effects. He publicly exposed them in British newspapers and set himself up as a magician, replicating many of their effects on stage.

Magicians were not the only ones who were keen to find out how mediums performed. In 1872, FLORENCE COOK claimed that she had produced a MATERIALIZATION of her 'CONTROL' Katie King for the first time. A number of séance appearances followed until Katie put in her final appearance with Florence in 1875. Throughout most of this time Cook was investigated by eminent chemist SIR WILLIAM CROOKES, who was also carrying out investigations on DANIEL DUNGLAS HOME. Crookes was satisfied that both were genuine and he even delivered a paper on the subject to the prestigious Royal Society. In 1882, several prominent scientists from Cambridge University formed the SOCIETY FOR PSYCHICAL RESEARCH (SPR). The SPR investigated all forms of psychic ability but they also took (and still do) a special interest in the claims of mediums.

In the 1890s, a new device was to make communication with the spirit world available in every home – the OUIJA BOARD, or spirit writer, was invented. This was an aid to automatic writing, a development of the PLANCHETTE, which did not seem to need to have an established medium present to produce results. But, although it seemed to make spirit communication available to the masses, the real stars were still the mediums, and in 1893 one of the most impressive took the world by storm. EUSAPIA PALLADINO, from Italy, alternately amazed and confused – it was claimed that she was the greatest medium who had ever lived, despite the fact that she was frequently caught cheating. Palladino argued that it was easier to cheat and that she did not want to disappoint an audience so, if the spirits were not performing, she would fake it.

Interest in spiritualism had been declining for a number of years until the huge loss of life associated with World War I temporarily reversed the trend. SIR ARTHUR CONAN DOYLE, creator of Sherlock Holmes, had been lecturing and writing on spiritualism for many years, and his second wife was a medium. Like many, he turned to spirit photography and the séance room for comfort after losing his son in the war. This put him in conflict with his friend the arch-debunker HARRY HOUDINI, who made a show of publicly exposing fraudulent mediums.

After the 1920s, spiritualism lost many of its converts, although belief in it as a religion and interest in attempts to communicate with the dead have never vanished entirely. In 1959, the Swede Friedrich Jürgenson opened a new chapter. While recording bird song he picked up voices which he believed were the spirits of the dead communicating with him – the study of ELECTRONIC VOICE PHENOMENA (EVP) was born. Between 1972 and

1982, George W Meek and William J O'Neil created the SPIRICOM machine, which supposedly allowed real-time communication with the dead.

Technology has not, however, replaced the medium and the séance. From 1993 to 1998, a series of scientifically designed séances were held by the SCOLE GROUP. Observation by the SPR yielded a 300-page report, covering 500 séances which included a number of APPORTs, a phenomenon which had been popular during the Victorian era.

Spiritualism is still practised today but on nothing like the scale that it was during the Victorian era. For the majority of those who attend séances, use ouija boards or call on the services of mediums, they are merely fun distractions – relatively few would now consider themselves to be involved in serious attempts to communicate with the afterlife. However, there are still a number of popular mediums, who appear in television programmes in which there are apparently attempts to communicate with the dead, helping to promote a continued interest in the subject. Whether this will be sustained remains to be seen.

spirit writing

Writing allegedly produced by spirits.

Spirit writing, within the context of a SÉANCE, can take one of two distinct forms: AUTOMATIC WRITING, in which

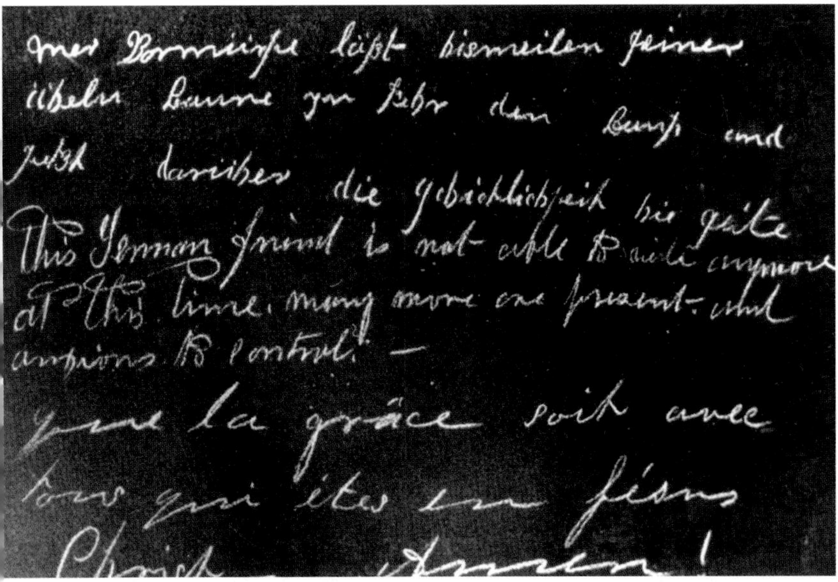

An example of spirit writing, produced during a séance conducted by medium Henry Slade. (©2004 Fortean/TopFoto)

the MEDIUM is in direct contact with the writing implement (or in some cases a PLANCHETTE) but their hand is supposedly guided by a SPIRIT, or versions in which the writing implement and media are isolated from human contact (for example SLATE-WRITING). In both instances, the medium is considered to be CHANNELLING the messages from the spirits.

Spirit writing also features in some cases of alleged hauntings or poltergeist activity. Such writing appears without its production being witnessed, often on walls, and supposedly without the involvement of a living person. There have even been cases where it is alleged that it was possible to attempt to communicate with the spirit producing the writing by adding written questions or responses. Spirit writing of this type famously featured in the HAUNTING of BORLEY RECTORY and the case of the HUMPTY DOO POLTERGEIST.

SPR *see* SOCIETY FOR PSYCHICAL RESEARCH

Stokes, Doris (May Fisher) (c.1920–1987)

English medium who did much to revive the popularity of spiritualism during the late 20th century.

Born Doris Sutton in Grantham, Lincolnshire, Doris Stokes was a noted MEDIUM during the latter part of her life. She claimed that her mediumistic abilities became apparent when she was a young child, when she both saw and heard SPIRITS, and she later became involved in SPIRITUALISM, joining a spiritualist church where she was encouraged to develop her 'talents'. In the mid 1970s Stokes became popular as a psychic medium in Britain, and following an appearance on Australian television, she began to tour widely in Australia and the UK, performing to sell-out audiences at the Sydney Opera House and the London Palladium. Allegedly using her powers of CLAIRAUDIENCE, Stokes would apparently deliver messages from deceased friends and family to members of the audience.

Sceptics claimed that Stokes's alleged paranormal abilities could be quite easily explained as trickery. Some claimed that those members of the audience that received messages from the spirit world were plants – ie people who Stokes already knew a great deal about. Others suggested that she used techniques such as 'cold reading': for example, fishing for information then repeating it back as though it was something the performer had been told by the spirits; bombarding someone with lots of information and watching to see which details they react to before elaborating on these elements; and making very general statements which could actually apply to most people while appearing to make them specific – this latter form of cold reading could be compared to the information given in newspaper horoscopes, where at least some of the details given will seem relevant to a lot of the population at any one time.

Stokes always claimed that her mediumistic talents were genuine, and wrote a series of very popular books outlining her life and work. Her frequent television appearances, and her notoriety in the press, led to an increased interest in spiritualism, and while many would dismiss her as a clever stage performer, others still believe that she genuinely communicated with the dead.

stone tape theory

A theory that suggests that recurrent hauntings are a form of recording on the material environment analogous to video or audio tapes.

The stone tape theory (or rather hypothesis) explains recurrent HAUNTINGS as recordings of scenes or events that are imprinted in the fabric of buildings and rocks, which are then played at intervals in the form of ghostly manifestations. If you accept this suggestion, ghostly manifestations have no consciousness and cannot interact with human observers – they are rather more like video clips.

It is thought that the term 'stone tape theory' comes from Nigel Kneale's television play *The Stone Tape*, broadcast on the BBC in 1972. In this play, the fabric of a room 'records' or 'stores' tragic or emotional events which are then replayed. Although a popular theory with many ghost researchers, proponents are unable to suggest any physical mechanism by which such effects might operate.

Some suggest that the term is best considered as a metaphor or analogy for certain aspects of place- or object-centred PSYCHIC experiences, including hauntings.

super-ESP

A term used to describe a possible explanation for supposed communication with the spirits of the dead.

In 1959 the US parapsychologist Hornell Hart coined the phrases 'super-ESP' and 'super-psi' to cover descriptions of possible mechanisms by which MEDIUMs can appear to be communicating with SPIRITS. Such descriptions were based on the theory that, rather than contacting some element of the self which has survived death, mediums might be inadvertently using extrasensory perception (ESP) to access information from the minds of the sitters. ESP is defined as the ability to obtain information without using the known senses, and includes CLAIRVOYANCE, telepathy and precognition.

This hypothesis introduces an additional difficulty for spiritists: even if obtaining information by normal means can be eliminated from an investigation, if that information is known to anyone present at a SÉANCE (consciously or otherwise) then it is still not necessary to admit the idea that it was provided to the medium by the spirits. In fact, the theories offered by a number of researchers went further, suggesting that the information could be gained from further afield than the séance room – mediums might effectively be creating 'pseudo spirit personalities' by unconsciously gathering information using a wide range of PSYCHIC faculties over long distances. The idea is related to similar theories based upon the idea that a whole host of paranormal phenomena, popularly attributed to spirits of the dead are, in fact, generated through supposed powers of the minds of the living (for example, see RECURRENT SPONTANEOUS PSYCHOKINESIS).

Sceptics would, of course, contend that super-ESP can only serve as a useful theory if and when uncontroversial evidence is produced to the effect that the pronouncements of any medium actually require a paranormal explanation.

super-psi *see* SUPER-ESP

T

table-turning

The supposedly unexplained, sometimes violent, movement of a table during a séance.

Table-turning or 'table-tipping' is one of the wide range of physical phenomena that are said to occur during SÉANCES. To achieve the effect, the participants sit around a table, with their hands gently resting on it. If they are successful, the table will begin to move without any apparent human intervention – the movement is then usually ascribed to the actions of the SPIRITS. In some séances the table moved very energetically – for example, the séances of EUSAPIA PALLADINO were usually characterized by quite violent movements of this sort.

Table-turning was a common feature of séances from the very early days of the SPIRITUALISM movement. By the mid-1850s it had become a popular pastime in the homes of Victorian Britain. Many were happy to accept that the movement was produced by the spirits, but a number of scientists and sceptics investigated further. Michael Faraday devised a system of two table tops, one sitting on rollers above the other. If even a small amount of pressure were applied to the top table, the rollers would move, telegraphing the fact that the movement had been produced by a push or a pull from one of the sitters.

The popularity of table-turning started to wane at the start of the 20th century and, while it is still reported in some séances, it is now more likely to be encountered as part of a stage magician's act.

In its broadest sense the phrase 'table-turning' can be used to refer to any movement of objects during a séance.

Tedworth, Drummer of *see* DRUMMER OF TEDWORTH

theatre ghosts

Apparitions associated with theatres.

Stories of haunted theatres are very common in Britain, the USA and elsewhere. London has many reputedly haunted theatres, possibly the most famous being the THEATRE ROYAL in Drury Lane, which is haunted by the 'Man in Grey', as well as by the ghosts of past performers. The ADELPHI THEATRE in the Strand is said to be haunted by the actor William Terriss who was murdered in 1897 – Terriss is also said to haunt the London Underground (see LONDON UNDERGROUND GHOSTS); it is claimed that the Haymarket Theatre is haunted by the former actor-manager John Buckstone; some say that the Sadler's Wells Theatre is haunted by 19th-century clown Joseph Grimaldi; and tales tell that the Old Vic is haunted by a woman playing the part of Lady Macbeth. Many English provincial theatres are also reputedly haunted, notably those in Bath, Brighton, Bury St Edmunds, Farnham, Margate, Portsmouth and Whitby. The haunting is not normally experienced when shows are taking place but rather when the building is quiet, either before or after performances. Examples of haunted theatres are also found in other parts of Europe, the USA and Latin America.

Theatre Royal

One of London's most famously haunted theatres.

The current Theatre Royal, in Drury Lane, London, opened in 1812 with a performance of *Hamlet*, but the history of the theatre dates back to 1663, when the first playhouse of that name was constructed. The present building is said to be haunted by a number of APPARITIONS, including the 'Man in Grey', often regarded as the most famous of all England's THEATRE GHOSTS.

The 'Man in Grey' is said always to appear during the day rather than at night, apparently attending either rehearsals or matinée performances. The apparition is described as wearing a tricorn hat, riding cloak and boots, and as having powdered hair or a wig. He either walks slowly along the balcony before disappearing into a wall, or takes a particular seat in the upper circle, leaving his seat at the end of a performance, and again disappearing into a wall. Some stories relate that the 'Man in Grey' seems so real that witnesses have been known to think him an actor in costume rather than a ghost. Unlike many other ghosts, a sighting of the 'Man in Grey' is said to be a good omen, and it is believed that if he is seen during rehearsals the play will have a successful run.

Legend claims that the 'Man in Grey' was a wealthy young man of the 18th century who was having an affair with an actress. He would meet her in the upper circle after performances, but was eventually stabbed to death there by a jealous rival. The murderer then hid his victim's body in a recess in a theatre passageway, and later returned to wall the recess up. This story seems to have arisen from an incident in the mid-19th century, when builders discovered a skeleton, complete with a dagger in its ribs, as they carried out repairs to the building.

Other Theatre Royal apparitions include the ghosts of past performers.

The actor Charles Macklin, who killed fellow actor Thomas Hallam there in 1735 during an argument over a wig, is said to haunt the backstage area; the comedian Dan Leno (1860–1904) appears in a certain dressing-room; clown Joe Grimaldi (1778–1837) is reputed to make his presence felt in helpful ways, guiding struggling actors around the stage; and 19th-century actor Charles Kean has been reported sitting quietly in the audience. A story also persists that the theatre was once visited by a royal ghost. Charles II, who licensed the original Theatre Royal in the 17th century, is said to have attended a performance of *Oklahoma* in 1948.

Thornton Heath Poltergeist

A 20th-century alleged poltergeist case from London, investigated by Nandor Fodor.

NANDOR FODOR became involved in what is now known as the case of the Thornton Heath Poltergeist in 1938. The case centred around Mrs Forbes, who was then 35 years old, and who lived in London with her husband and son. The family home was apparently plagued by POLTERGEIST activity – some objects mysteriously appeared, others crashed to the ground, and glasses flew from Mrs Forbes's hand. Mrs Forbes also reported physical assaults upon her person by mysterious forces – she claimed that something had tried to choke her with her own necklace, that the claws of a 'phantom tiger' left weals on her arms, and that a vampire had bitten her, leaving puncture marks on her neck.

Fodor witnessed apparent poltergeist activity at the house, but believing that she might be causing the phenomena by natural means, he suggested that Mrs Forbes be studied at the International Institute for Psychical Research, where it would be easier to establish whether she was choreographing the disturbances herself. Mrs Forbes was undressed to check that she was not concealing any objects about her person, but mysterious incidents still continued – objects from her house, some miles away, appeared, falling to the floor next to her. Fodor still believed that Mrs Forbes was causing the phenomena and, investigating her background, he concluded that she had definite emotional problems, and that the incidents with the 'tiger', the vampire and the mysterious strangler showed that she was harming herself. While she was being studied at the institute, he convinced her to have an X-ray – this revealed objects, missed when she had been asked to undress, which she was holding under her breast prior to their planned 'mysterious' appearance later on.

Fodor was convinced that Mrs Forbes had fabricated the haunting, but rather than simply dismissing the case, he believed it showed the need to include psychoanalysis in psychical investigation. Even fraudulent hauntings were worthy of study in order to examine the mental processes involved. He described the case in the *Journal of Clinical Psychopathology* in 1945.

Tighe, Virginia *see* MURPHY, BRIDEY

time slips

Experiences in which a person seems to be physically present in a different time.

A small number of APPARITIONS involve an apparent wholesale transformation in scenery and environment to that of an earlier time. Such incidents have been dubbed 'time slips'. In addition to percipients seeing detailed physical features which belong to an earlier age, they also have a strong sensation of being physically present in the past. In a small minority of cases witnesses also claim to interact with human characters. The classic example of a time-slip experience is the case of the VERSAILLES GHOSTS – in 1901, two Englishwomen walking near the château of Petit Trianon in the grounds at Versailles believed they witnessed scenes from the 18th century. Another example dates from 1957, and involved three young naval cadets – as they walked towards the village of Kersey, Suffolk, the season seemed to change from autumn to spring, church bells stopped ringing and everything became very still. The men apparently saw the village as it would have been hundreds of years earlier, before becoming afraid and running away.

Time slips have been the subject of relatively little study. Although a number of cases involving the apparent perception of historic buildings that are no longer extant have turned out simply to be cases of mistaken location, a small residue of cases remain where no obvious explanation is available. Despite the intensity of time-slip experiences, it seems likely that they occur only on a subjective level, involving perhaps either powerful hallucinations or an altered state of consciousness. Furthermore, cases are known where individuals encounter scenery which could never have existed in that location in the historic past. For example, in his book *More Things* (1967), the cryptozoologist Ivan T Sanderson described an experience shared with his wife while walking near the isolated Lake Azuey in Haiti. The couple suddenly became aware of houses on either side of the road and felt as if they were walking in Paris as it would have appeared some 500 years earlier, an experience which persisted until a companion raised a flame from a cigarette lighter, bringing their shared vision to an end.

Tomczyk, Stanislawa (Early 20th century)

Polish medium who claimed to be able to use psychokinesis to move objects and stop clocks.

Stanislawa Tomczyk was a Polish MEDIUM who was involved in a number of experiments into alleged paranormal abilities in the early part of the 20th century. Tomczyk claimed to be able to levitate objects without touching them, stop a clock within a glass case and influence the turning of a roulette wheel. In the early 1900s, her abilities were investigated by the psychologist

The Polish medium Stanislawa Tomczyk apparently using psychokinesis to cause a pair of scissors to levitate. (© Mary Evans Picture Library)

Julien Ochorowicz of the University of Lemberg. While under hypnosis Tomczyk revealed an alternative personality called 'Little Stasia'. Those who believed in Tomczyk's powers later took Little Stasia to be Tomczyk's CONTROL or spirit guide, and claimed that it was through her that Tomczyk was able to perform her amazing feats. Ochorowicz believed that solid rays could emanate from Tomczyk's finger-tips and it was these that caused objects to move, apparently by PSYCHOKINESIS. Sceptics counter that the 'solid rays' were fine threads that Tomczyk used to suspend items in an attempt to deceive people about her powers.

Tomczyk's skills were also tested by members of the SOCIETY FOR PSYCHICAL RESEARCH. In these experiments it was suggested that the medium was better able to control the movement of objects when under hypnosis. Tested again in 1910 by a group of scientists in Warsaw, Tomczyk was apparently able to produce remarkable phenomena under laboratory conditions. Although claimed by some to display the greatest proof ever of mediumistic ability, Tomczyk later took no further part in public life.

Tower of London

The historic medieval fortress in London that is reputedly the most haunted spot in Britain.

Often dubbed the most haunted spot in

Britain, the historic Tower of London is traditionally haunted by a wide-ranging collection of ghosts – apparently arising from its blood-soaked history as a fortress, prison and execution site. The first ghost reported in the Tower's history was that of Archbishop Thomas Becket in 1241, an apparition that was blamed for knocking down walls (even though Becket was murdered some distance away in Canterbury Cathedral). Other reputed ghosts include those of Anne Boleyn, said to walk headless at Tower Green; Lady Jane Grey, seen in 1957; Henry VIII; Margaret, Countess of Salisbury; Sir Walter Raleigh; and Edward V and his brother Prince Richard, who were imprisoned in the Tower in 1483 and most likely murdered.

Another famous sighting of an altogether more unusual apparition reportedly occurred in the early 1800s, when the 'Keeper of the Jewels', Edmund Lenthal Swifte (or similar), and his wife claimed that they witnessed a phantom object resembling a glass cylinder hovering in the air in their dining room in the Jewel House. According to Swifte, his sighting occurred within a few days of a sentry seeing a ghostly bear, an experience which induced a shock that allegedly proved fatal.

Over the last 50 years, clearly identifiable sightings of the historic ghosts have been few and far between, but reports continue of other, more anonymous apparitions and cold spots and strange noises in different parts of the Tower. In keeping with a number of historic haunted properties (see also HAMPTON COURT PALACE), efforts are now being made to record the ghostly experiences reported by staff and visitors.

trains, phantom *see* PHANTOM TRAINS

trance, mediumistic

A trance state apparently entered into by certain mediums as part of the process through which they claim that they communicate with the spirit world.

A TRANCE MEDIUM appears to be able to fall into a trance state at will, and once in this state they are apparently able to begin CHANNELLING messages from the spirits. The process often involves the MEDIUM appearing to fall into a deep sleep, during which they become possessed by a spirit which temporarily takes over control of their body. Such displays were particularly popular during the heyday of the SPIRITUALISM movement.

It has been suggested that entering into a mediumistic trance simply involves a form of self-hypnosis, during which the medium recalls knowledge they have gained by ordinary means but do not have conscious access to (see CRYPTOMNESIA). Some sceptics go further and suggest that mediumistic trances are nothing more than a stage act employed by mediums to lend authenticity to their fraudulent claims.

The cellar of the Treasurer's House, York, where Harry Martindale allegedly witnessed a procession of phantom Roman soldiers. (© 2004 Fortean/Trottman/TopFoto)

trance medium *see* MEDIUM, TRANCE

transfiguration medium *see* MEDIUM, TRANSFIGURATION

transmigration

The apparent movement of the immortal part of a human being from one 'host' to another after the death of the physical body.

Those who believe in the possibility of transmigration hold that the human soul or SPIRIT may be transferred from one body to another after death. The new host may be human or animal, and in some cases it is even claimed that it can be vegetable or mineral. The use of the word 'transmigration' differs slightly from that of REINCARNATION in that it describes only the process of the movement of the soul – it does not include the wider concept of progression or regression based upon the quality of, and actions during, the previous life, or the idea of an ultimate goal. Transmigration is sometimes also referred to as 'metempsychosis', which literally means 'change of soul'.

Treasurer's House

A famous haunted house in the city of York, England, where phantom Roman soldiers were allegedly seen in 1953.

The Treasurer's House, close to the

Minster in York, England, was the scene of one of the UK's most famous ghost sightings when, in 1953, Harry Martindale, a 17-year-old apprentice carpenter, claimed he saw a procession of Roman soldiers travelling through the cellars where he was working. Some noted that his description of the figures did not correspond to the image of Roman soldiers popularly portrayed in books and films – they were bedraggled and appeared to have little armour, although their weapons included spears and short swords and at least one round shield. They walked rather than marched and appeared to be extremely tired and dishevelled. The figures appeared thigh deep in the floor, indicating that the ground level had risen since Roman times. The unusual detail of round rather than rectangular shields was found to be appropriate to auxiliary soldiers who were garrisoned in York during Roman times. Harry Martindale later became a police officer and also a guide on ghost walks organized in the city; all who interviewed him were convinced of his sincerity. Other sightings of the Roman soldiers are reported to have occurred in the 1930s and at least one other witness, a former curator-caretaker at the Treasurer's House, reported similar experiences in the cellars there after Harry Martindale's experience was made public in 1974. See also SPECTRAL ARMIES.

Tregeagle, Jan

The ghost of a 17th-century Cornish lawyer, said to have been summoned from the grave and given a series of eternal and fruitless tasks.

Known as Jan or John Tregeagle or Tregagle, the historical Tregeagle was an unpopular lawyer known for his wickedness. According to legend, he used his position to amass a large fortune through forgery and bribery. Some claim that he married for money, then murdered his wives, and that he sold his soul to the Devil. It is also said that before his death he had to bribe a parson in order to secure a grave in consecrated ground.

The legend tells that some time after Tregeagle's death he was summoned from the grave when his name was spoken in court. In some versions of the story, this occurred when a dispute over a loan was heard at Bodmin Assizes. Tregeagle had witnessed a loan between two men before he died, but no documents had been drawn up. The lender then tried to get his money back, but the debtor claimed that the transaction had never taken place. In desperation the debtor declared in court that, 'If Tregeagle ever saw it, I wish to God that Tregeagle may come and declare it!' Tregeagle's ghost obediently appeared, and informed the court that the debtor had indeed had the money and, ominously, that while it had been easy to summon him from the grave it would not be so easy to send him back there. In other tellings, the case being heard by the court was that of a dispute between two families over the ownership of a piece of land. Tregeagle had acted for one of the families and had gained the land through fraudulent means. The defendant summoned the lawyer from his grave, and presented him as a witness – Tregeagle testifying to the defraudment. When the case was over, the defendant refused to return the ghost to its grave, attempting to wash his hands of the affair.

In both versions, Tregeagle's ghost torments the man who called for him, to such an extent that the clergy are called for. They decide that the ghost must be kept busy for eternity to save Tregeagle's soul from the Devil, and assign him the task of emptying Dozmary Pool on Bodmin Moor with a limpet shell. It was thought that the task would never be completed as Dozmary Pool was believed to bottomless, and the limpet shell provided had a hole in it. Again, different versions exist as to what happened next. In one, the ghost is chased from Dozmary by hellhounds, before being sent to Padstow to weave ropes from sand, then to Bareppa, near Helston, to clear the beach of sand, carrying the sacks across the Loe estuary and emptying them at Porthleven. One sack was dropped, giving rise to the legend that this was how Loe Bar was formed. Eventually, Tregeagle was banished to Land's End, to sweep the sand from Porthcurno Cave – his howls still heard when the winds blow and his work is undone. Another tradition is that the ghost was taken to Gwenvor Cove to weave the ropes of sand. Each night, the tide washed away his work until, on a night with a hard frost, Tregeagle used water from a nearby stream to cause the rope to freeze and complete his task. Finally, he was charged with starting the task again without using fresh water, and the ghost is still there, and can be heard howling before a storm.

Tunstead Farm

A farm near Chapel-en-le-Frith, Derbyshire, haunted by a skull known as 'Dickie'.

Tunstead Farm was home for many years to an old damaged skull known as 'Dickie'. Particularly famous in the 19th century, this SCREAMING SKULL was said to make knocking sounds and loud noises to warn the farmer when any strangers approached the farm, or when any of the livestock needed attention. Some claim that the skull could also predict imminent death in the family. Most famously, Dickie is said to have once diverted the path of a new railway line. It is claimed that in 1863 railway engineers planned a route through Tunstead's farmland, but Dickie caused the bridge foundations to sink. The engineers chose an alternative route.

Two distinct traditions circulate to explain the origins of the skull. Some say that it is that of Ned Dickson (or Dixon), who was the owner of the farm. He went abroad (possibly to war) but on his return he was murdered by his cousin, who wished to gain the farm for himself. He was killed in an upstairs room, and either his skull was left there, or he was buried in a local churchyard and the skull simply appeared there of its own accord, or (as in other screaming skull traditions) such moanings beset the house that Ned's body was disinterred and the skull retrieved in order to quieten the ghost. The second tradition says that Dickie is the skull of a woman whose APPARITION has been seen haunting the farmhouse. In both traditions the skull could not be removed from the farm without it causing intolerable disturbances.

The skull has not been seen since 1938, and some believe that it was buried in the garden by a farmer's wife who could no longer tolerate the constant stream of visitors who came to see Dickie.

U

Underwood, Peter (1923–)

English writer and investigator of ghosts and the paranormal.

Peter Underwood was born in Letchworth Garden City, Hertfordshire, in 1923. It is said that his first experience of the paranormal occurred when he was nine years old, when he saw the ghost of his father a few hours after his father's death. Underwood joined both the SOCIETY FOR PSYCHICAL RESEARCH (SPR) and the Ghost Society in 1947 – he was

The famously haunted Borley Rectory, photographed in 1929. Peter Underwood carried out extensive investigations into the paranormal occurrences at Borley, after visiting the site in 1947. (© 2004 Fortean/TopFoto)

later President of the Ghost Society, but left the group in 1993 and formed his own organization, the Ghost Club Society.

Underwood was associated with HARRY PRICE and the investigations at BORLEY RECTORY, tracing and interviewing those involved with the house. After Price's death, Underwood was named literary executor of his estate. Underwood has gone on to investigate numerous ghost cases, and has lectured and written widely on the subjects of ghosts and the paranormal. His published works include *A Gazetteer of British Ghosts* (1971), *The Ghost Hunter's Guide* (1986) and *Ghosts and How to See Them* (1993). His autobiography, *No Common Task: Autobiography of a Ghost Hunter*, appeared in 1983.

V

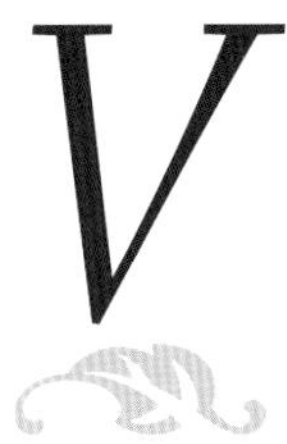

Vennum, Lurancy *see* WATSEKA WONDER

Versailles ghosts

Possible evidence of a time slip.

On 10 August 1901, two English women, Miss Annie Moberly and Miss Eleanor Jourdain, were visiting the 17th-century palace at Versailles, near Paris. As they walked in the grounds of the palace, near the small château of Petit Trianon, they wondered at the quaint, old-fashioned costume of the staff working in the gardens and also noticed that a fellow tourist, who sat sketching, was wearing a peculiarly outdated form of dress. The two women were impressed by their visit, although they had experienced a sense of oppression, which they felt was caused by the August heat.

On looking into the history of the palace after their visit, the two women came to a startling conclusion – that they had witnessed a series of apparitions and a wholesale transformation of scenery back to the 18th century. They claimed that they discovered that the grounds as they had seen them, and the buildings contained in them, had been those of the 18th century, not the early 20th century (by which time numerous alterations had been made). They also claimed that they could date the scenes they had witnessed more specifically – they believed that the tourist they had seen sketching was Marie Antoinette, who had last been at Versailles in 1789.

Each woman wrote a detailed account of her experiences, and their story was eventually published as *An Adventure* in 1911. The book included very precise details of the former garden design and architectural features at Petit Trianon, and of the costumes of the late 18th century. However, from its initial appearance *An Adventure* was criticized by many psychical researchers, although the work remained popular and was reprinted five times in the next 45 years. The case has continued to be the subject of much discussion since the last edition of *An Adventure* in 1955. Some credence was given to the account by the researcher Guy Lambert, who argued in 1958 that there

A 19th-century engraving depicting Marie Antoinette, dressed as a shepherdess, at Petit Trianon, Versailles. (© Mary Evans Picture Library)

were some 20 distinguishing features to their experiences inconsistent with 1901, and suggested that the two women had witnessed Petit Trianon as it had appeared in around 1770.

One theory proposing a natural explanation of the events is that the two women inadvertently observed a costume masquerade – although this would not account for the architectural discrepancies they described. Others have suggested that Moberly and Jourdain simply imagined their experiences, or built them up from subconscious recollections of books or pictures they had seen relating to the history of Versailles. Supporters of a paranormal explanation claim that the case of Petit Trianon is a genuine example of a TIME SLIP, and that the women really did witness 18th-century Versailles. Others have pointed out that Jourdain and Moberly were not the only people to see strange things there – in 1908 there were reports of a 'sketching tourist' near Petit Trianon, and a number of visitors reported seeing other figures in old-fashioned dress over the next few decades. However, hopes that there might be a repetition of the phenomena in 2001, on the hundredth anniversary of the famous Petit Trianon experience, were not fulfilled.

Wardley Hall

A 16th-century manor house in Lancashire; now the residence of the Catholic Bishop of Salford, it has been associated with the legend of a screaming skull since the 18th century.

The legend of Wardley Hall's SCREAMING SKULL was first recorded in the mid 18th century. It was said that the skull had been found bricked up in the chapel wall in 1745, and was then placed on display. The skull is still kept at the hall, in a glass-fronted niche.

There are two popular explanations for the origins of the skull. The more fantastical legend ascribes it to Roger Downes – the somewhat dissolute heir to the hall who died in 1676. It seems that Downes, during a day of drunkenness in London, vowed that he would kill the first man he saw. He did so, killing a tailor with his sword. Soon after (having apparently escaped justice, perhaps using his influence at court) he was involved in a disturbance on London Bridge, and a watchman used his weapon to decapitate Downes at one stroke. The head was sent to Wardley, where it was received by Downes's sister, and at some point afterwards placed on display. Unfortunately, Roger Downes's coffin was opened in 1799, and while the skull itself was not intact (apparently the top portion was missing) it was still attached to the rest of the skeleton.

The second, and perhaps accurate, explanation is that the skull is that of Father Ambrose Barlow, a Benedictine monk and priest who was imprisoned a number of times for saying Mass (often for the Downes family at Wardley Hall) and preaching Catholicism. He was eventually sentenced to death, and was executed in 1641, his severed head being afterwards impaled on a spike, as was the custom of the time. The Downes family then rescued the priest's head and placed it in the wall of their chapel, where it lay undiscovered for over a hundred years.

Some claim that during its time at Wardley Hall the skull has (in common with other screaming skulls) refused to be removed from the house and buried. Each time it is moved, moaning is heard and there are noisy disturbances throughout the hall. It has also been claimed that following attempts to bury it, the skull has eerily reappeared. Somewhat bizarrely, it has also been attributed with the power to cause thunderstorms if it is ill-treated.

Watseka Wonder, the

The name by which Lurancy Vennum, an American teenager who was allegedly possessed by a series of spirits, came to be known.

Lurancy Vennum lived in the town of Watseka, Illinois. From July 1877, when she was 13 years old, she apparently fell into a series of trances and suffered from a complete change of personality. At times she was quiet and sullen, and on other occasions she reported ecstatic visions. She was heard to speak in a variety of voices and to converse with 'angels' or the SPIRITS of the dead. Within a few months her parents were considering having her committed to an asylum. In January 1878, Vennum was visited by Dr E W Stevens, a medical practitioner and spiritualist, at the suggestion of one Mr Roff. Roff had heard of Vennum's condition, and believed that she did indeed communicate with the spirits, as he believed his own dead daughter, Mary, had done. Vennum was initially quite violent towards Dr Stevens and warned him to stay away from her, but she later revealed to him that she was actually several different people. It was claimed that Vennum was possessed by, among others, a 63-year-old woman called Katrina Hogan and a young man called Willie Canning.

Under hypnosis, Vennum apparently revealed that a further spirit wished to come into her, and when asked for a name she revealed that it was Mary Roff. Soon after this incident, Vennum began to act as if she was the dead Mary Roff, begging her parents to be allowed to leave their house and 'go home'. The Roffs agreed and for over three months Vennum lived as Mary in the Roffs' house, allegedly able to recognize Mary's friends and relations and to recall many incidents of Mary's life. After this period of time Vennum's own personality returned and she moved back home, although Mary would periodically 'return'. Some commentators believed that the level of detail that Vennum provided regarding the life and habits of Mary Roff proved that she had indeed been possessed, or even that Mary had temporarily been reincarnated in the body of Vennum. Others suggested that a psychological explanation was more likely, and that Vennum perpetrated a hoax simply because the idea of living as a guest in the Roffs' home was an attractive one. In either case, Vennum became known as the Watseka Wonder, and had either successfully carried off an elaborate deception, or had truly been possessed.

White Lady

Archetypal phantom of a woman clad in white.

White Lady apparitions are common throughout Great Britain, the term coming from the colour of their attire; variants include Grey Ladies

A 19th-century etching of an apparition of a White Lady. (© Mary Evans Picture Library)

and, particularly in Scotland, Green Ladies. Many ancient manor houses, castles, monastic ruins, roads and open spaces are said to be haunted by White Ladies and there are many well-attested sightings outside folklore. The costume of White Ladies is usually historical but of no particular period; occasionally they manifest in modern apparel. While many White Ladies are identified by folklore as historical characters, such attributions are often dubious; the majority seem wholly anonymous. PHANTOM HITCH-HIKERS and many SPECTRAL PEDESTRIANS may also be seen as an aspect of the tradition.

Outside the British Isles, White Ladies are said to haunt rural crossroads and bridges in France; castles in Germany (where they are often taken to be an omen of death); and a number of sites in Switzerland; They are also known in Eastern Europe and Latvia. White Lady apparitions are also common to both North and South America, with many Latin American countries having a screaming White Lady apparition known as 'La Llorona'. The ubiquitous nature of sightings encourages the view that White Ladies represent an archetypal feminine figure emanating from the unconscious mind, or that they are a form of 'genus loci' or 'spirit of place' manifestation, linked with certain landscapes. A number of theorists link them with female gods and spirits from classical or Celtic mythology and even with visions of the Virgin Mary.

Wild Hunt

A spectral hunt which appears in folk myths across Northern Europe and Britain; anyone who sees it is said to be doomed to die.

The folk myth of the Wild Hunt is prevalent all over Northern Europe and Britain. This noisy and riotous band of spirits is accompanied by a pack of ghostly hounds, and is said to ride out most commonly at Hallowe'en, Yule and New Year's Eve, when the souls of the dead are traditionally allowed to return to earth, thundering across the sky amid raging winds and striking terror into any below. To hear the sound of the Wild Hunt is taken to be an omen of strife and disaster, and those who are unlucky enough to see it will either die or be caught up by the hunters and swept away. In Norse mythology, the Wild Hunt's leader is Odin, or Wotan to give him his Teutonic name, and he rides his eight-legged steed, Sleipnir, with his pack of black dogs, hunting the spirits of the dead. In Celtic countries, the hunt was sometimes thought to consist of a fairy host, whose leader was variously identified as Gwydion, Nuada, King Arthur, Cernunnos or HERNE THE HUNTER; the quarry was said to be a boar, a wild horse, the damned, a ghostly deer or female fairies. In some areas the hunt leader was a goddess, and the riders were female, and were known as the 'Hag Riders'. The hounds were often believed to be the souls of unbaptized children. In Wales and the West Country, the leader of the hunt was said to be Gwyn ap Nudd, the fairy 'Lord of the Dead', accompanied by white hounds with blood-red ears. In the Middle Ages, the Wild Hunt became more and more associated with witchcraft, and it was believed that witches participated in the hunt, gathering the souls of sinners and unbaptized infants, and led by a demonic spirit and sometimes by the Devil himself; this was one of the main charges made in witch trials during the Middle Ages. But in later times, the Wild Hunt lost its associations with evil and witchcraft and became a popular literary and artistic device, featuring in many paintings, poems and books. See also AERIAL PHANTOMS.

Winchester Mystery House

A bizarre Californian mansion; according to popular belief, it was built on the advice of a medium to appease the spirits of those killed by Winchester rifles.

The Winchester Mystery House is now a popular tourist attraction. It is a 160-room mansion in the Santa Clara Valley, south of San Francisco, which was under construction continuously for 38 years from 1884. Its continuing popularity derives from the bizarre nature of its structure – some doors open onto ten-foot drops, others open onto blank walls, and stairways lead to the ceiling.

Originally an eight-room house, the property was bought in 1884 by Sarah Winchester, heir to the Winchester rifle fortune. Sarah had lost her only child, an infant daughter, in 1866, and her husband died in 1881. Although left an extremely rich woman, Sarah was greatly troubled by her grief, and is said to have turned to SPIRITUALISM to find some solace. She apparently invited MEDIUMS to conduct SÉANCES in her home, then in New Haven, in the hope that they would be able to contact her husband. Legend has it that these séances were generally unsuccessful, but one Boston medium claimed that he was able to contact Sarah's husband, and that he had learned that Sarah was under a curse – the souls of all those people who had been killed by Winchester rifles had taken revenge upon her with the deaths of her child and her husband, and these souls needed to be appeased

Sarah Winchester's 'mystery house', San Jose, California.
(© 2003 Charles Walker/TopFoto)

The medium told her to move west and build a home for herself and the ghosts, so that she might escape the curse. Some claim that when Sarah first saw what was to become the Winchester Mystery House, she heard a spirit voice say 'this is it'.

Sarah immediately began building work on the house, employing a team of builders to extend it and a team of servants to look after it. She did not employ an architect, or draw up any blueprints for the work, but gave instructions each day, sketching plans on paper bags – some claim that she was working to the dictates of the spirits. The workmen were employed seven days a week, and for every week of the year. Her piecemeal instructions often meant that they had to destroy the work they had recently done in order to implement the new plans, but money was no object. She also employed a team of gardeners, and had them plant a high hedge to keep her work secret from the outside world. She rarely left the house, and when she did venture to the shops, she stayed in her car and had shopkeepers bring their goods to her. By 1906, when the house was damaged by an earthquake, it was seven storeys tall. Work continued after the earthquake, and by the time of Sarah's death in 1922, it was said that she had acquired enough building materials to continue work for a further 38 years.

Local legend claims that when she was alive Sarah regularly entertained ghosts in the house, and that she truly believed she was building a haven for the souls of those killed by Winchester rifles. The house includes a séance room, where Sarah is said to have communicated with the spirits each day in order to receive her instructions. There are claims that she was also obsessed with the number 13, requiring rooms to have 13 windows, stairways to have 13 steps and chandeliers to have 13 lights – a sink in the house, hand-painted in Venice, has 13 drain-holes. Spiders' webs are also a noticeable motif in the house – some believe that a window depicting a spider's web with 13 droplets of water was designed by Sarah herself.

Sarah left the house to a niece, apparently with instructions that the ghosts should still be welcomed and cared for, but within weeks the contents had been cleared and the house was then sold. Modern visitors still report various ghostly phenomena, including phantom footsteps, cold spots and odd noises.

Woburn Abbey

An English stately home, residence of the Dukes of Bedford, said to be haunted by a number of ghosts.

Woburn Abbey, in Bedfordshire, was rebuilt in 1746 on the site of a 12th-century Cistercian monastery. It has been the seat of the Dukes of Bedford for nearly 400 years.

A number of ghostly figures are said to haunt the abbey. The APPARITION of a monk in a brown habit, suggested by some to be the ghost of a lay brother at the original monastery (as the Cistercian habit was white, it would seem unlikely that he had been a member of the order), has reportedly been seen in various parts of the house. The Woburn Abbey Antiques Centre appears to have its own ghost – the apparition of a tall man in a top hat has been seen there – and the summerhouse in the private gardens is also said to be haunted, this time by an unseen presence. Some believe that this latter 'presence' is the ghost of Mary du Caurroy, wife of the eleventh duke. Known as the 'Flying Duchess' because of her skills as an aviator, she died in 1937 when the plane she was flying was lost off the English coast.

The final ghost associated with Woburn also takes the form of an 'unseen presence', this time one that enters a room by one door then leaves it by another – the mysterious opening and closing of the doors being a great annoyance to any family member using the room. While some claim that the disturbance is caused by the restless soul of a young man who was murdered at the abbey, there is no documentary evidence to support this. However,

Woburn Abbey remains one of Britain's famously haunted houses.

Worth, Patience

The pseudonym of US writer Pearl Lenore Curran, who claimed that she was not responsible for her written works, but that she channelled them from Worth, a 17th-century Englishwoman.

Born Pearl Lenore Pollard in Illinois in 1883, Curran showed little interest in writing in her early life. Although she had demonstrated an aptitude for music, she had shown little interest in other subjects and had not done particularly well at school. In 1913, Curran was shown a OUIJA BOARD by a neighbour, and although she was apparently sceptical, thinking that such parlour games were silly, and her first attempts at using it were not successful, she persisted and eventually claimed that she received the following message:

> Many moons ago I lived. Again I come. Patience Worth my name … If thou shalt live, then so shall I.

Following this message, Curran began to ask specific questions of the spirit of Patience Worth, and claimed that she received coherent answers. Worth had supposedly been a 17th-century Englishwoman who had lived in Dorset before travelling to America, where she had been murdered by Native Americans. Soon Curran felt that the ouija board was no longer needed for her communications with Worth, as she could anticipate Worth's responses. Curran claimed that whole sentences from Worth would form in her mind – and a series of books were published setting out Curran's claims. Curran went on to publish a great many works – novels, poems and a play – which she claimed were composed by Worth. Sceptics pointed out that one of the novels supposedly by 17th-century Worth was set in the Victorian era, but the books were very popular, and many were fascinated by Curran's claims. Her supporters insisted that Curran could not have written the books herself as she had not received enough education to enable her to do so, and a 'ghost' truly was responsible for them.

By 1922 it seems that Curran and Worth had apparently fallen out, and by the time of Curran's death in 1937 she no longer claimed further communication.

wraith

An apparitional double; also a general term for a ghost of the dead.

In Celtic folklore, a wraith is an apparitional double or ghost of the living (a DOPPELGÄNGER or FETCH) that is said to herald death. The appearance of a wraith is generally taken to indicate that the person it represents has either just died or is about to do so. The word 'wraith' (originally Scottish, and perhaps from the Old Norse *vörthr*, 'a guardian') is also used more generally to refer to an APPARITION or GHOST of any kind.

X

xenoglossy

A phenomenon in which a person is said to speak or write spontaneously in a foreign language that is unknown to them, an ability which they could not have acquired by natural means.

Xenoglossy, also known as xenoglossia or xenoglossolalia (from Greek *xeno-*, meaning strange, and *glossa*, meaning language) is an apparently miraculous phenomenon in which a person demonstrates the ability spontaneously to speak or write in a foreign language that is unknown to them, and which they could not have acquired by natural means. This ability is sometimes said to be demonstrated by MEDIUMs and clairvoyants who claim to channel spirits who speak or write in a language that is unfamiliar to the channeller. Xenoglossy has also been cited by some as proof of REINCARNATION, the argument being that the only way a person can speak a language unknown to them is if they have retained knowledge of it from a past life. Some people who have undergone the controversial process of PAST-LIFE REGRESSION are said, while under hypnosis, to have spoken in languages which they no longer know when they are awake.

There has, however, been no scientifically proven case of xenoglossy. Sceptics hold that in most, if not all, alleged cases, the knowledge of the 'unknown' language displayed is minimal, and could have been learned by casual exposure – as, for instance, in the case of the subject whose ability to speak Russian was the result of his having overheard, as a child, a language tutor teaching students Russian phrases in the next room, and having unconsciously memorized some of what he heard.

Z

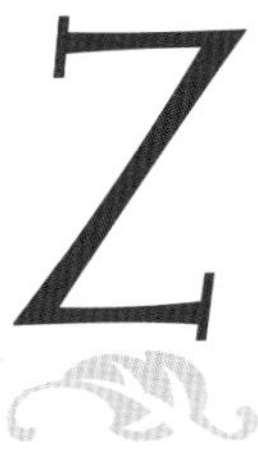

Zugun, Eleonore (1913–late 1990s)

Romanian girl who was the focus of a biting poltergeist and believed she was possessed by the Devil.

Born in the northern Romanian village of Talpa, Eleonore Zugun became famous as the Romanian peasant girl who was the centre of attention from a so-called biting POLTERGEIST between 1925 and 1927.

In 1925, Eleonore found a coin by the road when she was on her way to visit her grandmother. It was a folk belief in that area that such coins were the property of the Devil, and when her grandmother discovered that Eleonore had bought sweets with the money and eaten them, she told her granddaughter that she had swallowed the Devil. That night Eleonore became the focus of poltergeist disturbances, including stone-throwing and object movements. These incidents were attributed to an invisible entity dubbed *Dracu*, or Devil in Romanian. Eleonore was placed first in a convent and then in some form of institution. Her case attracted attention, and she was investigated by psychical researchers, including Fritz Grunewald of Germany, who made an extensive record of the apparent poltergeist incidents surrounding her, although he died before he could complete his observations.

Another interested investigator was the Countess Zoe Wassilko-Serecki. In September 1925, she arranged for Eleonore to be taken to Vienna. In the months that followed, hundreds of strange events occurred, and it became clear that Eleonore believed she was possessed by Dracu. In 1926, the Countess published a short book on the case, *Der Spuk von Talpa*. In April of that year, Eleonore was taken to London to be studied by HARRY PRICE at his National Laboratory of Psychical Research. Price observed the mysterious movement of objects in Eleonore's presence, and at this stage it became apparent that if Dracu was insulted or made angry, scratches, weals and bite marks would appear on Eleonore's arms, hands and face.

Eleonore Zugun was the focus of poltergeist disturbances and believed she was possessed by 'Dracu', the Devil. The marks on her face were said to appear when Dracu was angry. (© Mary Evans Picture Library)

Although there was some evidence that in the latter stages of the investigations Eleonore resorted to fraud, many of the incidents surrounding her remain difficult to explain. All phenomena ceased entirely on Eleonore's reaching puberty and she grew to adulthood without any further repetition of the manifestations. She was traced by Harry Price after World War II and reported to be running a hairdressing salon; she lived on in Romania into her eighties and died in the late 1990s.

Glossary

This glossary contains additional terms that do not directly relate to ghosts and spirits, but that may nevertheless assist readers in their use of the book.

cryptozoology

The study of unexpected animals whose existence or identity is currently undetermined by science.

exorcism

The performance of a ritual, usually by a priest or other religious authority, to drive out a spirit or demon believed to have possessed a person or place.

extrasensory perception (ESP)

The claimed ability to obtain information without using the known senses, using techniques such as **telepathy**, **precognition** and CLAIRVOYANCE.

macro-PK (macroscopic-psychokinesis)

Large scale demonstrations of PSYCHOKINESIS that can be observed by the naked eye, for example, metal bending.

magic

May be defined as the influencing of events and psychical phenomena by humans using mystical, **paranormal** or **supernatural** means.

magic, black

The use of **magic** with the intention of harming others, or for personal gain.

magic, stage

A form of entertainment in which illusions, sleight of hand and conjuring are performed to make the audience believe they are seeing something which is apparently impossible.

magic, sympathetic

A type of **magic** that depends on the belief that one thing which resembles another in some way, or which was once in physical contact with it, can be used to influence it. An example would be burning a lock of a person's hair in order to cause that person harm.

Marian apparitions

Visions of the Virgin Mary experienced by people throughout history, from the early days of Christianity to the present.

micro-PK (microscopic-psychokinesis)

Demonstrations of PSYCHOKINESIS that produce effects so slight they cannot be observed by the naked eye, and require statistical analysis for their evaluation.

paranormal

Something that cannot be explained in terms of the laws of nature and reason as we currently understand them.

precognition

Prior knowledge of future events, gained by PSYCHIC means.

psi

A general term covering all areas of **extrasensory perception** and PSYCHOKINESIS.

psychometry

The supposed employment of PSYCHIC powers to gain information about an object's previous owner or its history by handling it.

random number generator

Any device which is used to produce a series of random numbers in tests for PSYCHIC ability. The devices can take various forms, ranging from dice or coins to complex electronic instruments.

rapport

The connection between a MEDIUM and a CONTROL (spirit guide).

soul

The inner essence of a living being, thought in many religions and belief systems to be immortal. The soul is thought to be self-aware and to be the true basis for sentience in living beings. It is widely held that the soul can exist separately from the physical body and survives after death.

supernatural

Something that is above or beyond nature and any naturalistic explanation or understanding. The word differs in use from **paranormal** in that it is often understood to mean that the phenomenon concerned is not amenable to a scientific approach.

telekinesis

The movement of objects through **paranormal** or PSYCHIC powers. It was the original term for what is now known as PSYCHOKINESIS.

telepathy

Direct mind-to-mind contact with another individual so that thoughts and images can be shared.

Index

researchers and research organizations

screaming skull cases

Chambers Unexplained

Chambers Dictionary of the Unexplained

Chambers Dictionary of the Unexplained is a fascinating and illuminating book, and an essential reference for anyone with an interest in unexplained phenomena. Written in consultation with experts in their field of study, its carefully researched, balanced entries cover topics ranging from alien abductions to the zodiac. Special panels are devoted to topics of particular interest, while numerous colour photographs and illustrations make the book a joy to browse.

ISBN: 978 0550 10215 7

Chambers Myths and Mysteries

Discover a world of secrets with this guide to ancient and modern mysteries, including legends, superstitions, folk tales and age-old beliefs. *Myths and Mysteries* sheds light on everything from Stonehenge and Atlantis to Amelia Earhart and Elvis Presley.

Drawing together selected entries from *Chambers Dictionary of the Unexplained*, and including new material, *Myths and Mysteries* is a must for anyone interested in strange and extraordinary stories.

ISBN: 978 0550 10394 9

Visit **www.chambers.co.uk** for further details, or call 0131 556 5929 for a Chambers catalogue.